# A Small Place in Galilee

# New Perspectives
## Jewish Life and Thought

*Berel Lang,*
series editor

Zvi Sobel, *A Small Place in Galilee:
Religion and Social Conflict in an Israeli Village*

Jonathan Boyarin, *A Storyteller's World: The Education
of Shlomo Noble in Europe and America*
Foreword by Sander L. Gilman

Judith Baskin, *The Midrashic Woman*

# A Small Place in Galilee

## Religion and Social Conflict in an Israeli Village

Zvi Sobel

**HM**
**HOLMES & MEIER**
New York / London

Published in the United States of America 1993 by
Holmes & Meier Publishers, Inc.
160 Broadway
New York, NY 10038

Copyright © 1993 by Holmes & Meier Publishers, Inc.
All rights reserved. No part of this book may be
reproduced or transmitted in any form or by any
electronic or mechanical means now known or to be
invented, including photocopying, recording, and
information storage and retrieval systems, without
permission in writing from the publishers, except
by a reviewer who may quote brief passages in
a review.

Book design by Irwin Wolf

This book has been printed on acid-free paper.

**Library of Congress Cataloging-in-Publication Data**

Sobel, Zvi.
    A small place in Galilee : religion and social conflict in an
Israeli village / Zvi Sobel.
      p.    cm.—(New perspectives)
    Includes bibliographical references and index.
    ISBN 0-8419-1342-0 (alk. paper)
    1. Judaism—Israel—Yavne'el.  2. Yavne'el (Israel)—
Religion—20th century.  3. Yavne'el (Israel)—Ethnic relations.
4. Orthodox Judaism—Relations—Nontraditional Jews.  5. Jews—
Israel—Yavne'el—Identity.  I. Title.  II. Series: New
perspectives (Holmes & Meier)
BM392.Y39S64  1993
306.6'095694'5—dc20                                      93-10994
                                                                             CIP

Manufactured in the United States of America

Man's path through life is
over a very narrow bridge.
Be strong and believe that
God's mercies fill the Universe.

                        Rabbi Nahman of Bratslav

# CONTENTS

INTRODUCTION ix

## Chapter 1
### A SMALL PLACE IN GALILEE 1
- The Village 3
- Population: Veterans and Newcomers 9
- Work 12
- Agriculture 23
- Agricultural Beginnings 25
- "Lords of the Earth": The Emergence of a Jewish Yeomanry 28
- Two Yavneelim 41

## Chapter 2
### AND PROPHECY DEPARTED FROM ISRAEL: YAVNEEL'S RELIGION 53
- The Popular Religion of Yavneel 56
- The Religious "Ground Bass" 64
- An Emerging Religion of Place 75
- Sephardi Folk Religion 80
- Pork Is Not Tasty, It's Also Not Proper: Religious Beliefs and Practices 95

- Atheists and Believers: Together and Apart … 105
- We Are Here Only Because We Are Jews: Religion as a Legitimating Force … 118

## Chapter 3
### A CITY OF BRATSLAV: THE HASIDIC INVASION … 135
- The Whole World Is a Very Narrow Bridge: Goals of the Hasidim … 141
- The Hasidim and the "Ethnics" … 156
- Two Hasidim … 170
- Worldviews in Conflict … 177

## Chapter 4
### WHATEVER HAPPENS HERE WILL HAPPEN IN THE WHOLE COUNTRY: IT'S NOT WHAT WE HOPED FOR … 190
- Memory and Continuity: Memorial and Independence Days … 190
- Can We Live with Stones Being Thrown in Wadi Ara?: The "Day of Peace" … 199
- Bringing Back the *Galut*: The Pull of Exile, the Push of Zionism … 208
- The Decline of Commitment: Israel as a Failed Utopia … 215
- And What of the Village? … 224

NOTES … 229
GLOSSARY … 237
INDEX … 245

# INTRODUCTION

YAVNEEL, which in the time of the Judges and the Prophets was called Yama, is a small place in a small region of a small country. It is not an important center of culture, a focus of industrial or, for that matter, agricultural production, or an axis of political power. It is not a place of strategic or military importance, it boasts no major educational institution, neither secular nor religious, and is, in fact, somewhat out of the way. One doesn't have to pass through the village in order to reach another place: there are ample alternatives. One would not consider a move to Yavneel to seek employment, or to get rich: neither is very likely. Nor would one choose Yavneel as a place of residence because of the services available or for benign climate unless, in the first instance, one preferred to cope with minimal public intervention and, in the second, enjoyed long periods of great heat and a quite merciless and relentless amount of sunshine. For those seeking night life or a vibrant street scene, they would do well to seek elsewhere. Yavneel is a quiet place where people tend to take their pleasure in the bosom of the family or in subdued social evenings spent with friends, spiced by a very occasional night out at the cinema in Tiberias, or the celebration of some festival. It is a community where anonymity is neither a virtue nor a permitted refuge, and where a stranger is quickly recognized as such, receiving instant appraisal and, if possible, placement in the scheme of things. People, as they do in small places, acknowledge each other, greet each other—at times with a slight wave of the hand, at times with the exchange of a few words. Sometimes it is done on the move and at other times people will stop, perhaps sit and talk a bit. To pass one by with no notice being taken is a sure sign that some irritation has arisen, or perhaps a long-time feud continues to flourish—or otherwise it could only mean that one was not seen and chances are that notice will be demanded.

As with all such places, Yavneel is ingrown and often focused on petty grievances or marginal jealousies encapsulated in long memories which just don't let go. Though memory of insult or injury is long, there is a correcting and salving inclination to set everything aside in time of trouble or of separation, where the defining factor will likely or not be whether or not you are one of us, a *Yavneeli*. Yavneelim seek each other out when involved in long separations from the village, and for those who have left permanently there remains an indelible sense that they not only come from some place very special but that in large measure they are who they are as a result of having lived in this place. People tend to have their characters weighed and measured against presumed resemblance to that of their grandparents—for better or for worse. Not only those who live or have lived in Yavneel, *Yavneelim,* but veteran Israelis and students of the pre-state Jewish community, the *Yishuv,* will be heard to argue that there is a Yavneeli "type" or "character." It is a picture of a plodding, phlegmatic farmer—a mule for work, a bit slow on the uptake, quick to anger and quick to forgive, a courageous fighter and a crafty manipulator of his environment, social and physical—in short, the salt of the earth.

Though a small place, Yavneel is not unknown in the country at large, either because of who comes from the village or because of events that took place there. In the struggle against the British mandatory regime Yavneel was a center of the Haganah, the major underground arm of the Yishuv. The Golani Brigade, one of the most distinguished divisions of today's Israeli Army, was founded and organized in Yavneel. At least two of Israel's most daring generals were sons of the village, as were a host of other leading soldiers and fighters from the formative days of the state. Others who distinguished themselves in art, literature, politics, and popular culture were either born in the town or trace their roots in the country to forebears who had settled and lived there.

Together with a few other communities in the Galilee, Yavneel has emerged as an incubator and framework for the development of family agriculture and the life-style and value system that accompanied it. The drama of return and rebuilding and reclaiming that underlies the core myth of the Zionist enterprise echoes in the history of the village and has deep resonance beyond its borders. Indeed, in an almost uncanny fashion, this small place in Galilee seems a microcosm not only of the early history of settlement in the land, but of what has resulted and emerged in the country itself as it appears today.

Yavneel is a small place but in at least one sense it is a major place and that because of the role it fills as a repository for the memory and explication of events that have shaped contemporary Israeli society in a whole host of ways. It is a place that in some curious fashion seems to represent an unplanned and unsought-after gathering together of the scattered fragments of the House of Israel, so that in this modest enclave one finds Sephardim and Ashkenazim, nonbelievers and believers, Hasidim and *misnagdim,* as well as converts from and to Christianity. Its politics ranges from far right to moderate left; its occupations include farming, work in light industry, small business, as well as the service sector and the free professions. Its population is comprised of "veterans" whose roots in the country go back a hundred years as well as "newcomers" who appeared in large numbers as a result of the mass immigration in the early fifties and whom fate has decreed to remain "newcomers" forty years after their arrival. The problems that occupy center stage in the life of the community are in large measure the problems that confound the society at large: tension between the dominant Ashkenazim (those Jews who have lived in Europe and the West), and subordinate though numerically larger Sephardim (the eastern, or Oriental, Jews); the perceived threat of being once and for all overcome in the ongoing struggle with the Arabs in their midst; and, far from least in importance, the place and role of Jewish religion and the nature of this religion in its individual and communal expression.

If Yavneel merely reflected a set of norms or central features prevalent in Israeli society it might prove of ethnographic interest, and study of the community would no doubt enlarge our understanding of aspects of this particular place over time, allowing here and there for modest generalization. The examination, for instance, of what has happened and is happening to agriculture in the country could profitably be based on a detailed analysis of this question in the village and does in fact have applicability in a rather far-ranging fashion. But the focus of such an undertaking need not have been Yavneel; it could have been almost any similar community and the results would have been quite circumscribed, reflecting what happens in the normal course of events. Things change—but when they change because of a shock to an apparently normally functioning system, sharpened sensitivity leads to heightened visibility, which in turn exposes much more than is commonly the case. Victor Turner, following Freud in this, has observed how "disturbances of the normal and regular often give us greater insight into the normal than does direct study," for what has happened is that "deep structure may be revealed through surface anti-structure or counter-structure."[1] And what has elevated Yavneel—this small place in Galilee—to an importance belied by its size and its distance from the heart of the country where decisions are taken and events shaped is to be found in its having been selected as a place of settlement, ninety years after its founding, by a Hasidic group that follows the teachings of Nahman of Bratslav. Not only has it been chosen as a place of concentrated ultra-Orthodoxy, or the *haredi* way, but also "targeted" for the eventual dominance of this ultra-Orthodox perspective in the community—and beyond. Given the fact that Israeli society as a whole is being confronted by questions revolving around matters such as the place and nature of religion, political power and religious authority, societal legitimation and its anchorage in the biblical "title deed," and conflicts between the contrary value systems of secular Zionism and religious traditionalism, one can easily surmise what levels of threat and concern were elicited by the rather sudden appearance of Bratslav Hasidim in the village. It should also be apparent how the events in Yavneel are being watched and weighed by forces ranging over the entire ideological and social landscape of Israel for signposts pointing to the future contours of the country's inner and outer *gestalt.*

Religious traditionalism and secular Zionism have coexisted in Israel since the beginning of the state and before. It is, however, only over the last two decades or so that anyone in the non-Orthodox camp thought of the possibility of seeing in the *haredim* a living, competitive entity that could or would exercise power beyond the limited confines of its adherents. It was widely thought that the world of ultra-Orthodoxy representing no more than 6 percent of the population was a fading artifact of a world that had been in decline for generations and had received its final devastating blow at the hands of the Nazis, with only a sad remnant to remind us of what was no longer. Indeed, at least one reason for the openness and generosity extended to this ultra-Orthodox sector on the part of those who were far from its life-style or belief system was the desire to demonstrate that Hitler and his evil minions did not, in the end, succeed.

But willingness to underwrite religious ultra-Orthodoxy went beyond this symbolic *ex post facto* victory over evil and reflected certain truths about this society not easily articulated or, indeed, cognitively embraced by its majority non-Orthodox population. One is that in the search for continuity, which is a basic element in state building, and societal maintenance, there exist no models from the past—distant or close—other than those anchored in the unique religious/ethnic mold that has characterized the Jewish world for two millennia. Beyond the past four decades or so there are no Jewish heroes standing at the head of an army of liberation nor are there Jewish universities spreading light in the world, or Jewish parliaments legislating guidance for the people. There was only the memory—fabricated and real, enhanced and unvarnished—of the shtetl or the mellah or the ghetto to provide a skein of continuity and a program of action for the Jewish people, and in those places it was traditional religion and faith that enveloped, defined, and dominated. Another "truth" that when spoken aloud is often denied by many Israelis is that for whatever reason—the proximity to the past, the absence or weakness of replacement values, a kind of historic filial piety—Israel is a religious society. In this it reflects to some degree the same ironic paradox that Everett Carll Ladd attributes to Americans when he refers to them as both a religious and secular people: "My argument is that America is today what it has always been: a highly religious, intensely secular society. Nothing much seems to be happening on either of these fronts—the latter because we have gone about as far as we can go; the former because we see no reason to back away from the point we long ago arrived at."[2]

It is not possible to understand Israeli society without serious and extensive analysis of the religious factor. Religion, Jewish religion, whether of a folkloristic, popular variety or a traditional canonical variety, is deeply ingrained in the consciousness of Israelis, as well as in the formal structures that frame their lives. It touches the ridiculous, as when dust from the area of the Western Wall of the Temple is spread at the feet of a leading soccer star in an effort to improve his goal production, to the more sublime of Army-sponsored seminars for soldiers at ultra-Orthodox centers of learning. It includes laws about personal status as well as those dealing with the raising of pigs on holy soil. Religion embraces celebration of holidays, and the national calendar records only one "secular" occasion (Independence Day) in a long list of observances. It includes as well a goodly portion of religious television programming, and the dispensing of religious guidelines through the general media; for example, when the Sabbath begins and

## INTRODUCTION

ends in all major centers, the counting of the Omer (the forty-nine days between Passover and Shavuot) and when businesses and services will be open or shut on this or that religious occasion. For most Israelis—and most see themselves as nonobservant if not secular—these processes not only are unopposed but seem to be welcomed. Not only is there space for the sacred in their lives but a felt need for the richness and comfort of ritual, a need shared with others in a postmodern age that extends beyond narrow national confines. "When there are few rituals to mark the turns in the wheel of life, if all events become the same with no ceremony to mark the distinctions—when one marries in ordinary dress, or receives a degree without a robe, or buries one's dead without the tearing of cloth—then life becomes gray on gray and none of the splashiness of the phosphorescent pop art can hide that grayness when the morning breaks."[3] "The sacred," Daniel Bell continues, "is the space of wonder and awe," and mankind seeks a new vocabulary to express it that inevitably pays homage to the expressions elevated by that which was. What was— the past—has resonance and meaning for all people, and not just Jews. But Jews have made remembrance numinous with little parallel among the nations: the command to remember, whether historical event, sacred chastisement, characterological peculiarity, communal destiny, or personal sanctity, runs deep in Jewish consciousness and occupies the center of Jewish spirituality and faith.

The recognized keepers of the flame and still the current interpreters of this message for large numbers of Israelis are those who uphold Orthodoxy in the country, which includes the ultra-Orthodox wing notwithstanding their anti-Zionist stance and their stalwart inclination to oppose Zionism in a forceful and active manner. Despite the espousal of an anti-Zionist worldview and indeed often expressed disdain for its message, the ultra-Orthodox minority has achieved a position of major importance in the political life of the country, which has led to ever-increasing demands for financial support of their institutions *and* vociferous assertions that it is *they,* rather than the Zionist usurpers, who represent legitimacy and continuity in Jewish life. Rather than change, they uphold the old and the traditional; rather than evolved prescriptions for chastisement, they point to eternal revelation; in place of individual choice they subscribe to ironbound authority; rather than work in the temporal arena of the here-and-now, they embrace the time-honored holy labor of study and prayer. Thus, when a group bearing such a message arrives in a community that sees itself and is seen by others as the embodiment of the opposing message of pioneering Zionism, the level of culture shock can easily be imagined.

With the appearance of the haredim or ultra-Orthodox Bratslav Hasidim in Yavneel, the inclination prevalent in the country to accept the claims of these protectors of the sacred flame to legitimacy was put to the test in very actual, here-and-now terms. In Yavneel it was no longer a matter of exaggerated claims on the national treasury, or the passage of religious legislation by the Knesset, quickly followed by clever maneuvers as to how these could be circumvented, but the very real possibility that a rooted life-style would be upset. Would streets be roped off and closed to traffic on the Sabbath and holy days? Would the swimming pool and sports fields be segregated by sex and also closed on holy days? Would rigid standards of kashruth be instituted to replace the mild level of dietary-law observance now in force in the shops and public institutions of the village? Would values so laboriously and valiantly achieved such as labor in field and workshop, self-defense, political and social pluralism, be overshadowed by patterns reflective of the Diaspora rather than Zion reborn?

In Yavneel, what had previously been viewed as perhaps unaesthetic departures from established communal norms, or annoying peccadillos of an Orthodox minority living apart in very specific and far-off centers of concentration, was transformed into a direct threat to the village itself. In a village consisting of slightly more than four hundred households, the newly arrived Hasidim boldly asserted that they hoped to eventually bring in two hundred additional households of haredi believers that, if achieved, would transform Yavneel from a veritable symbol of Zionist pioneering values to a replica of the East European shtetl from which the pioneers had fled in more than just the geographic sense. Slowly—and soon in increasing tempo in the streets of bucolic Yavneel—one witnessed two distinct worlds converging, and the encounter was marked by paradox and contention. Here burly farmers eyeing the heavens for signs of rain or intensifying sun walked alongside bearded, side-locked Hasidim who looked to the heavens for other omens promising firmer direction. Earthy villagers, not averse to a good mid-morning belt of Arak or a smoke over a cup of coffee and the hearing or telling of a ribald joke, jostled mystical Bratslav Hasidim who neither touch alcohol (except once a year on the festival of Purim) or tobacco, and are given to nocturnal wanderings in the fields where they devote themselves to meditation and talking with God and release all inhibitions in shouts and screams to the heavens. Individualistic yeoman who are unable or unwilling to identify who among them enjoy informal leadership roles, who wields greater or lesser influence, are cast together in one small place with disciplined believers who follow the authority of one man—the *rebbe*—without question or reservation. In short, a concatenation of outlooks and loyalties suggests the inevitability of an explosive encounter in the charged meeting of disparate worlds.

Both outsiders and many among the villagers themselves foresaw bloody encounters occurring between what was perhaps too easily viewed as an unbridgeable chasm separating the forces of belief from those of unbelief. The existence of the chasm is clear and undeniable. Hostility to the Hasidim and fear concerning their ultimate goals is palpable among the villagers. Although violence of any serious kind has not yet occurred, it is entirely within the realm of possibility.

Indeed, in the weeks following my first visit to the community, in the spring of 1986, most veteran villagers with whom I spoke assured me that "blood will flow." Many saw in the decision of the Bratslav leader and his followers to come to Yavneel an act of aggression that was putting to the test the outer limits of non-haredi patience and tolerance. My initial (mistaken) estimate was that violent encounters would indeed take place and that the Hasidim would be sufficiently discouraged to abandon their plans for settlement. But rather than abandon the notion of settling in the face of strong local opposition they have persisted in bringing more and more families to the community, thus posing their image of Judaism against that which has emerged in Yavneel over the nearly one hundred years of its existence.

But there are other than surface forces at work here and in the country at large. Powerful undertones are present that assiduously work against the outbreak of violence or the development of an exclusionary or separatist policy that would guide the relationships between the very Orthodox and those following a different path of Jewish life. On the level of rhetoric one might well imagine the worst—widening and deepening of the gulf separating the champions of what appears to be traditional Orthodoxy and those either seeking, or as is more likely, slipping into new, still rather inchoate patterns of a rooted popular religiosity. But on the behavioral level, attention is inevitably drawn to the fact that there exists a seeming refusal or inability to cut the ties binding this generation no less than others in the past to the deeply embedded kernel of authoritative revealed faith and to its guardians and interpreters who are still perceived as bearing the mantle of legitimacy.

It is, however, not only legitimacy and continuity that are being upheld in the village. There are, in addition, practical factors involved that tend to dampen enthusiasm for the pursuit of a full-blown *Kulturkampf.* It is understood among the more level-headed and responsible people in both camps—the haredi and the non-Orthodox—that in addition to tensions among Jews based on origin, class, religious outlook, and political inclination there is also the "Arab question." In Yavneel, indeed in Israel as in other places and other times, the perceived sense of threat from "outsiders" acts to bring about a closing of the ranks. However powerful the factors acting to create a chasm between those who uphold ultra-Orthodoxy and those who pursue a different path, a sense of threat emanating from the camp of the "other" can open channels of cooperation that, in a more peaceful arena, would not have been predicted.

Perhaps, as is often enough the case, the sages have provided us with a most pointed and seminal caveat when they declaimed (in Talmud *Berachot* 45a), "Go and see how the people are behaving," suggesting in this a twofold course: do not impose burdens that the people are unable or unwilling to bear and do not presuppose an outcome on the basis of abstract logic or convention. "Go," rather, and "see how the people are behaving."

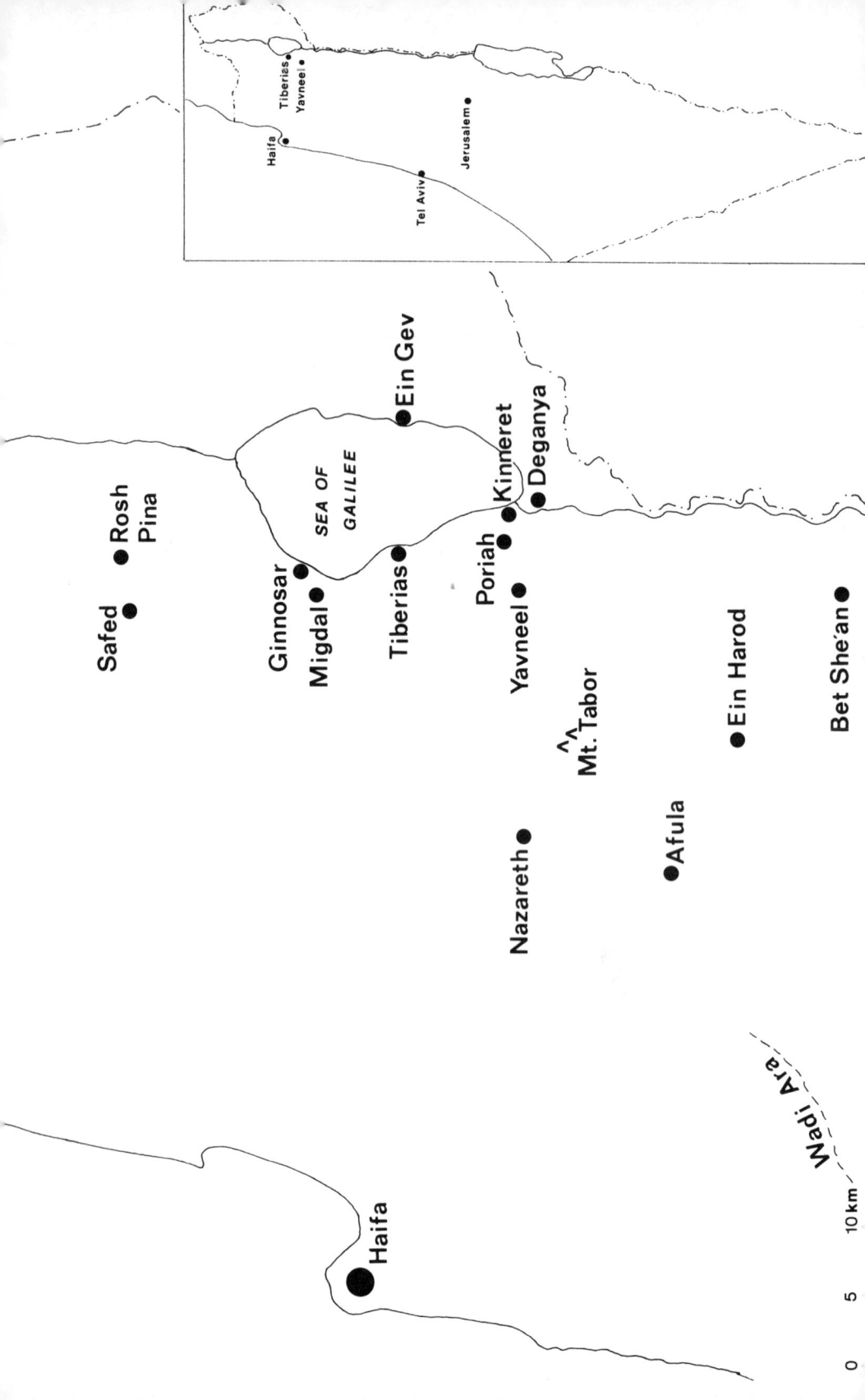

# A Small Place
# in Galilee

# 1

## A Small Place in Galilee

YAVNEEL CAN BE REACHED from two directions: one going down and the other going up.

The temptation to see in this geographical circumstance something of a paradigm of Jewish historical relatedness to Zion is great and has about it a certain seductive simplicity. But in another sense this view represents a continuation of a symbolic mode that the life of Yavneel, and indeed aspects of a Zionist vision, have somewhat abrogated. Traditional modes of thinking about and interpreting Jewish experience have tended to symbolic abstraction, to abstract interpretive antics, to a sort of reductionism where the surface and obvious phenomenon, the *p'shat,* took second place to deeper meaning, usually of cosmic dimensions. The Song of Songs could not be a tale of love, but must represent the relationship between God and His people Israel. Jerusalem could not be *only* a city in the stony hills of Judea, but has its heavenly corollary, the upper, or higher, Jerusalem. The victories and defeats of the ancient Israelites could not be profitably interpreted in political terms, but had to assume transcendent value as part of a divine order.

But this sacred interpretation of history tends to crowd out and indeed eliminate all attempts at understanding events that are clearly the result of temporal circumstances. As in Chagall's vision of the shtetl, with its floating, ethereal figures fiddling in a dream world of blue cows and houses on an impossibly precarious slant, the suggestion is always that there is more, much more than "up and down." The possibilities of the Jewish vision consider "up" as possibly "down," and "down" as conceivably "up," and both are in flux and movement and pregnant with still other and only hinted-at possibilities. For most of us, however, Yavneel can be reached only in two ways and in a manner that can be understood and agreed upon by all. Yavneel is not a symbol either distorted or expanded, but a *place,* a space in the very tangible here-and-now. There exists no heavenly corollary to the earthly Yavneel.

From the east the road winds up toward a plateau overlooking the Sea of Galilee and the fertile fields of the Jordan Valley continuing on for some miles past the village of Poriah and Kibbutz Alumoth, beyond which one comes first to the fields of Yavneel and then to the town itself. From the west one descends from Moshav Sharona, again on a serpentine rather dangerous road, this time facing the Golan and the mountains of Gilead in Jordan, arriving first at Yavneel's outer communities of Smadar, Bet Gan, and Mishmar Hashlosha, and then into the center of town. Coming from the east, one's attention is drawn constantly back toward the great lake, and the verdant valley spreading out to the south. One's attention is drawn quite naturally to the proven opulence of what lies *behind* rather than to the unhinted-at promise further on. The vision of the already experienced lingers and satisfies as it dulls expectation or yearning for the as-yet unseen.

From the west, however, Yavneel shows a different face. Almost immediately after the descent begins from the edge of Sharona, the village comes into view set in the valley basin among trees, gardens, and fertile fields. Stopping somewhere midpoint in the descent, the vista is one of bucolic gracefulness and quiet. The town nestles in a basin, and the light reflected from the white- and beige-walled homes and their red pitched roofs changes radically with the passing of the day from its morning revelatory blaze, to a midday stillness, to the afternoon and early evening softness. From within the town the eye is constantly lifted up but always to a view that is defined and limited: the fields and orchards of Yavneel to the north with the village of Poriah stretching along the spine of the hill; to the south and behind the town, the towering mountain from which it is said the Messiah will first appear but for now barren and stony, casting its late afternoon shadow on the valley; to the west the olive groves of Sharona that stop abruptly on the upper ridge, forming a separation, a boundary between plateau and valley; while to the east the mountains of the Golan and Gilead that, as the day wears on, turn pink with hints of blue and ocher. This latter view provides the only suggestion of beyond, of distance, of openings that can be breached; the others all contain, delimit, and circumscribe.

## The Village

Yavneel can be reached by going up or coming down, and once you are there its substantiality allows little opportunity for Chagallian indecisiveness. It is evident that the struggle with this soil that began almost a hundred years before has been won, but not wholly, not completely. The fields, although rich and extensive, stop at different points along the northern wall of the valley, exposing a gravelly unfruitfulness which had been its face for centuries before the coming of the first Jewish settlers, who brought it to life and took their life from it. The exposed edges of the uncultivated lands hint at only a partial victory and also serve as a reminder, always in sight, of struggles not yet undertaken and defeats, potential defeats, which can drag this people back to the earlier and well-trodden path of their forebears for whom time rather than space formed the context and crucible of existence.

On the mountain lying behind the town or, more correctly, on its slopes, there is very little in the way of agriculture, it being too steep to work and to irrigate, and it has become a sort of corridor to the past in two ways. Here is the first and main burial ground of the community, a serene and beautiful space in a magnificent copse of high pine trees planted early in the century by the original settlers. Here, the community gathers to bury its dead and to carry forward, to enhance and embellish memory, history in Bernard Lewis's sense of "remembered" rather than "recovered" or "invented."[1]

It is a place, following Elias Canetti, that induces in the visitor the feeling that "all the centuries he knows of are his,"[2] where deep values and great aloneness are recorded in stone. "He was a good and loyal worker" is the message flashed back to the visitor from innumerable tombstones in the local cemetery of the early settlers, leaving little room for doubt as to the importance then of this fundamental pioneering ethos. As a seeming counterpoint to this sense of rooted place—and embraced by an ethos of commitment and change—are the forlorn graves of nameless refugees from the coast who died of typhus during their sojourn in Yavneel during World War I, who remain anonymous, who are unremembered, who to this day seventy-five years after the event seem misplaced even in death.

But the mountain also is used as pasture for herds of sheep tended by hired Arab shepherds, whose presence demonstrates yet another link of continuity to the valleys farther in the past when they were sparsely inhabited by Arab pastoralists, and perhaps for some to a still more distant past when the tribe of Naftali dwelt here.

Yavneel's 460 households are clustered into five units: three of them—Bet Gan, Mishmar Hashlosha, and Yavneel itself—are contiguous, flowing into one another in a seamless fashion, while the other two are separated by open areas both spatially and in other ways more telling and less forgiving. One of the units, Smadar, on the western entrance to town, was established as an agricultural settlement for new immigrants located in Yavneel's transit camp; after the initial shakeout when Europeans tended to leave, they were largely Sephardi Jews from North Africa. It failed as an autonomous settlement, and was ultimately incorporated as part of Yavneel. Now it is a suburb that provides expansion space for younger families of veteran settlers and for some of the earlier failed moshavniks who lingered on.

In appearance, Smadar is a curious mixture of neglect and great artifice. Not yet reflecting the organic rootedness of Yavneel, some of its houses are in a dilapidated state, with overgrown not-quite-gardens, while others show care and investment. In some ways it represents the raw, the new, the anti-aesthetic of the immigrant *moshavim,* the communally run settlements of independent farmers, jerry-built in their dozens by the Jewish Agency in the 1950s. In other ways it holds forth promise of melding with time into the flowing rootedness of old Yavneel.

The other unit, at the opposite end of Yavneel, is called simply *Shikun,* or "housing project." In a word, it is nameless. It is here that the bulk of the Sephardi newcomers who arrived during the early and mid-1950s were provided first with temporary and then with permanent housing forming a sort of ethnic enclave or ghetto. It is here that Yavneel's "social problems," Yavneel's poverty, and according to some, Yavneel's shame is concentrated. Here, too, the house roofs are red-tiled, and the sun's reflection on the distant Golan is seen along with the shadows of the Messiah's mountain; but somehow its image is closer to the mundane and the haphazard rather than the essential and expansive.

In the three "core" sections of the town—Bet Gan, Mishmar Hashlosha, and Yavneel itself—there are distinctive elements which set them apart from each other, but the end impression is one of fluid, indeed organic, wholeness. Yavneel is laid out on a north-south axis, with houses and outbuildings of stone that were constructed at the turn of the century with an equal eye for defense and agriculture. In a few remaining home sites one can still see the "escape" door built into the stone compound-wall for flight in extremity. A perpendicular branch to the north-south line lies to the west, and both enclosed the original settlement of forty homesteads that, on the basis of early, grainy photographs, looks like some unnatural growth on the barren landscape. The houses lined up on both sides of the main (and only) street look like tents made of stone, a statement of wished-for permanence spoken in some doubt. With the passage of time this starkness—both of landscape and houses—has softened, expanded, assumed confidence, so that now, clearly, the image of rootedness, place, permanence has totally overcome the earlier doubt.

Bet Gan, originally built as a sister community two years after the establishment of Yavneel, begins on the east-west perpendicular fanning out in the direction of the southern mountains and reflects the same architectural tradition as Yavneel, but with a seemingly greater measure of flexibility. The horizontal linearity of Yavneel is broken here by curves and softened by smaller clusters of dwellings, suggesting more of the shtetl than the settler compound. Indeed, among veteran Yavneelim, as the residents of Yavneel are called, its people are thought of as being a closer replication of the *muzhik,* the Russian peasant, than are the Yavneel settlers; they are a cut below, as it were, reflecting stolidity, a strong work ethic but with a plodding inclination to unimaginativeness. Here, as in Yavneel, the harshness of the gray-black building stone of Galilee has been softened by a patina brought by decades of sun, wind, and rain, and by the abundance of flowers—hibiscus, bougainvillea, geraniums—that surround most of the houses against the backdrop of palm and eucalyptus trees.

Mishmar Hashlosha, named in honor of three settlers murdered by Arab marauders, was established in 1937 on lands partially provided by the settler families of Bet Gan and Yavneel in the expectation of settling refugees from Nazi Germany. It is located on the same perpendicular line as Bet Gan, but on the northern side. Unlike Bet Gan and Yavneel, the buildings here are more in keeping with the style of the period of the later Yishuv and early independence (the 1930s and early 1940s). They are built of buff stucco, most with small, well-tended gardens and utilitarian asbestos and steel outbuildings looming up behind many of the houses for agricultural machinery and, in some cases, milking herds. Mishmar Hashlosha suggests a sort of midpoint between the otherness of Shikun and the in-placeness of Bet Gan and Yavneel. It hints at the same ideological thrust of the early settlers, based as it was on a return to the land tinged by a feeling of hesitant uncertainty about its status. The residents, very few of whom are the original settlers from 1937, are a mixture of old-timers and some of the Sephardi "newcomers" and old Yemenite community who have moved up the social and economic ladder; they form a part of core Yavneel in all respects but somehow are a little less vibrant, a little more tenuous in their claim to full inclusion.

It is at the center of town that one comes upon the institutional structures of the community which in their differing ways reinforce and emphasize the challenge of rootedness to its opposite. The modernistic town hall with its angular thrustings is trying to make a statement but still unsure about the message—not quite certain about the desirability of having abandoned the stone-block structures of old Galilee for the contemporary steel, glass, and concrete of post-independence Israel. Watching Yavneel's farmers and workers in their mud-clogged boots and rough clothes walking through its corridor, one senses that they seem somehow to have lost their way, to have come here in error. Yavneelim who are not in their nature or behavior reluctant or hesitant seem here to be unsure of themselves, even somewhat sheepish. The building is, in some fashion, an attempt to pull Yavneel away from its insular particularity and move it into a more anonymous mainstream—and it is resented. Located nearby is the health clinic, a functional, almost aggressively institutional, structure, alongside of which lies an equally one-dimensional building housing the regional labor council. Here, too, is the main synagogue built in the 1930s, which like the town hall must be viewed, albeit differently, as a transitional structure.

If the town hall haltingly inches toward Israel's brash modernity, the synagogue stolidly insists on a statement of continuity with the East European origins of the founders. It is a homely, stucco structure with a main entrance flanked on both sides by tiny study rooms; and a main hall with six large opaque windows to the north and the south, with its ark and central reading platforms facing east to Jerusalem. It has no architectural interest whatsoever, but nevertheless it invites; it raises no questions, it underpowers, it holds no awe; it is simply a *shul,* a gathering place where gossip and politics are as likely to be pursued as prayer, where a catnap is a more likely event than religious ecstasy, where believers, scoffers, and doubters can share a space ample enough in its memory dimensions to embrace them all on their own unstated and unchallenged terms. It is comfortable in its stark discomfort. It is as familiar as a "racial" memory. But Yavneelim do not depend, as Jews traditionally have not depended, on memory, "racial" or otherwise, for transmitting the heritage from generation to generation. One does not absorb the nature of Jewishness in some mystical and certainly not in any genetic fashion. One must be taught, and for this one must build schools.

A few meters beyond the synagogue one comes upon another homely, rather functional structure—the public school. The original school, built of the same black Galilee stone used in the construction of the early homes and still standing, has been incorporated into the newer building dating from the establishment of the state. The original structure has about it a lovely gracefulness missing in the modern annex, but growth and expansion have done their work in moving the old school to its fate of sedate obsolescence, still another vessel of communal memory.

Beyond the school one comes to the original crossroads, with one turn leading down to the sea of Galilee, another up to the mountain and Shikun, while the third moves toward what is fatuously termed the industrial zone. Here one sees in concrete and steel a series of workshops reflecting Yavneel's reluctant lunge into the post-agricultural periods of the country's development. Most of the twelve units are empty, with only a *bureka* bakery, a carpentry, and a metal shop functioning with some degree of success, the others either never having been rented or already failed. Expectation here is on hold, and the very silence of the compound resounds as a commentary on having crept away from the agricultural raison d'être of the village toward a destiny never embraced but halfheartedly pursued—a bow to what was said to be inevitable, but which adamantly eludes.

Here, too, one sees the houses where the Yemenite settlers were originally concentrated and where the older folk among them still live in modest homes of stucco and concrete block, whose low roofs seem to have been designed with their diminutive inhabitants fully in mind. Here one witnesses a sort of demographic footnote to Yavneel: inhabitants almost from the start, but never fully taken seriously, never completely taken into account, always echoing the larger events taking place in the black stone houses and abundant fields surrounding them. In the marginal location and design of their houses which hug the ground, one sees a reflection of their timorous nature, of an unshared vision of Zion that, for them, only led upward, to the "heavenly" Yavneel, while for the others went in both directions, up and down, thus exposing a chasm as yet unbridged.

## Population: Veterans and Newcomers

Yavneel is only a small corner of a small land. But it is one of the oldest Jewish settlements in the country, settled at the turn of the century, and in a circumscribed but defensible fashion reflects much that characterizes Israel as a whole. It is circumscribed because Israel is highly urban, and Yavneel is rural; although the typical Jewish Israeli is at most the second generation born in the country, Yavneel is into its third and fourth generation of native-born. Although the vast majority of the population is concentrated on the coastal plain, Yavneel is in a valley basin in Lower Galilee far from the "action" of the center. Notwithstanding these important differences, Yavneel reflects the Israeli reality in a startling array of ways. Like Israel as a whole, its two thousand citizens include a majority of Sephardi Jews, the so-called "eastern" or "Oriental" Jews who had lived in the Middle East and North Africa, and most of whom had arrived in the great immigration wave of the 1950s. It has an establishment core of settler-farmers whose forebears arrived at the end of the nineteenth century from Russia, Romania, and Bulgaria, and included religious traditionalists and so-called radicals or freethinkers. It has a small group of people whose grandparents converted to Judaism in Russia, two Hebrew-Christian families, and a Yemenite community that settled in 1912. Its middle-class core is Ashkenazi, the "western" Jews who came from Europe, with a sparse addition of upwardly mobile families from among the "new immigrant" "easterners," or Sephardis, while its substratum of poor industrial and agricultural workers is drawn overwhelmingly from Sephardi background. Its religious range includes Hasidic families, traditionally Orthodox, partially traditional, and secular groupings. Like most of the country, Yavneel had been formerly aligned with the Labor party and has moved steadily right since 1977, with a majority opting for the Likud in the last national elections. While once farm-oriented to the virtual exclusion of other occupations, it is steadily moving away from agriculture, with less than 20 percent of the households farming exclusively at present.

There is, however, a factor characteristic of Yavneel and about a dozen similar communities that highlights an important difference between it and the larger society: Yavneel has a rooted yeomanry with ties to the land and a relatedness to place not readily found outside these few settlements. This core group of old settler families sees matters through a prism unfamiliar and, in many respects, incomprehensible to the majority of their fellow citizens not only in the community itself, or in Israel, but in the Jewish world at large. It is a core group that sees itself, if not divinely appointed, at least cosmically guided to provide the spearhead for a return to roots and values previously understated, ignored, or obscured in the Jewish praxis.

One might see in Yavneel something of a microcosm of Israeli society after forty years of evolving statehood. In Yavneel the paradoxes, conflicts, absurdities, and something of the mystery of renewed Jewish sovereignty in Zion emerge to exaggerated and thus, for the analyst, highly useful prominence. A small corner perhaps, but as Eudora Welty observes, "one place comprehended can make us understand other places better. Sense of place gives equilibrium; extended, it is a sense of direction."[3] As noted, Yavneel is not Israel and Israel is not Yavneel. Distinguishing and unique features abound, and delineate both the larger and smaller canvasses. But having stated the caveat, one is struck by the usefulness of the smaller entity as a sounding device for analyzing and understanding, whether in opposition or fit, some prominent and dominating features of the larger context. In the very smells and sights of the town, in its human geography and its history, one is constantly made aware of what I have elsewhere called the paradoxes and confusions of Israeli society and, in no small measure, the conflicts that undergird and define its reality.

A stroll through the town exposes one to an almost promiscuous heterogeneity of people that startles, almost unnerves. It is as if a crazed impresario had made an attempt at portraying the "ingathering of the exiles" as set pieces in a tableau dramatizing this theme of national rebirth—and presented it on a small stage where everything could be seen simultaneously, replete with entrances and exits. The impact is powerful and yet not incoherent; jarring, but not quite as much as one might expect. At any given moment one might observe on Yavneel's main street Hasidim in black garb, bearded and earlocked, passing gnarled farmers driving by on their, more often than not, battered tractors, or the sons of farmers on newer equipment sporting aviator sunglasses and peaked caps emblazoned with advertising for Caterpillar or John Deere farm machinery. Housewives in tight jeans or short shorts pushing perambulators alongside ultra-Orthodox women in wigs or covered heads and ankle-length skirts over black cotton stockings. Gaggles of small Hasidic children with ice-cream smeared faces watching the "secular ones" kick a soccer ball about or shoot baskets near a tennis court where mini-skirted girls bang tennis balls over a net. Dark-skinned, wiry Yemenite shopkeepers passing Moroccan or Tunisian workers returning from long days in the fields and factories of the Jordan Valley kibbutzim. Weathered, leathery-skinned older farm women with the look of Central European stolidity marketing alongside black-eyed, worn immigrants from the mellahs of North Africa or the alleyways of Baghdad and Djerba. "Modern" Orthodox young men wearing the knitted mini-skull caps, which set them apart in more than the devotional sense as part and parcel of a comprehensive vision of renewal, studying the rules of the biblical agricultural sabbatical year with haredi newcomers whose vision is that of an older dispensation abstracted and detached from the touch and smell of turned furrows and clipped orchards. Old, retired farmers who have passed their lands along to their sons sitting on benches in the strong sunlight of the valley, passing the time of day with the only partially acclimatized former merchants and craftsmen from Tunis, or the everpresent village phenomenon in every place and every time, the *batlan,* or ne'er-do-well, who seems to survive all vicissitudes with aplomb and not a little mystery. Ashkenazim and Sephardim, European, North African, and Asian, religious, ultra-religious, traditional, and secular, light-skinned and dark-skinned, workers and farmers, newcomers and veterans, old and young, the productive and the failed, the rooted and the marginal—all are cast together in a small space they share in many aspects while still maintaining their distinct and separate ways.

## Work

It is in how Yavneel works, and how Yavneel looks at work, that we see these shared and separate visions testified to in a most salient fashion. Yavneel began as an agricultural community whose first settlers enjoyed minimal farming experience at earlier sites in the Galilee such as Metulla, Rosh Pina, and Huran, but who for the most part were not agriculturalists in their countries of origin. Many were not strangers to hardship, but for most the back-breaking work involved in premechanized farming as well as deep funds of inherited skills and knowledge were absent from their makeup. They came not with a well-articulated ideology of "the conquest of labor," but more of the benign, suggestive goals of the early *Hovevei Tzion,* the lovers of Zion, who sensed more than they could explain about the importance of Jewish labor in a Jewish land. While they had gained some agricultural experience in other settlements in Galilee there was general agreement among them that the "best" farmers were the *sabotnikim,* peasant converts from Russian Christianity who formed part of the group of first settlers. "They," it would appear, "had it in their blood," whereas for the others it was a most difficult taste to acquire. In the beginning, Arab farm laborers helped not only in teaching the settlers about the secrets and idiosyncracies of the land, but about the nature of hard physical labor as well; and with time the lessons were absorbed. The idea of work on the land, on which the Bilu movement* had focused as a core value of Jewish national renewal, became with the passage of time a key element of self-definition and a measure by which one's worth and communal standing was determined; this judgment went beyond life into the grave, where generations to follow could learn from the very tombstones that "He was a good and loyal worker." For the early settlers their achievements as tillers of the soil were not exclusively in the nature of a personal goal, but were additionally a warrant for their claim to the land and an aspect of communal renaissance. Their joy in the success of the enterprise suggests a certain astonishment in the achievement, a feeling of triumph at the results that are expressed in memoirs, celebratory speeches, and commemorative local histories. Shmuel Zimmerman, a second-generation

---

*The first modern movement for agricultural settlement in Palestine, the Bilu was founded in Russia in 1882.

settler, typifies this pattern of near awe and quasi-religious fervor when he writes:

> We were blessed in having achieved in this region of the land in the Lower Galilee and the Jordan Valley a new and special area of settlement both in its destiny and in its spirit: Hebrew peasant villagers, genuine workers of the land who draw bread from the earth. Descendants of exiles from myriad communities, a mixture of languages and customs have been gathered in one spirit to be attached to the arid lands of Galilee which were covered by the tents of Kadar [Bedouin]. A voice calls from the depths of the earth—conquer it and rule.[4]

"Hebrew peasant villagers, genuine workers of the land" has about it a tone of wonderment going far beyond reportage of simple fact. Even among second- and third-generation settlers one hears reference to work and, specifically, work on the land expressed with so much rhetorical conviction as to raise questions with regard to how naturally steeped the value had become in actual fact. It seems to be a battle still being waged and perhaps in some ways less successfully than hoped for. More and more, in the streets of Yavneel one hears the claim being made that "we don't work hard enough," or "the Arabs do all the manual work and we become more the intermediaries just like we were in the Diaspora." One hears in these comments the other side of Zimmerman's poetic triumphalism, namely the fear that the conquest of labor, the return to the values of a life based on agriculture, are, at best, tenuous.

> It's not only in agriculture that we have stopped doing our own work. Who builds the buildings, works in the factories, cleans the streets? We work less and less. Maybe it's the future, but it is not what we wanted or needed.

Often a value in decline or in question is clasped that much closer to the breast and proclaimed with greater enthusiasm and commitment than one that is unchallenged or comfortably realized. Thus, one of the most often aired complaints about out-groups or marginal residents of Yavneel is that they "don't work," or "don't work well," the first generally said of the Hasidim, and the second about the Sephardim. Perhaps underscoring the importance of the charge, the centrality of the question is seen in the fact that the accused deem it necessary to counter the accusation in some way. Itai, of North African parentage, but born in Yavneel, defensively observes that the main reason for the farmers' current economic difficulty is to be found in the fact that "they are not particularly hard workers. By hiring outside labor, instead of doing what they need to do by themselves, they have worsened their economic situation." For their part, the Hasidim lay claim to being hard workers "on the spiritual side of things," claiming that "if the farmers worked as hard at what they do as we do at what we do—the Messiah would have arrived."

Work in the village is plainly classificatory, and goes beyond its prosaic aim of providing sustenance. It is freighted with ideological and historical meaning, revolving around the attempt to distance the "new" Jewish man and woman in Zion from the perceived degradations of exile, where an unnatural, indeed unsavory, economic scaffolding held sway. Work among Yavneel's settler-farmers was not, in Maurice Godelier's term, "work in general," a discrete activity as it were, which is characteristic of the modern western context, but part of a more ancient, primitive if you will, web of experience involving politics, kinship, and religion.[5] It was and still, to some extent, is what Everett Hughes called "one of the most important parts of his [the individual's] social identity, of his self; indeed of his fate in the one life he has to live."[6]

Clearly, work and more specifically work on the land was for the early settlers a form of dialogue with a history and a destiny being denied. It was furthermore an attempt to leapfrog centuries of Diaspora separation from landed rootedness to a new affirmation of "in-placeness." The miracle, if one is to be found here, is that this revolution succeeded as much as it has. The fact that it is perceived as incomplete or threatened by a return to earlier, more deeply embedded values is not surprising. But the fear among many that they are slipping into a rejected past forms an active ingredient in the web of antipathies that flourish among the town's citizens. In commenting against the presence of Hasidim in Yavneel, a third-generation farmer bitterly observes that the world of the haredim is "a different world which expects the Messiah. They come here dressed in black, bent over. Our fathers came here dressed like that as well, but they folded their *kapotes* [black overgarments worn by the ultra-Orthodox] and went out to the fields to work. We left the Diaspora because we wanted a different life here." And indeed the vision of a "different life" is, in fact, not shared by all the town residents, and in their attitudes to work and all that is associated with it the differences run deep.

On the surface and at first meeting, Yavneel is a village of farmers and those involved with working the land. Yavneel rises early. At 5 A.M., as heavy mist still covers the valley, lights snap on in the houses of hired workers and independent farmers alike. At 5:45 the first bus leaves the town for the Jordan Valley with agricultural workers from Shikun going to the moshavim and kibbutzim where they work as hired hands. The first few tractors are taking to the fields with sleepy farmers on top. The synagogue has begun the morning *minyan*, and by 6:15 the first few women are visible dealing with household tasks. At 6:30 another Jordan Valley bus enters the town, and this together with trucks, pickups, and a few private cars successfully completes the morning start-up for work.

Between 9 and 10 A.M. and depending on the season farmers return home for breakfast, while other workers take *aruchat eser*, the ten o'clock tea break, wherever they are. Some farmers follow by going to the feed and fertilizer warehouse, which has become a sort of club or putative village square where they exchange banter, information on prices and other agricultural conditions, and a bit of hand wringing about the depressed state of agriculture and the "abased" state of the farmer. A return to the fields for most is concluded by lunch— the main meal of the day—an afternoon rest in the deep heat of Yavneel's summer, and a return to the fields when some late afternoon cooling sets in. In high season, work often continues after dark by the light of tractor and combine headlights, both to avoid the heat and to complete the task within a reasonable time.

Howard Newby has observed that agriculture is one of the few undertakings that despite technological change still remains distinctive in at least one important respect: "the length of the production cycle and the rhythms of working on the land remain largely governed by the seasons of the year."[7] Spring, summer, and fall are the seasons of heavy work in the fields, varied, multifaceted, intensive, and, even with the most advanced equipment, physically demanding. Winter is a time of slowdown, repair, planning, expectation, and recovery. Rains can be a blessing or a ruination; heat can be too intense, and can begin or end too early or too late; plant diseases, soil depletion, market rises and falls all set their stamp not only on the "rhythm" of the farmer's work, but on his life as a whole.

In their sense of work, or what they do, Yavneel's farmers are part of a shared universe of farming wherever it might exist. One might say that they share more with a farmer in Norway or France than they do with an urban dweller in Tel-Aviv, but having said this I recognize its inadequacy, perhaps its falsity. The ever-present sense of the work as in some fashion "holy work," redemptive work—a sort of wager with history where winning underscores victories well beyond good crops or higher yields—sets the Yavneel farmer and others who share this vision and this condition apart, which in the end perhaps brings them nearer to the Tel-Aviv urbanite than to their confreres in other places. Work, in the Zionist ethos, while having undergone change over the decades since the concept of renewing the Jew while building Zion, remains, though substantially weakened, a prime value, at least for that part of the population which can be seen as its inheritors. It is a prime value, but not necessarily, it must be emphasized, a universal pattern of action.

But Yavneel, and, indeed, Israel as a whole, is not comprised solely or even in its majority by East and Central European Jews and their descendants. The majority in both are now immigrants and the children of immigrants from North Africa and the Middle Eastern countries. Additionally there is now the strengthening or reemergence to importance of traditionalist groups who never shared the Zionist vision or this value. Finally, there is the element of change, perhaps decline, visible on a generational plane, where the young of both Sephardi and Ashkenazi background view matters of all kinds, not least their attitude to work, through a changing prism.

For that minority among the Sephardi residents of the town who have successfully moved into the status of independent agriculturalists—and here only two extended and about nine nuclear families stand out—there has taken place, to a large extent, an assimilation of the older settler convictions and behavior regarding the work ethic. Not coincidentally, these people are pointed out as examples of successful integration because they have adopted proper values and as proof of the fact that prejudice against Sephardim due to origin or other cultural factors does not play a key role in their low placement on the status ladder. Insofar as Sephardim are not integrated into the community and not successful, it is said to be a function of their refusal or inability to assume the burden of a work ethic thought to be the very foundation of the community. When I asked a second-generation Yavneeli of Yemenite background if his father held a conception of work as a holy undertaking, he answered that for them "work was a living and no more. In my family, success was not determined by how hard or how well you worked, but by whether you were paid more." A successful farmer of Moroccan background who is also religiously traditional observed that "we must work because we cannot rely on miracles," which also reflects an instrumental and pragmatic rather than ideological or romantic notion of work.

Given the fact that most of the Sephardim are wage laborers, both agricultural and industrial, and were not prior to their immigration in the early 1950s bearers of a secular Zionist ideology, their attitude is not surprising. For this segment of Yavneel's population work is indeed an undertaking to be measured in the hard coin of remuneration rather than in any more elevated sense. Watching Yavneel's "working class" moving off to work in the early morning hours does not inspire reflection on the joy to be gained through the "conquest of labor." For these men and women a more prosaic muse is at work.

Among the Hasidim who have moved into Yavneel since 1986 we witness even a more profound dissonance with the prevailing value structure than among the Sephardi population. Whatever the actual and ideological difference that exists between the old farmer-settlers and their descendants and the Sephardi "newcomers" and theirs with respect to any number of questions including that of work and its place in their lives, a powerful difference is perceptible among the Hasidim. Central to the different outlooks of the farmer-settlers and the Sephardim is the active presence of an ideology of labor in one group and its absence in the other. Additionally, and not to be neglected, is the conflict of outlook that exists between the propertied and the unpropertied, those with a stake of significant proportions in how they labor and those with relatively little to gain or to lose as a result of work done or undone. A worker, after all, tends to be paid the same whether or not the enterprise that employs him is making $x$ profit or only $y$ profit.

Thus, one can view the differences between the settler-farmers and the Sephardim in terms of differing practical interests, as well as cultural and, ultimately, historical contexts. With the Hasidim, however, there is in effect a contrary view of the world based on an ideology no less comprehensive, compelling, or insistent on actualization than that of the settlers with respect to labor as well as a variety of other fundamental concerns. The Hasidim embrace a theological model of life in which there is a kind of holy division of labor: the tribe of Zevulun is to work while the tribe of Issachar is to be supported by them while they do the Lord's work, or to put it more plainly, while they study Torah. This is the response, the defense most readily resorted to by Hasidim when challenged by cries of "parasitism," a term that in Hebrew takes on a veritable sneering, hissing resonance. This, together with the accusation that they do not participate in the defense of the country, are the two most damning charges aimed at the Hasidim by almost all segments of the otherwise heterogeneous non-Hasidic community and that seems to elicit reactions of pure fury among many. Fury is compounded when the rejection of these two values—work and defense—is explained in terms of a putative laboring model widely expressed by the Hasidim which states that "the society needs light and the haredim who don't work or serve in the Army take care of the generator which supplies that light while the others do the work and the fighting. When all are proper Jews, when all are haredim, some of us will work and fight. But until then, we have our holy task and it doesn't include physical work or the Army." And indeed, while other segments of the town's population are to be seen at work in the stores, fields, offices and workshops of the community, only the elderly, the very young, nonworking mothers, and the Hasidim can be seen in the streets, or in the synagogue study-hall, or at home, at all hours of the day. Clearly, this is a sector of the population not seeking renewal through labor, or the creation of a new type of Jew through a bonding process with the soil. In their total rejection of the work ethic, the Hasidim in this more than in any other way have established the reality of their "otherness," of their marginal and ultimately troubled standing in the community.

While not in opposition to the work ethic *per se* but rather in practical terms at least with respect to agricultural work, the town's non-Hasidic youth—those currently in high school and doing their army service—are closer to the haredim than to their grandfathers. Farming is in decline here as elsewhere in the country, and only a small minority of the town's youth will be able to be absorbed in this endeavor. Ironically, and in a fashion only peripherally sensed rather than expressed, an explicit cause of the opposition to the Hasidic invasion—the fear that they will change the basic agricultural tone of the town—has already taken place, and without any perceptible intervention from outside forces, certainly not the ultrareligious newcomers. With regard to work outside of agriculture, the young people of Yavneel seem to reflect the attitude of their city-bred compatriots so that they fit more comfortably into the future than into the past. One is hard pressed to conclude whether the struggle of the early settlers has been realized or perhaps lost, whether the circle has been squared or closed. Clearly a sense of mission attaching to work in general, not just farming, is absent among most of the town's young people.

The grandchildren and great-grandchildren of the founders and early settlers are focused on career rather than redemption either of a personal or collective nature. Most of those between the ages of fifteen and eighteen speak of a desire to somehow continue living in Yavneel, but are unsure how or if this will be possible in a capacity other than farming. The early settler Shmuel Zimmerman's romantic conception of working the land is as foreign to them as it is to the Hasidim, although the sense that Yavneel is the product of labor rather than revelation still acts to distinguish between the two. The fact that they are there because of what was *done* before their birth, rather than what was *revealed,* colors their sense of personal identity as well as their sense of place and belonging. They recognize the fact that they are heirs to a demanding tradition but the rhetoric as well as the reality recedes into a past which is not as easily embraced as it was by their parents' generation. The traditional phrase has it that "from generation to generation a message will be brought forward," but in the movement from ideology to pragmatism the question of "message" is, at best, obscured and, more probably, lost.

In a commemorative volume celebrating the eightieth year of the village's establishment it is noted that "in the course of Yavneel's growth, the young people fulfilled many important tasks in the life of the settlement. These revolved around four central axes: school, defense, community life, and labor."[8] However, with the radical changes introduced since 1948 and the post-independence era, only the school remains as a central "axis" of life for the town youth, their involvement in farm and workshop having declined precipitously. Work, as "a central life interest," in Lee Braude's terms,[9] continues to be honored but is decidedly peripheral as a context for self-definition. Until the 1950s, going on for a high-school education rather than working on the family farm was considered something of an affection for the children of the old settlers, and unimaginable for the children of the Shikun and the Yemenites. This is no longer the case for any of the town's subgroups, and its implications for work and attitudes to work are wide. If work in a traditional system was "at the same time an economic, political and religious act"[10]—and in some ways though radically new Yavneel was in its origins and early development an attempt to embrace a form of pastoral traditionalism—for the town's youth of whatever background it is only the economic dimension that remains viable. When asked how they viewed the future of the town, the town as it would appear in the twenty-first century, youngsters tended to speak about "maintaining its special character as a farming community," but emphasized the social, aesthetic, and visual aspects rather than the tasks they might perform. "We want to raise the level of pride in our town," said one. "Yavneel should be a clean place with low buildings and gardens." "It should remain and retain its standing as an agricultural settlement and not adopt urban ways," said another. "We need more integration between the groups which compose the town, more understanding and more cooperation." Clearly there is a prevailing sense that what could be accomplished by hard work on the land has already been achieved, and it remains for succeeding generations to reap the fruits, protect the gains (presumably through understanding and cooperation), and heal the wounds inherited from the time of the founders.

Prominent among these wounds is the persistent gulf between those whose grandfathers were among the original and early Ashkenazi settlers and those whose parents literally "found themselves" in the town when they arrived from North Africa during the great immigration of the 1950s. The comments about the town's future all come from members of the former group, descendants of the original settlers. Young people in the second group do not see themselves as inheritors either of a space or a doctrine. Work, and indeed a sense of relatedness to the community, is experienced in a manner that is much more consistent with their parents' generation. It is among these youngsters, and these alone, that I heard a desire expressed to leave for other parts, to find a trade that would liberate them, to improve their situation. Here one does not hear pious reflection on the achievements of the founders, awed respect for their presumed capacity for endless, backbreaking labor in the fields and orchards. Rather they express a desire for higher-status employment than was the lot of their fathers and mothers, a "better life" in short, to be grasped wherever it can be found—here or elsewhere. Both groups of young people are, in fact, oriented to a more individualistic conception of work, with the difference that for the Ashkenazi youth there is a perception of change as "moving on" while for the Sephardi youngsters there is more a sense of "moving out." For the children of the original settlers, the hallmark is fulfillment and changed emphasis, not actual rejection of their parents' values, while the children of Sephardi immigrants seek to dissociate themselves from a past which did not ennoble, which could not satisfy on either a personal or communal level.

## AGRICULTURE

Though the future of agriculture in Yavneel appears bleak and unpromising, the town still sees itself and thinks of itself as agricultural in nature. This perception seems to be shared by most residents, whether Ashkenazi old-timers, Sephardic "new immigrants," or Hasidic "newcomers," despite the widely understood circumstance that only 20 percent of the households earn their livings by farming and an additional 40 percent are part-time farmers. And even among the farmers few families are able to make ends meet without additional income from wives who work in nonagricultural occupations as teachers, clerks, or in various service undertakings both in and outside of the town.

The period from the late 1960s to the early 1980s is spoken of as Yavneel's "golden age" of agriculture, as it was for the country as a whole. During this time incomes were high, and expansion both in terms of farm investment and family life-style in fact exacerbated tensions between farmers in the community and nonfarmers, who clearly were not enjoying anything approximating the former's general prosperity. It was during this period that those without land most pressingly experienced the significance of this fact as setting them apart from and "lower" than the veteran settlers and the few newcomers who had farms of their own. It was also during this period that great bitterness, with its roots in a variety of causes and coming from many directions, tended to focus on this central, singular issue of the landed and those without land, which tended more often than not to correlate with being an Ashkenazi or a Sephardi, and thus provoking still an extra measure of anger. Agriculture, and more precisely agricultural ownership, signals position and status in the town, as well as demarcating between those with deep roots and inviolable attachments and those who cannot make these claims in this universally accepted coin.

On entering and moving about the town one gains the unmistakable impression that agriculture is *all* that involves its residents. The "industrial zone" is off in a corner and not really visible unless it is deliberately sought out. The few shops and services are spread out, and tend to leave visitor and resident alike with the impression that the less said about their existence the better. In any event, they do little or nothing to broadcast their existence, so that if one knows about them, well and good; and if not, you are probably not in need of their services or—you're a complete stranger in town. The characteristic odors hanging over the community and varying with the seasons are of manure, fertilizer, and cut field crops, while the sounds are those of agricultural machinery or, on the outskirts, the tinkle of bells on lead sheep or the barking of dogs busily guarding the herds. Heavy lorries moving through the town bear immense loads of tomatoes being trucked to canneries, or peppers and Chinese cabbage to be prepared for export. The busiest focal point of daytime socializing is the seed and fertilizer warehouse of the Farmers Union or the office of *Eli Bare,* the organization responsible for local water allocation. The time frame in which the town lives is heavily, if not exclusively, influenced by the agricultural cycle, both seasonally and on a daily basis, with little to suggest that only a minority of the town residents are fully engaged in that occupation. Similarly with the tempo and rhythm of daily activity, which bear about them the unmistakable mark of work on the land: a certain slowness of movement, a kind of deliberative attitude to challenges and questions of present time which have been posed and answered in myriad past times and will be addressed again in future time.

The agenda of Yavneel, the rhythm of the town, are today, as in the past, set by the dominant ethos of an agricultural community, which may be a misleading reflection of the village's demographic reality although not its chosen symbolic character. The agricultural life-style is one that the town embraces as most aptly descriptive of itself as it is and as it wants to be. Those who fall outside its parameters are less Yavneelim, if Yavneelim at all, while those within are the true progenitors of the founders' vision as well as bearers of the banner of the Jews' new relatedness to space and rootedness. And for those who are not farmers, which here means owners of farms, there exists a decided sense of being *less* of the place itself, and less in perhaps other ways, a judgment that tends to be shared by both camps. The message delivered, as well as the message received, is that being a farmer means truly being a part of the society, of arrival, of acceptance, and ultimately even of "Israeliness," whereas not being a farmer suggests the opposite. Given the utter centrality of this attitude, it is in no way surprising that land ownership and working the land have become levers of conflict and struggle between the "haves" and the "have-nots," the veteran Ashkenazi settlers and the more recently arrived Sephardim, with the Hasidim occupying a space somewhat on the fringes.

## Agricultural Beginnings

Conflict over land and the status hierarchy based on land and land ownership has characterized the community from its very beginnings and is *not* an outgrowth of the gulf between Ashkenazim and Sephardim. Although the actors and other elements of the conflict have changed over time and a new "ethnic" valence has been introduced, nevertheless land—how much and by whom it is owned and how successfully it is worked—has provided a backdrop to interpersonal relationships among the residents from the very inception of the *moshava*. During the very first years of settlement a status hierarchy emerged that had at its apex the Ashkenazi farmers sharing high status (but at a recognizably lower level) with the guards *(shomrim)* and the ritual slaughterer, who was seen as *the* local religious authority. A notch below was the doctor, who joined the moshava at the end of its first decade, and below him hired agricultural laborers, teachers, a baker, plumber, and shopkeepers. The Yemenites were also at the bottom end of the scale, but here it is not entirely clear whether their low status was a function of ethnic distinction or the fact that they were all hired agricultural laborers.[11]

Yavneel was one of a string of towns established in the Upper and Lower Galilee by Baron Rothschild, and was administered through an organization established by Baron Hirsch known by its initials as ICA (PICA as of 1924), whose purpose was the settlement of Jews on the soil of the Holy Land.[12] Baron Rothschild was a figure of considerable weight and gravity who saw himself as a patron in the full meaning of the term, interjecting himself through local agents responsible only to him in all the affairs of the settlements. The relationship between the Baron and the settlers as filtered through his agents had about it a decided feudal or, more correctly, monarchical cast; and numerous conflicts emerged between patron and farmers although in most cases it was manipulated such that disputes tended to be seen as between the Baron's local agents and the settlers. Criticizing the Baron himself was a form of *lèse-majesté* and was rarely, if ever, expressed in any public way.

Between the years 1901–4 ICA established four Jewish colonies in the lower Galilee—Yavneel, Kfar Tabor, Menachemya, and Bet Gan—that were planned to be centers for the growth of field crops. But from the very outset, problems with water, pests, soil salinity, internal rivalries, external attacks, and a further list of almost biblical woes beset the settlers. Many left in the first years, but a constant stream of replacements assured continuity and a slow, often painful, growth. Dry farming failed for lack of rain, almond groves suddenly died, tobacco growing proved inadequate, springs dried up, locusts and then mice decimated fields. But the settlers were flexible and willing to try replacement crops and a deep water source was tapped, although water remained problematic until a branch of the national water carrier was shunted to Yavneel as late as the 1950s. In 1934–35 Yavneel was hooked into the national electricity grid, and also in the 1930s the farmers finally obtained full title to their lands from PICA.

Yavneel's agricultural development can be divided into three periods. The first—from 1901 to 1932—was the period of large-scale farming, with each farmer working large areas of up to 300 dunams.* This was the period of "dry farming," with each farmer planting field crops such as wheat and barley and also maintaining a small area for home use consisting of vegetables, a few cows, goats, and chickens. This was the period when the community experimented with tobacco cultivation and other crops, but in the absence of adequate water resources most such experiments failed.

The second period began in 1932 with the drilling of a deep well, thus easing if not solving the problem of adequate water supply. This was the period of irrigated as opposed to dry farming and constituted the first "promising" era for Yavneel's agriculture. This period, too, witnessed a strong growth of an organizational infrastructure supportive of agriculture and agricultural settlements, including a co-op for collective purchasing and marketing, a framework for the control and distribution of water resources, and the cultivation of large areas devoted to orchards and citrus groves.

The third period is marked by the hook-up to the national

---

*A dunam is approximately ¼ acre.

water carrier as well as the general economic growth and demographic expansion of the country as a whole from the end of the 1950s to the start of the 1980s. During the decade of the eighties Yavneel had 170 farms with 14,000 dunams under cultivation, one-half of which was being irrigated. Farm size averaged from 60–120 dunams, with some below and a few in excess of 200 dunams. Some 2,000 dunams were devoted to winter crops; 1,100 dunams to tomatoes, mostly for industrial use; 1,000 dunams of almonds; 400 dunams of olive trees; and 300 dunams of citrus; and the remainder to mixed farming, feed crops, herds, and the like. This was the period in which Yavneel developed export crops—sweet pepper and Chinese cabbage—which enlarged not only its economic base but its sense of outreach as well. This was the time when land truly became translated into treasure, and the reality of ownership, *ba'alut* in Hebrew, turned struggling farmers into "lords of the earth."

## "Lords of the Earth": The Emergence of a Jewish Yeomanry

"Lords of the earth" is a term of opprobrium often hurled at the veteran settlers, the "core group," by those residents who see themselves as marginal or as outsiders. They are the descendants of the original or early settlers, Ashkenazim, owners of the larger farms in the community, or closely associated to farmers by descent and self-definition. They are considered by others as well as by themselves to be "true Yavneelim," in contrast to those residents of Yavneel who do not share these characteristics and thereby are relegated to partial inclusion or, in some cases, exclusion from the community. They share a belief that work on the land is, in Howard Newby's term, "a qualitatively different experience" from any other kind of work, and that "it defines for the farm worker what he *is*."[13] They are comfortable in their skins and in their place, and indeed find it difficult to think of themselves as living elsewhere or in doing other than what they do. So powerful are their ties to this particular, unique place that for many a possible move to other parts of the country is equated with leaving Israel altogether, and for a smaller minority even visiting or traveling outside the community is thought of as superfluous. Over and over again I was told by Yavneelim, "I can't exist anywhere else but Yavneel." For Yair, a fourth-generation Yavneeli, the fact that he lived in Bet Gan, some 50 feet removed from the center of Yavneel where he and his father before him were born, was "jokingly" equated with living in the Diaspora, in *Galut.* His uncle Shimon, something of the town character and a robust 80-year-old man, has never been to Elath and last visited Jerusalem in 1936. "Why do I have to go to these places," he said, "when everything I need is here." Yair's father, Joel, returned to Yavneel alone, leaving his wife who was on a two-year government contract in Copenhagen, so that he could "breathe again" in his valley. Eliezer went to Ramat Gan to seek his fortune following army service, and, as he put it, "lasted two months until I realized that this is no place for me." Yaakov, whose father left Yavneel to join a kibbutz where Yaakov was born and raised, returned to the town with his wife and children, saying "I have come home."

Yavneel's farmers know their land in a way familiar to rooted agriculturalists in other places, but which is foreign, almost incomprehensible, to most of Israel's Jewish population that was and is largely an urban one. Young people, the sons and daughters of the town farmers, can identify sections and plots of land by name, usually by their Arabic names like the *didabar,* or the *falka,* as if these clods of earth lived and breathed. For most of us this kind of knowledge is nothing short of uncanny, magical, and certainly far from the "packed suitcase syndrome" that has characterized so much of the Jewish Diaspora experience. For Yavneelim there is no sense of their bags being packed, of moving, of leaving. Indeed, one of the striking features of Yavneel is its sense of rootedness, which is clearly a factor making for a lack of communication between the farmers, the residents of Shikun, as well as the Hasidim, who bear a more traditional *Galut* set of responses to place. Even when compared to the much celebrated kibbutz pioneers, one sees a difference from the kibbutznik who tends to be a "born-again" farmer or, among latter generations, a seeker after economic and social relevance, fitting into the current social trends toward the large-scale move to industry or even outside business investment. The Yavneel farmer is not a convert; he is to the manner born.

However, the Yavneel farmer is not a peasant, but rather closer to the idea of the yeoman farmer, a freeholder, or as Webster has it "a man of commonality of the first or most respectable class." Crucial to the definition of peasantry is that they "support, through their agricultural production, not only themselves, but superimposed classes and institutions such as landlords, churches and towns that dominate them politically. . . ."[14] The Yavneel farmer bears responsibility only to himself and his family in a practical sense, although within a context of commitment to a larger entity and even to an idea of national and cultural renewal. Because of this larger commitment the image of yeomanry is somewhat tempered, but nonetheless remains strong and distinctive. The most popular film seen by a large number of Yavneel's farmers in recent years was *Jean de Florette,* based on the Marcel Pagnol novel that tells the tragic story of an obstinate farmer and his brother-in-law who make life miserable for a hunchbacked tax collector who returns from the city to his rural roots. Yavneelim saw in this drama a portrayal of their own story, their own town, and they tended to identify with *both* sides in the conflict. Although they fully understood the wish of the tax collector to leave the decadent and unfulfilling life of the city and return to the liberating, life-enhancing framework of farming, they also identified with the crafty peasant who lusted after his land and would stop at nothing to prevent the tax collector's successful homecoming. While they might balk at the tragic consequences of his actions, Yavneelim respect and elevate just those qualities of cunning, combativeness, and all-around toughness portrayed by the villain of the film at the same time that they admire the romantic, homing impulses of the hero.

Land—ownership of the land, working the land—has, from

the community's beginning nearly a century ago, been the central concern of their lives. Conflicts about land ownership and cultivation, such as water allocation, grazing rights, purchase and sale, make up a considerable proportion of the town's archival records, clearly demonstrating its centrality. Land is property, land is wealth, and those who had it did whatever had to be done not only to protect what they already had, but to enlarge it, to keep it within the family as defined both by blood and group. Thus, land is more than property; it is also a metaphor for belonging, for being part of a select group that presupposes a "within" and "without." For those who have land, there are shared memories associated with place, with struggle, and for those who don't, there is a sense of confusion—of unfulfilled longing for inclusion that cannot come about because of the unshared past whose hallmark is a very real deed of possession of rock, tree, and soil.

When speaking of the past, of the experience of their fathers and grandfathers, the core group of Yavneelim emphasizes collective struggle—struggle with PICA, the British, the Turks before them, the Arabs, as well as the conflicts among themselves. They also speak of collective suffering—heat, disease, locusts, drought, failed crops, poor markets. But the embracing framework of their memory is of having overcome, of having conquered. Loss occurred frequently; defeat never. When the Sephardi "newcomers" relate the past, however, they tend to speak of relationships to family, to non-Jews, to personal histories involving various levels of success or lack of it; and their narrative invariably sounds flat and one-dimensional, without sweep or grandeur, defeat or victory. Both groups are fully cognizant of the fact that here in Yavneel a person's worth and value is intimately tied to ownership and working of the land, and to the collective memories associated with the land.

Those members of the core group of settlers who failed to achieve ownership, and thus did not succeed as participants in the collective struggle and in the creation of a communal myth, either left the town or were relegated to a marginality no less comprehensive in its impact than what befell the Sephardi immigrants, suggesting once again that land rather than ethnic factors determined placement in the Yavneel firmament. Menashe Ben-Shimon, a frail old man of eighty-nine, is one of the very few "failed farmers" to have remained in Yavneel; and his moving account of travail, defeat, and misery has about it an almost biblical cadence that sets him apart from the yeoman pride of Yavneel in a most poignant fashion.

*Author:* Mr. Ben-Shimon, where were you born?

*Ben-Shimon:* I was born in Russia.

*Author:* In which part?

*Ben-Shimon:* In Kavkaz [the Caucasus].

*Author:* And at what age did you immigrate to Palestine?

*Ben-Shimon:* A young age, when I was six. With my family.

*Author:* How many members were there in your family?

*Ben-Shimon:* We were eight children and my father and my mother.

*Author:* Which place in Palestine did you immigrate to?

*Ben-Shimon:* We came to Yaffo, to the Yaffo port.

*Author:* And how old are you?

*Ben-Shimon:* I'm now eighty-nine.

*Author:* And after you got off the boat in Jaffa, did you and your family come straight to Yavneel?

*Ben-Shimon:* We then came to here, to Beit Gana. Yavneel did not yet exist.

*Author:* So you came straight here to the Arab village?

*Ben-Shimon:* To Beit Gana, to the settlement on the hill.

*Author:* And what was it called?

*Ben-Shimon:* Bet Jen.

*Author:* Bet Jen, that is the same as in Arabic?

*Ben-Shimon:* Yes, the same.

*Author:* By the way, do you speak Arabic?

*Ben-Shimon:* I understand Arabic. When I came, I lived among the Bedouins. When we came to Jaffa, an Arab approached us and wanted us to buy a vineyard of 10 dunams from him. And . . . and so my father said, what will we plant there? We'll plant wheat, we need to have flour to eat. And so we came to Migdal and there was no water tower, and there was a lot of malaria; we were burning up all the time and so what were we to do? So we moved to Rosh Pina. In Rosh Pina we received a farm.

*Author:* Were you given a certain number of dunams and a plot of land?

*Ben-Shimon:* In Rosh Pina? We were given a wooden shack, it wasn't a real plot, but the land was at a distance of about 4 or 5 dunams from the moshava and so we would sleep there in the field until we had finished reaping and harvesting and then we would return to the moshava. And there was nothing to eat, the Arabs would steal what we had planted in the night, so what were we to do? We were in Rosh Pina for three years, with nothing to eat, and they started building Migdal, and so father said that we should move to Migdal, we'd all have bread, so we moved to Migdal and worked there. My father was a carpenter, my older brother worked in agriculture. My sister worked in the garden, and so we had some bread to eat. And then we said there is no school in Migdal in which to study, and so we moved to Sejarah, and we were there for three years as well and then we moved to Petah Tikva. In Petah Tikva, I had another brother and we studied at a Talmud Torah. And then the World War started, and there was no bread, what to do, no bread at all, there was none to be found with the war and so I was there for a while, and then a great many locusts came and ate everything, all the orchards, and everything was left bare. Especially bad were the small ones that came out of the eggs, which were worse. And then what were we to do? We sat there for about a week, and then we were told to collect the eggs. Their eggs are sort of long. In each egg there were one or two hundred, and so I was a young boy and I would go around collecting these eggs, a *rotel* a day, you know a *rotel* is 2.5 kilos, it was a Turkish weight. The Turks were here then. And so I'd collect a great many for ten *grush,* and so we were there for a long time, and there was no bread, nothing to eat. Then I moved and started working for a farmer.

*Author:* There in Petah Tikva?

*Ben Shimon:* No, here in Bet Gan.

*Author:* Did you come here alone or with your family?

*Ben-Shimon:* With my family. My mother would collect bales of wheat in the field and she would beat it in the field and sift it for wheat. So each time she would go and each time she would

|  |  |
|---|---|
|  | collect a sack. And so we had food to eat. And so I moved here and worked for a farmer for eight or ten years—just for a little bread. |
| *Author:* | Is your family known around here? |
| *Ben-Shimon:* | They were here. |
| *Author:* | Are they still here? |
| *Ben-Shimon:* | Father left here, he went somewhere else, mother lived here. |
| *Author:* | Your father left the family? |
| *Ben-Shimon:* | Yes, because there was no family peace. And so he went to Ein Harod, with the *g'dud* [early Zionist labor battalion], and he worked there, and he worked on the Haifa-Hadera road and then in Migdal, and then in Jerusalem making stones for construction with the *g'dud*. So it was just mother and us. I worked for the farmer, I worked hard. |
| *Author:* | You mean *your* father left the family. |
| *Ben-Shimon:* | Father left, he fought with mother. |
| *Author:* | I thought you meant the father of someone else for whom you worked. |
| *Ben-Shimon:* | No, it was my father, and so I worked for the farmer for eight years just for bread, he didn't have anything in the field; then there was no combine, we did everything by hand, and I would do the raking and we would get up early in the morning and come with a cart to collect the wheat and take it to the silo. Each farmer had his own silo and then we would thresh the wheat, using horses. And so I worked for eight years. I had to work, there was nothing to eat. And what more is there to tell? |

This unedited account of personal, social, and physical hardship, which conveys a mood of almost unrelieved marginality more reflective of the experience of Sephardi newcomers than of the Ashkenazi settlers, provides a striking counterpoint to the yeoman experience of the core group. Contrastingly, in early accounts of the first settlers who arrived at about the same time as Ben-Shimon, we again hear biblical cadences, but with significant differences. Ben-Shimon has resonances of a poor and threatened tribal patriarch, Jacob sending his sons to Egypt to "search" for bread, while the coming of the early settlers to Yavneel Valley vividly recalls the tenacity of Jacob's descendants coming out of the desert to lay claim to the land of Canaan, after first "spying it out" and seeing that it was good. The latter impression emerges from the following account of the settling of Yavneel as told by Avraham Kosnitsky in his book *B'terem Ha'ir Ha-Boker* (*Before Daybreak*):

> The Baron's agents in Palestine received a message from Paris that no more land was to be purchased in Metulla, but that for farmers who were willing to settle in the Lower Galilee there would be support. Settlers from Rosh Pina and Sahem Julan had already visited the area, and after a long night of discussion and debate, it was decided that ten farmers from Metulla and two other settlements would be sent to look around and to collect impressions and gather information about the area. They were told by the ICA agents that the land was very promising with ample water from springs flowing from the mountains. They were told about the goodness of the land by settlers in Rosh Pina and by a local Arab who praised Yama [Yavneel] highly and they decided to go to this place. Within one week of arrival three huts were built and the men of Yama immediately set about cultivating the land.[15]

For those who remained and those who followed in the formative period of the community, there emerged a bonding process with the land along with a type heretofore unknown in the Jewish constellation of *Galut*. Instead of wealth or learning as the standard of excellence, skill with a plough or scythe and tenacious defense of property and other rights assumed the position of a higher value. In place of resignation before events determined elsewhere and by others, whether by the Baron, the Turks, the British, or the Arabs, the Yavneeli struggled forcefully to impose his will and protect his place. A fierce sense of independence, of autonomy, grew to replace a felt historical dependence, so much so that Yavneelim to this day refuse to identify leader figures among themselves, answering "we are all about the same." Being born in Yavneel, being a native son or daughter of the place, carries with it an ennobling quality, a birthright, which can be lost but would be difficult, if not impossible, to earn.

The Yavneeli is a bucolic figure, even phlegmatic, but, as the following anecdote shows, a person given to quick action in the face of danger or challenge. In dramatizing the distinction between the heroic Yavneel veteran and the fearful Sephardi newcomer, the story also points up how deeply embedded are ethnic stereotypes in the myth of the founders.

## A Yavneel Story

> Recently, a town resident of Sephardi background was driving from Smadar toward the center of town. As he slowed to make a turn onto the main road, three men waiting by the side of the road mistook his slowing as an offer of a hitch. One opened the door and two proceeded to enter the car, whereupon the driver, realizing that the hitch-hikers were Arabs, panicked, struck one of the men, and fled from the scene, leaving the car with the motor running to run off the road and into a tree. The driver yelled that terrorists were in the town and even identified their weapons as the favored Kalashnikov. A call by radio and telephone quickly went out to the effect that terrorists had taken a car and driver hostage. Yavneel sprung into action. Within minutes townspeople appeared in the streets with their weapons, the police sealed off the entire valley, sappers and dogs were brought to the scene. When everything was in place, one of the town's leading farmers showed up in his car together with the three putative terrorists who, as it turned out, were none other than an Arab shepherd and two of his sons (one a soldier in

uniform carrying his M-16 and *not* a Kalashnikov). They had worked in the town and been known to its residents for many years. For the veteran settlers who recounted the story the message was clear: there is a true Yavneeli who *acts* firmly, quickly, and with great vigor, in contrast to those given to unfounded and crippling fears.

The Yavneeli is a hunter, a stalker. He loves the wadis, the fields, the mountains, all that is weather and earth—all things powerful. Like the one who is *not* his ancestor, he is a wild ass of a man. This is the mythic Yavneeli, the Yavneeli celebrated and upheld as an example of historic liberation from an equally mythic and rejected past; and as with all such constructs the detritus of reality, of wide difference, litters the edges of myth—tempering, softening, leveling. One can tell much about a society from the characterological types it elevates and those which it denigrates, but it is, of course, not the whole story; the interstices as well as the bold verticals and horizontals form no less an important part of the tale. The talents of Esau might be valued, but the figure of Esau is not. The Yavneeli is ever conscious of a tie to a past that is not utterly rejected, not completely without grace, in which the commitment to word and precept holds a place of honor, and continuity rather than change is pursued.

Change for the yeoman farmer is to be embraced in matters of technology, but eschewed in other domains. For the true Yavneeli, the past is sacred. "This is our home; our fathers and grandfathers came here and we don't give up easily. We want to keep the place as it was and as it is. We have roots here. The others [the Sephardim] want to advance and to climb up socially, those who don't have the land—they want factories and jobs so that they can prosper. I understand, but I don't want it to change." Eva Tokatly is the great-granddaughter of a founder and in her comment there is an innate understanding of the tie to the land from which a life-style established in the far past flows into the present and into the future. As Jamaica Kincaid rightly observes, "to the people in a small place the division of time into the Past, the Present, and the Future does not exist. An event that occurred one hundred years ago might be as vivid to them as if it were happening at this very moment."[16]

The importance of freeholding is understood not only by the core group of veteran settlers. Those without land, or who have only in the last few years managed to put together a small farm of 40 to 60 dunams, are no less keyed in to its ramifications. Roni, who is not a farmer but is something of a spokesman for his fellow Sephardim, observes that "land is property. A person who works the land or wants to work on the land believes that this country belongs to us all and wants his share too. Why should land go only to those whose parents already have land enough of their own? The veterans do not give an inch, they will not divide the land." Moshe, also not a farmer and of Sephardi origin, accuses the Yavneeli farmer of having a mean streak: "They are vicious; they withheld land that should have been distributed in order to have it for their own sons. They didn't help us, they didn't give us instructions in farming, so that we would fail. They let us flounder and sink." Yaakov, a Yemenite handyman and a third-generation Yavneeli, concurs, asking, "Why did they want us to fail? How would it have hurt them if we had succeeded?"

While those outside of the core group understand that freeholding is *the* major factor in the local status hierarchy, and in the holding and wielding of power, and while they understand yeomanry as a metaphor of arrival, they tend not to share nor really to fathom the depth of these ties which not only characterize but have shaped an identity—an identity still foreign and elusive to them as it is to most of the country's citizens for whom land is property and little else. "This land, this land you are standing on now was first ploughed and planted by my father before I was born. My father's generation were heroes. They were the originators of Hebrew pioneering labor." While this statement of the founding myth may be trite and sloganeering in tone, it is nonetheless deeply felt as a defining context *and* a heavy responsibility. Among Yavneel's yeoman there exists a firm commitment to hold the land and to pass it along to the following generation, a desire that is bound by both personal and wider national constraints. "A disaster awaits us as a result of the move to the cities," observes one of the farmers. "We as a people are surrounded by enemies and land is our only hope, our future. If Jews will live only in cities they will cease to live there too. I love the land, I love to be in the fields and even now I work as much as I can [the speaker is partially disabled as a result of a work accident]. My sons too want to work the land. . . . A people without land is not a people."

Yavneelim are among the few in our midst who have had the necessary time to form this rather "foreign" relatedness to place. Time and a relationship to space are ineluctably tied one to the other. One or two generations in place are, it would seem, not enough for the creation of memory of a rooted kind. The Jewish sense of national memory, other than in an ontological sense, has been underexercised for millennia, and no artificial construct based on the needs for group survival or myth creation can replace the natural passage of time in the formation of deep memory. Jewish Diaspora culture is epiphenomenally one of eschatological time, where space is abstracted, whereas that of a farming community, where generation follows generation and land is passed from old to young, is, perhaps, above all, one of space. Here time and space are intimately linked, bringing a sense of security that has so often been absent among Jews. Jews have represented in history a near-classical formulation of cultural portability, a culture which has demonstrated continuity and tenacity in the *absence* of rootedness in place.

Most of us are still edgy, still uncomfortable with this new formulation of place and time. We tend to nervousness over its inevitable toll on the web of familiarity that every culture with a hold on its bearers must claim in order to function. "What connection is there between space awareness and the idea of future time and goal?" asks Yi-Fu Tuan. "How do we describe 'familiarity,' that quality of 'at homeness' we feel toward a person or a place?," he continues. "Are space and place the environmental equivalent of the human need for adventure and safety, openness and definition? How long does it take to form a lasting attachment to place?"[17] Answers are tentative, inexact with regard to Yavneel, but one nevertheless senses outline and direction in the simplicity of spoken experience and the boldness of behavior. The Yavneeli farmer strides his earth with a sense of ownership and deep familiarity enveloping his existence with a cloak of adventure and yet providing an overarching feeling of safety. Here is his place of nurturance—as it was for his father and his father before him.

## Two Yavneelim

Asa is in his middle sixties and Shimon is eighty. They are both grandsons of farmers, and although Shimon no longer farms, their personalities and even values tend to be closer than either would admit, given that Asa is a rabidly religious born-again Jew while Shimon sees himself as an unreconstructed atheist and spiritual cynic; and while Asa is a dedicated and outspoken political reactionary with strong racist leanings, Shimon tilts toward the traditional labor-socialist perspective that dominated the town's politics and outlook until relatively recently.

### Asa

Asa is a picaresque character whom only a novelist could do justice in describing. He is immediately recognizable riding through the town on his beat-up old tractor, white beard, and earlocks blowing in the wind with a faded old work hat, the *kova tembel*, on his head. He generally seems to be going somewhere, but he's never rushed and is invariably willing to set aside time for a tipple of Arak or a coffee. He is *always* ready to engage in what passes for conversation, which for him is generally either a monologue or a prepared grilling of his interlocutor, where there tend to be right and wrong answers, very little in the way of ambiguity, and at times, as follows, a rather surprising denouement.

*Author:* Where is your family?

*Asa:* Traveling.

*Author:* Switzerland? [His wife is Swiss and she visits family there.]

*Asa:* No! No! It is forbidden to leave Israel now. The Messiah is about to come. Right away! Now!

*Author:* How are things otherwise?

*Asa:* Flowers, he [the mayor] plants flowers all over town while ignoring the only true and real flowers—our children.

In addition to preparing me for the immediacy of the Messiah's coming, which he is wont to do on innumerable occasions, Asa in his rather telegraphic and seemingly disconnected fashion was also calling my attention to the general skewing of values in the town, where resources are expended on the ephemeral and superficial rather than, as the Torah counsels, on the permanent and elevated. Asa is an extremely physical type—lean, muscular, and strong. He is a fighter, a soldier, which in the Yavneeli constellation is a placement rather high on the ladder of achievement. He has been a fighter since his teens, when the British were the enemy, having any number of successes of derring-do to his credit. In his youth, and because of his hell-raising attitude to life and his demonstrated courage, he was known to the townspeople as "Black Asa," a name that followed him into World War II as a soldier in the Jewish Brigade and later in the War of Independence as an officer in Moshe Dayan's famous elite strike force. Although a notorious cut-up and rake throughout his early years, he seemed to embody the most dearly held values of Yavneel yeomanry—courage, strength, chutzpah, love of the land, and commitment to farming as a way of life and as a channel for personal and communal fulfillment.

After the failure of his first marriage, Asa seemed to go to pieces, withdrawing into himself until he came close to death as a result of a motorcycle accident that took place on the holiest day of the Jewish calendar, Yom Kippur. When he recovered, "Black Asa" put aside the life-style of his youth and became deeply religious and, most uncharacteristically for the newly observant, the born-again, he contracted a marriage with a young, deeply religious Swiss Christian volunteer, who converted to Judaism and with whom he has raised a family of five children.

In addition to field crops, Asa's farming consists of a large stand of olive trees, fruit orchards, and a substantial herd of goats and sheep with whom he is not loath to converse in a combination of Hebrew, Arabic, and Yiddish, along with a range of guttural sounds seemingly understood by the beasts in his care, but mysteriously unfathomable to the casual bystander. For Asa, any learning, any study not connected to Torah, is not only unedifying, but also a distraction from the pursuit of true understanding. I would invariably be greeted by his challenging "Nu, sociologist, have you learned anything worthwhile today?," which left the unmistakable impression that the work of the sociologist is no proper work at all and, even worse, without redeeming value.

Asa is a man of great passion and utterly tenacious with respect to his beliefs and prejudices, which are legion. In his lexicon Arabs are interlopers, "Johnny-come-latelys" with no legitimate claim to any part of "Eretz Yisrael," the Promised Land of Israel. "It would," he avers, "be best for all if they would leave and go to a place of their own," but he feels no need to identify that place. He would not hesitate to forcefully remove the Arabs, but in any event is certain that with the imminent arrival of the Messiah that particular problem will be dealt with by a higher authority. He will not compromise with the forces of irreligion or violators of what he considers religious law or propriety. For example, when a number of Yavneelim who were in conflict with the local rabbi called in an army chaplain to officiate at the graveside ceremonies in honor of fallen soldiers on Memorial Day a few years ago, Asa demanded that the community's properly empowered rabbi be allowed to act, with matters almost coming to blows. While

Asa wants and looks forward to the time when all Jews will take upon themselves the "yoke of the Torah," living lives of religious punctiliousness if not perfection, he has only one real test for determining whether or not he can relate to you prior to this divine hope being realized; and that is your response to the question, "do you accept that Eretz Yisrael is the land of the Jews?" If the answer is "yes," sufficient common ground has been established for carrying on the conversation. Discussions with Asa can be both mentally and physically exhausting. Asa shouts, looks to the heavens for corroboration, all the while pummeling his adversary, grabbing him by the arm or shoulder in a vise-like grip, presumably for emphasis, that carries with it a sort of mild menace. "Does it not say in the Torah that the land should rest on the seventh year," he asks, "and is there therefore any reason not to insist that this is how we are intended to farm?" "Do you agree that this is written," he asks, or glaringly, stepping back a bit, "do you have a different Torah?"

Thus, farming for Asa is not only a way of life to which he was educated, but it also frames for him the biblical past of his communal and personal sacred history, placing him within a context of religious legitimacy. One labors because one must earn one's bread by the sweat of the brow; and it is not without significance that traditional Judaism—the Bible, the Mishnah, the Talmud—apotheosizes agricultural labor rather than any other kind. Quotes from the Bible, the Sages, the Talmud spring readily to his lips and the sources are a constant font of contemporary and, often, still meaningful folk wisdom. Things happen today and will occur tomorrow because of what took place in the past.

There is an earthiness about Asa which somehow doesn't quite jibe with the picture usually associated with his kind of aggressive religious orthodoxy, among those who share his religious beliefs and practices but not his tie to land and place. In this he is unselfconsciously a throwback to the Israelite of old, the bearer of sword and book, a man for whom time had both a "canonical" and a "natural or seasonal" dimension.[18]

Contrary to what might be expected given his seeming obsession with the coming of the Messiah and the need for *t'shuvah,* or return to the faith, he is anything but dour and stiff; instead, he is always ready to joke, breaking forth in Rabelaisian laughter with only the slightest provocation. However, his humor tends to the ironical, and requires a fair amount of "insidedness" to fully or even partially fathom. In this he is rather like "Tevya," and to miss the reference in tradition or the source in Bible or Talmud is to be left somewhat befuddled.

Asa's material life-style is one of simplicity, indeed involves a certain spartan rejection of the rather gaudy aesthetic that dominates in the society at large. It is a life-style that rejects ostentation in favor of even a certain seediness; and one would be hard-pressed to know from his surroundings whether he was a successful or failed farmer. For him, success clearly is to be expressed and demonstrated in ways other than the purchase of a new automobile, or Scandinavian furniture, or even a new tractor.

Asa is one of those absolutists who see the world through tinted spectacles in which there is good and bad, true and false, success and failure, us and them; where lines of demarcation are clear and unsullied by hesitancy or compromise. It is a guided world, a world amply provided with direction through the singular device of God's Revelation in His Torah as interpreted by the rabbis, the sages, the forefathers. It is not for us to tamper or to change, but rather to hear and to obey.

## Shimon

Shimon, a spry eighty-year-old with twinkling, cold blue eyes set into a weather-beaten face, is seemingly the mirror opposite of Asa. Where the one is deeply religious, the other is a militant atheist and scoffer; where Asa revels in a sort of stygian political conservatism, Shimon adopts a rather attenuated liberal and mildly socialist outlook; where the one sees authority in legal-traditional terms, the other favors cold rationality. As might be expected, they barely speak to each other. But putting this existential curiosity aside, an observer cannot help but be struck by the degree to which both express the nature of the Jewish yeoman of the third commonwealth, and by how their shared characteristics must be seen as greater than their very real and significant differences.

Shimon, though now in his ninth decade, goes to work every day in the metal shop, which produces farm carts of various sizes and types, run by his nephew Oren. He wears shorts and British colonial-style knee-socks the year round, taking pride in his immunity both to the ravages of time and the demands of the seasons. Shimon proudly observes that he doesn't own a coat, a suit, or a tie. The only difference between his "dress wear" and his work clothes is that the former is crisp khaki while the latter are "yishuv" blue. He doesn't own a car, doesn't know how to drive, and rarely leaves Yavneel. When he does leave, the parameters of his excursions tend to be Tiberias, in order to lodge some complaint about the local rabbi with the police or other authorities, and Afula, for medical treatment of a kind unavailable in the village. He can be seen riding his bicycle at very specific hours of the day: in the early morning from his house on the main street to his workshop, about 200 meters away; at 10 A.M. to the grocer's for the purchase of the day's modest food needs for himself and his wife; and again at 1 P.M. when he returns home for lunch and an afternoon rest. His afternoons are generally spent in his extensive and cluttered garden, where in addition to fruit trees he raises a wide variety of flowers and plants of which he is very proud.

Shimon did not inherit the family farm. He remained a bachelor until rather late in life, whereas his younger brother had already married and raised a family, thus leveling a claim that seemed fair and logical in the context of inheritance as practiced in the town. But he still sees himself as a farmer and a descendant of farmers, and indeed his life-style, his values, his perceptions, as well as the tempo and rhythm of his life are those formed in the crucible of an agricultural culture. "I started to work when I was eleven years old and now I am eighty and still working and will continue until I die. I can't stand it when I see people who don't work. It doesn't *have* to be farm work; it can be anything, but if Jews come here and don't work they have no place among us." While defending work in general as a fundamental value, Shimon clearly sees nonagricultural work as something of a compromise. He is proud of his grandfather and father because of their achievements as agriculturalists and encourages the nephews who have inherited his family's lands to stay in agriculture even though the economics of the undertaking are far from promising. As proud as he is of his family's agricultural commitment, he takes no less pride in his background as the *rabash,* or security officer, of the town for many years, including the period of the War of Independence.

Shimon, too, has a ready sense of humor, although, unlike Asa, his tends to the passing along of corny jokes and childlike riddles, almost always pointed and having current local implications, and thus generally grasped only by initiates. His material life-style is that of a poor man. His home is dark and dank, the plaster peeling from the walls in many spots, and the furniture looking like it was donated by a social service agency or, at best, purchased as very extensively "used." He and his wife are vegetarians, and for this reason as well as for more symbolically laden ones, they eat sparingly and simply. He jokes that the rabbi and the Hasidim can eat in his house, the house of an atheist and scoffer, more readily than in the homes of more traditional Jews because of the total absence of meat or flesh in any form.

As Asa is tenacious and unyielding in his commitment to religious orthodoxy, Shimon is no less so in his dedication to the role of the antireligious *apikoras,* defender of the community's values from what he views as the inroads of a parasitical religion that aims to undermine insidiously what prior generations had so laboriously created. Asa legitimates his value structure in terms of continuity with the religious beliefs and practices of the founders, whereas Shimon, using as it were the same data base, claims legitimacy on the basis of historical continuity. One sees the generation of the grandfathers as men of faith, the other sees them as heralds of change, and of secularization, and both can become enraged when challenged in their assumptions. As Shimon argues:

> There were religious people among the founders—my grandfather was religious, but my father was not and others were *hofshim* [free thinkers] or, as they were called, "radicals." They throw sand in our eyes when they claim Yavneel was always a religious community. We respected the needs of the religious like not riding past the *shul* on horseback on Shabbat, or not going demonstratively to the fields on holy days, but that was it. This place was never a religious settlement.

Both Shimon and Asa cultivate a widely shared perception of their fathers' and grandfathers' generation as larger than life, heroes who were able to turn wasteland to value, lives of sedentary apathy to ones of active self-definition. Andrew Delbanco saw a very similar process at work among the descendants of the Puritans in America, noting that "it was the founders' children who began to transform them from full and feeling human beings into simplified figures of inimitable heroism." He suggests that the sons dealt with "feelings of smallness" beside their larger-than-life fathers "by exalting the fathers extremely and by appointing themselves guardians of their patrimony."[19] Shimon guards not only the memory of immediate predecessors, but through his love and involvement with archaeology, and specifically the archaeology of ancient Yama, he joins himself to the far as well as the immediate past "when giants strode the earth." His sense of deep attachment to place is reinforced with each crumbling stone wall excavated in the unprepossessing *tel* that was prebiblical Yama; and where others see the remains of a rather unimpressive site, Shimon speaks of the place as a possibly important way-station between the sea and Mesopotamia, and later, after the conquest by Joshua and on into the Talmudic period, a place of significant Jewish settlement. Pointing to probable grain storage remains at the excavation, Shimon observes:

> This is Judaism for me; not all that mumbo-jumbo of the rabbis and the other parasites. And I am no less a Jew than they are; I say I am a better Jew and closer to the real Jews than they are. In my house the Bible is no less read than in that thief's house [meaning the local rabbi] but I'm looking for something else there than he is.

Both Shimon and Asa hold their fathers' and grandfathers' generations in awe and seek to extend even beyond their ancestors' ties to the past, but each in a different way: Asa through traditional religion and Shimon through what he thinks of as secular archaeology. However, the end result is remarkably similar: a binding tie to place and a sense of time that is, in David Graybeal's term, "durational and qualitative."[20] Things happen when they *should* happen, response must be forthcoming, and although the tradition is interpreted or read differently, it is from this fount that any event or action will be determined. Asa sees in the coming of the Hasidim to Yavneel a strengthening of these ties to the past; although he accepts the value of labor as a personal commitment, which he could no more easily shed than he could his deep traditional religiosity, he also accepts the notion of a sort of sacred division of functions, as in the Zevulun-Issachar model. For Shimon the arrival of the ultra-Orthodox is viewed as a breach with and rejection of the community's values, to be opposed in the most forceful manner.

It is, in the end, how both relate to the newcomers, the Hasidim, that we recognize a very significant difference between the two men. Asa, while a Yavneel yeoman in almost all important respects—the temporal time sense, commitment to farming and rootedness in place, tenaciousness, physicality, and courage—ultimately resorts to a traditional religious yardstick to determine affiliation and belongingness. For him, it is Jewishness as expressed in a commitment to traditional, Orthodox religious beliefs and behavior that determines inclusion in the world of Yavneel, which in the end is only *one* place and not the whole of the map of Jewry. Asa's religious convictions have pulled him back to a traditional calculus of involvement, which does not permit the exclusion from full participation of any Jew, whether newcomer or veteran, worker or *batlan* (ne'er-do-well). On the surface, he is in most ways a classic example of the new Jewish farmer in Zion, but in his actions and conviction he demonstrates a skein of continuity with Diaspora models of Jewish identity as they have emerged in history.

Shimon, on the other hand, distinguishes between natives and outsiders such that the stranger is rarely "fully accepted into the heart of village life and knowledge."[21] In his rejection of religion, to say nothing of Orthodoxy, Shimon has adopted a new yardstick for measuring degrees of inclusion or exclusion whose parameters are local birth, Zionist conviction, labor on farms and in workshops, love of place, and a sense of tie to the deep past of the biblical Israelite.

Asa's and Shimon's views of the world meet at any number of points, bound together, as are the two men, by a high degree of commonality and more shared experiences than otherwise. But in the end their distinct and opposing religious outlooks highlight the existence of a chasm typical not only of Yavneel but of the larger society of which it is a part. In affirming traditional religious Orthodoxy, Asa represents a pulling back to the outlook and values of Diaspora Judaism, albeit with a new overlay of rootedness to place and commitment to a life of labor on the land where rhythms are determined not only by nature but by divine precept and biblical precedent. Here the early Zionist vision of a revolution of consciousness is transposed into a correction, an addition, but hardly a rejection. What was, was good; what is, is better. For Asa, being a Jewish farmer in the Jewish land is necessary but hardly sufficient.

Perhaps because he so naturally fits into his environment—both physical and psychological—Asa is unconcerned by any fear of slipping back into a cultural mode sneeringly referred to by many as *Galutiut* or "exileness." But for Shimon, who seemingly is no less comfortable in his skin, this threat hangs like a sword of Damocles over both the community and the country at large. As he sees it, traditional religion carries with it the threat of return to values rejected by his forebears because, among other reasons, they had failed as a context for a "normal" configuration of Jewish peoplehood as well as a pattern of daily existence for the individual Jew. All the paraphernalia of Jewish Orthodoxy, from distinctive dress to involvement with Talmud study, to de-emphasis of physicality, are to him not merely unacceptable but repulsive, to be rooted out or at least forcefully isolated if woe is not to befall the common enterprise. Asa hears the echoes of Sinai, of divine commandment—thou shalt, thou shalt not; everything in its season and a season for everything. For him God speaks through his prophets and sages and wise men about what is to be done, and by whom, and when and how.

For Shimon, God is mute; it is nature that communicates. Not prophets but stones and wind bear a message of uplift and liberation, if not direction, and it is this voice that must be heard if we are not to slip once again into a void of "holy dependency" and ultimately shameful irrelevance. Shimon's voices come not from Sinai, but rather from the less majestic, less awe-inspiring wadis and hillsides that form the physical crucible of his life, and the voice heard is not God's but the poet's whose remove from God, like Shimon's, was less than met the eye.

In a letter to Yaakov Fichman, the great Hebrew poet Chaim Nachman Bialik described a night in Yavneel, which he had visited in 1909:

> In all my days of wandering in the land I don't remember one moment in which I was more in touch with my soul. It was a night in Yavneel which has become etched in my memory. Not really a night, but the moment that comes with the beginnings of dawn. It was the eve of Sabbath; I woke from my sleep and managed to distance myself at that last moment when the fading stars were hanging over the abyss and when the air had a sharp metallic feeling and at the same time a deep, delicate flavor of ambrosia.
>
> Suddenly, I heard a sound of singing in the distance. Beyond, I saw a moving shadow, a man from whom the singing came. This melody I shall remember until my last days. It floats

lightly and clearly merging with the landscape enveloped in a bluish twilight as if coming not from the soul of man but from the depths of the mountain. I was overcome. I wanted that moment to last forever.

This unique and secret hour I took with me from the land of Israel.[22]

# 2

## And Prophecy Departed from Israel: Yavneel's Religion

THE BREAK-OF-DAWN activity typical of Yavneel during the week is absent on the Sabbath, although a goodly number of tractors can be heard leaving to perform pressing tasks in the fields. Chaim Nachman Bialik would not have witnessed that sight for two reasons, the most obvious of which is the absence of tractors until the forties and, more importantly, nobody— even the most "radical" deniers of traditional observance— would have dared to publicly violate the Sabbath. In rare instances when an attempt was made to transgress the Sabbath, the community would close ranks to bring the miscreants to bay "for the sake of peace" if not for deeper concerns of a residual religious nature being infringed upon. Misha, a third-generation resident who thinks of himself as an atheist and, more importantly, the son of parents whom he describes as being far from Orthodoxy in both behavior and belief, observes that "when I was a kid we went to shul every Saturday; we tended to observe the Sabbath." He continues:

> I will tell you a story. In the period 1936–39 we used to work in the fields in groups because of the security factor. One year (I don't remember which) we had a big problem with mice eating the crops so we younger fellows decided to stay in the fields over the Sabbath in order to watch and also to work. Just before sunset and the onset of *Shabbat* my father rode out on his horse and ordered me back. I could not work on Saturday even if it meant considerable loss. I don't know if it was religion, but it was certainly tradition at work here.

Wandering about Yavneel on a Sabbath day in 1991, I ask myself the same question posed by Misha as to what "is at work here." Clearly, the fact that some farmers have set out for their fields, and that music can be heard coming from radios in some homes, and automobiles are fairly extensively in use puts Yavneel at some distance from an "observant community." No one would mistake Yavneel for Mea Shearim or B'nai B'rak,[1] or dozens of moshavim and other settlements that define themselves, identify themselves as *dati,* or Orthodox.

But neither would one come away with the impression that Yavneel is totally secular, or religiously neutral. Little Yavneel with a population of two thousand has within it no less than seven synagogues. At no spot inside the community can one fail to hear the sound of prayer emanating from a variety of buildings ranging from the main community shul to the tiny concrete-block room that is home to the Yemenite minyan. All, it is true, are populated by small groups ranging from the twenty to thirty or so worshipers at the main synagogue to barely a quorum of twelve at both the central Sephardi synagogue in Shikun and the Yemenite shul and the dilapidated house serving as a synagogue in Smadar. In all, the seven synagogues probably account for no more than one hundred worshipers on any given Sabbath, almost totally male and in large measure comprising only the middle-aged and the elderly. From this observation one could assume that traditional religion is in retreat here. Places of worship that draw upon so limited a segment of the population—limited *and* unrepresentative—suggest at the very least a low level of involvement with the formal religious structure. And, indeed, with the exception of the newly arrived Hasidim, who are not included in these numbers, this is a fairly accurate account of what in fact is the case in Yavneel.

Yavneelim are not overly involved with formal worship or the life of the synagogue. The larger synagogues reverberate with the echoes of empty places while the smaller ones give off a flavor of sectarian otherness, or in some cases even defeat. On the Sabbath Yavneelim are primarily to be found at home puttering around the house or performing homely tasks of one kind or another. But it would be incorrect to assume that Shabbat is comparable to Sunday in European or American society, although on the surface the comparison is inescapable. This is so not because the comparison would not hold on a house-to-house or person-to-person basis, but because it does not hold in a collective, communal sense. When taken together, there are signs, signals, and behavioral patterns that suggest continuity, albeit changed, of a group-oriented celebratory framework.

*Shabbat* for most Yavneelim might not be holy in an accepted Orthodox sense, but it is certainly other than profane. From Friday afternoon as the town begins to close down and slow up until the close of Sabbath, one cannot escape the sense of changed rhythms and altered agendas. Bustle is absent, shops are closed, houses are cleaned, flowers cut for the table, main meals for the family and, in some instances, the clan are prepared; the aroma of cakes being baked seems to permeate the air. With sundown the last of the young soldiers on leave for the weekend have managed to reach home, mixing with the observant on their way to synagogue, and a general sense of ease, of corrective retreat from the mundane, prevails. Friday evening and Saturday are the only days in the week when Yavneelim take a stroll as well as visit with each other and with family. In many homes candles are lit and in some the blessing over wine is recited. It is, in fact, the rare house in town where the day is not marked in some fashion, idiosyncratic though it might be.

Saturday morning marks a parting of the ways more abrupt than Friday evening in the way the different groups within the community observe the day. For the Orthodox and the more observant the morning is taken up with synagogue services, followed by the noon Sabbath meal and then the long afternoon of visiting, study, and napping that is a replica of observance to be found in the many places where Jews have lived. For the non-Orthodox the day is spent in a variety of ways, but the emphasis is on family and separation from routine and those acts and behaviors typical of the workaday world.

## The Popular Religion of Yavneel

Over the years a modus vivendi has emerged in the town so that both the religiously observant and the nonobservant are able to inhabit the same space, and an unspoken agreement allows wide latitude to the individual so long as the overall context can be seen to reflect the lowest common denominator of Sabbath distinctiveness. Even in those cases where farmers go out to the fields, in most instances this takes place before the start of synagogue services, and, most meaningfully, the farmers going to the fields do so with a rather apologetic nod, hurrying to complete their work both in order to limit offense and to be able themselves to join the altered atmosphere of a communal Shabbat. Somehow or other, although the full range from punctilious observance to near total violation of religious law regarding the Sabbath can be observed within the small space of the town, the overall "gestalt" is one of observance rather than its opposite.

Can Yavneel therefore be said to be a largely observant or at least a traditionally oriented community? If by "observant" one means strict adherence to the *mitzvot,* to the rules and regulations for behavior prescribed by *halakha,* the religious laws, then Yavneel in its majority is not observant. Indeed, if religious observance can be measured against a continuum from "full" to "none," then the general trend from Yavneel's beginnings to the present reflects a movement from "more" observance to "less."

As early as 1903, which was a year of *shmita,* when the land according to religious law is to remain untilled, the farmers of Yavneel did not take it upon themselves to decide the issue without rabbinic sanction. They feared that if they did not till the land, this might be exploited by local Arabs as a sign of abandonment, and difficulties would ensue as to ownership and title. Officials in the Paris Office of ICA, the administrative arm of Baron Rothschild's settlement program in Palestine, sent instructions that the land was to be ploughed and sowed, but still the Yavneelim hesitated to violate the halakhic dictum that the land must lie fallow every seventh year: even though their dependence on ICA and the Baron was nearly total they deemed it necessary to get a rabbinic judgment on the matter. Permission to set aside the law of *shmita* was sought from the rabbinical authorities in Tiberias who proceeded first of all to check on the Orthodox bona fides of the Yavneel farmers, who were asked whether the community had a ritual bath [*mikveh*], a ritual slaughterer, and a scroll of the law. The latter two were, in fact, in place and the Yavneelim explained that since many families still lived in Tiberias, the ritual bath of that community was used until their own facility could be constructed. The rabbis were further assured that the farmers behaved as "religious Jews," but even after this was established it was necessary to gain the approval of the Sephardic religious court, the *Bet Din,* which took time and at least one additional opinion from a leading rabbinical authority from abroad. Permission was granted, the land was ploughed and sown, and the authority of religion as well as the needs of settlement were upheld.[2]

Similarly with respect to another requirement of observant Jewry—religious instruction for the young—Yavneelim were careful to establish a *heder,* or religious primary school, even before permanent housing was built. A *melamed,* or teacher, was engaged; and each farmer was expected to provide him with food and a place to live for one month, and the children were moved with the instructor in a monthly rotation from house to house. In addition to food, lodging, and a tobacco ration, the community undertook to pay the teacher a salary, which, given the rather skimpy and austere financial situation, suggests something of the high level of importance attached to this essentially religious undertaking.[3] Even though a minority among the original settlers was considered nonreligious, there is no evidence of any opposition to this traditional religious instruction, although pressure for secular or "modern" education soon developed. As a result there emerged a two-track educational system in which boys continued to study in the heder, in Yiddish, while girls attended "school" where they were instructed in Hebrew and taught nontraditional subjects in addition to a core program of religious studies.

It is around the issue of education that we are able to observe the crystallization of the movement from "more" to "less" on a scale of religious observance. Strict traditionalists among the settlers were willing to live with a "two-track" system; but over the years pressures in the direction of modernity, if not secularity, foreshadowed a move toward a unitary school system, resulting finally in the closing of the heder during the 1920s, with all of the children attending the public school. Religious subjects continued to be taught, morning prayers of an attenuated kind were said, but clearly the movement was in the direction of a weakened role for tradition in its strictest formulation. This trend was visible not only in Yavneel but in its sister communities as well, which also were undergoing a shift from the values and patterns of the "Old Yishuv," the religious non-Zionist, Jewish community of nineteenth-century Palestine, to those expressed in the new vision that underlay the settlement movement taking root at the end of the century.

An attempt to close, or at least bridge, the gap is to be seen in the famed "journey of the rabbis," which took place over a monthlong period in 1913: five distinguished scholars, led by the then Chief Rabbi of Jaffa and later Chief Rabbi of Palestine, Abraham Yitzhak HaCohen Cook, traveled from

Hadera to Metulla. The purpose of the journey was to attempt to mobilize support for a spiritual awakening among the settlers who were perceived as slipping away from the "paths of pleasantness" in their relationship to religion and religious observance. The rabbis at each stopover in their mission stressed the holiness of the Sabbath, the importance of religious education and duties, and the need for close observance of halakhic strictures regarding the tilling of the land. In Yavneel they heard complaints from the settlers about the decline in the level of religious education, and the disgraceful behavior toward religion of some of the farm workers and guards, the *shomrim*. Shockingly, among the acts attributed to them included the holding of a feast on Yom Kippur, the slaughtering of sheep on Shabbat, and the absence of *mezuzot* on their doorposts. Given the fact that there were twenty workers in the town at the time, as against forty farmers, violation of religious propriety must have been palpable.

Most interestingly, the people of Yavneel in reacting to the rabbis took upon themselves the burden of correcting certain lacunae in the observance of tradition, including the strengthening of religious education, careful observance of *halakha* with regard to agriculture, and protecting the sanctity of *public* Sabbath observance.[4]

Here again the emphasis is clearly on the communal and the public, rather than the individual and the private. Clearly we see here a group of people growing somewhat detached from strict observance of religious duties, but still strongly linked to their roots in this tradition and retaining, on the whole, a positive attitude toward it. One would probably not be stretching matters in also seeing a bit of guilt at work within the collective conscience of the settlers over the inevitable erosion in their relatedness to a key element of their identity—the faith of the fathers as *practiced* by the fathers. Thus, one can readily understand the relatively strong emphasis placed on the development and maintenance of the educational system that provides the mechanism for the transmission of culture as well as its preservation. Especially where faith and ritual are weakened or undergoing change, the schooling of the new generation can represent either a last gasp or an attempt at salvage. But, even more importantly, the emphasis on the educational framework and the collective or communal dimensions of religiosity, rather than the individual or private, allows for a heightened level of community control, at the same time assuring that both religion and the tradition will reflect a desired level of continuity as well as legitimation for the common enterprise.

Over the years Yavneel has undergone a shift from a situation where a majority of the residents could be said to have been religiously observant on both a personal and public level to one where a majority of residents are not personally observant, in a halakhic sense, but where the framework of Judaism, especially its system of symbols, remains highly integrated in the life of the town. These symbols, as Liebman and Don-Yehiya have asserted, for the society as a whole have undergone a process of reinterpretation "which points away from God and towards the Jewish people, the Jewish state and the particular needs of the state."[5] Perhaps this reflects not so much a movement away from God as a movement away from the traditional concept of God and a passage toward a form of popular religion or "religion as practiced and experienced and not merely as defined and prescribed."[6]

Though selectively observant, Yavneel has not rejected religion. On the contrary, religion as understood by the majority of the town's residents is an integral part of their individual and collective makeup. Repeatedly I was assured that the town (and the Jewish people generally) harbored no atheists. "When the shells begin to fall around us we are all reaching for our *Sefer Tehilim* [Book of Psalms]." The farthest most Yavneelim with whom I spoke were willing to go on the subject of God was "I don't know if He exists" or "I believe in some higher force"; but outright denial of a supreme power was rare indeed. Those who denied a belief in God almost always qualified the assertion with some modified deist conception; while not Jewish in a normative sense it nonetheless preserves—at least for the respondent—some anchorage within the tradition.

What has been largely rejected—and this is highlighted by

the manner in which Yavneelim express their Judaism—is the concept of *Ol Ha-Torah,* the heavy burden of Torah, as a system of the permitted and the forbidden, and of rigidly defined ritual acts surrounding these prescriptions and proscriptions. Yavneelim characteristically seek from religion a blessing for what they do rather than a judgment upon that which is done or not done. In this, although always shocked when reminded of it, they are closer to contemporary mainline Protestantism or American Reform Judaism than to either East European or Sephardic Jewish Orthodoxy.

From an early pattern of normative religious Orthodoxy in the East European pattern Yavneel has moved toward a kind of popular religion which is often distinct from as well as in opposition to this normative mold. Yavneel in 1991 would not respond to the visit of the rabbis in 1913, or the question of *shmita* in 1903, as those earlier generations did, just as they do not observe the Sabbath or most other holy days as did their forebears.

I don't believe that this reflects so much a process of secularization (although this is decidedly present) as it does a development associated with the changed nature of the tie to place, the growth of rootedness with its accompanying sense of comfort and ease, and the resulting need for a sanctifying framework responsive more to civic need rather than authoritative fiat. Whereas Liebman and Don-Yehiya are in large measure correct in asserting that "God has reentered the civil religion, but only as a name, not as an active agent who confers legitimacy or to whom one can appeal for help," it is not quite so clear-cut as that.[7] Most Yavneelim with whom I spoke actually coalesce around just this normative feature of an interceding God that plays so central a role in Judaism and most other historic world religions. When pressed as to whether or not they ever prayed, almost all the nonobservant answered "only in time of travail," "tragedy," or "deep disappointment"; and then prayer tended to be directed rather than unguided and, most importantly, tended to assume at least some of the traditional forms. While there is *no* evidence suggesting any presumed victory for traditional religion and its concept of a transcendental God, it might be somewhat premature to suggest that God in Israel's, and Yavneel's, civil religion is "only a name."

Whatever the prevailing notion of God, it is evident that a different kind of religion has emerged here from that with which most Jews are familiar—at least in the Diaspora. Rootedness in place has seemingly brought about a lessened degree of compartmentalization associated with religion as an affair of rabbis and synagogues, which has allocated to it and in turn allocates sacred time frames and fixed and more or less inviolate rules. In the context of the village, religious adherence is celebratory rather than judgmental, communal rather than individual, mild and intimate rather than strenuous and formalistic.

"I'm not against religion," states a third-generation seventy-three-year-old Yavneeli who defines himself as secular or *hofshi* (free), "because I know what our origins were." He continues:

> Nor am I ignorant of the literature of the Mishnah and Talmud. I don't know this as well as a yeshiva student, but I know how the Talmud is structured, and I know many chapters, and I can even recite certain parts of it: none of this is foreign to me. And I think that in order to be loyal to our origins, or let us call it roots, our youth must know these things. But why all this emphasis on laws which no longer make any sense? Why can't I turn on a light on Saturday when all it involves is flipping a little switch? Why should I let the land lie fallow every seventh year when we have modern chemicals and fertilizer making this formerly intelligent rule obsolete and ridiculous? How can a modern country have religious law? Religion must be a matter of feeling!
>
> I'll tell you a story showing how far from our lives these Rabbis are and proving not only their uselessness but their insolence. Rabbi Porush [an Agudath Israel member of the Knesset and Assistant Minister of Labor and Welfare in the Shamir government] came to visit. His mother is buried here, you know. His father taught in our *heder* many years ago. I asked Rabbi Porush a question in front of an honorable and distinguished audience which came to hear him, and after he finished listing

our sins and explaining that we have juvenile delinquency in the country because we don't observe *shmita* properly. You, Rabbi Porush, know that during the time of the first and second Temple the *kohanim* [priests] filled the same functions the rabbis and teachers do today. During the year of *shmita* when the farmers had no income, neither did they, and all lived from *ma'aser* [tithe]. So tell me, during the year of *shmita* do you cut your income in proportion to the cut the farmers must take? All he could say was "if you find it so difficult financially I'll help you." So I said, "Thank you very much, but I can help *you* and two more like you. You cannot tell me to return to the period of the Second Temple while you stay put in this century. If you have a right to a regular income so do I." Religion cannot be forced. It must be voluntary and it must provide a link to the Jewish people.

The views of this third-generation Yavneeli reflect key aspects of a broadly accepted Yavneel outlook on religion. For this man, the religion of the fathers is an immutable part of one's makeup, and to know the sources of one's religion is incumbent upon everyone, although specific religious behaviors are negotiable. The formal religion—halakhic Judaism—must be responsive to immediate, temporal situations in a manner supportive of individual needs and communal goals. Religious authority must demonstrate *au courant* orientations and commitments if it is to fulfill even a ceremonial representational role in the community. "Feeling," or the affectual, takes precedence over the abstract, the cold "letter of the law." Voluntarism supersedes authority. The religion of the fathers was true, unsullied by profane and temporal concern; if only it could be recaptured, and even if we experience difficulty in carrying it out, it would be awarded a place of respect.

One might rightly ask if this is Judaism or rather a heavily syncretistic concoction involving modernism, reform Jewish practice, if not theology, as well as a weighty dose of self-serving sanctification of accepted norms? Does it have more to do with the religious values carried to Yavneel by the founding settlers or with Durkheim's conception of a moral community where rites and beliefs serve to unite a society around a certain conceptual base?

## The Religious "Ground Bass"

What appears to have emerged in Yavneel's village society is akin to what Robert Bellah refers to as a "religious ground bass," a concept he derived from his study of Italian religion. He defines the matter as "those loyalties to family and clan, to pseudokinship groups like the mafia, to village and town, and to faction and clique that so often in Italy, as elsewhere, ultimately define reality more significantly for their members than all the formal religions and ideologies combined. The musical metaphor of the ground bass is meant to suggest a deep and repetitious sonority, a drone bass that continues in spite of all melodic developments in the upper registers, the more formal theologies and philosophies, and not infrequently drowns them out altogether."[8] Bellah asserts that the notion of "ground bass" was developed in an attempt to get beyond what is subsumed under broad religious headings, and, taking the example of Japanese Shinto to grasp the matter, "at the point where . . . it shades off into the religion of the basic social structure itself, the religion embedded in the family, village, work group and so on."[9]

In Yavneel this "shading" came from a most unlikely source—the representative of the formal "legal" religion itself. The most popular religious leader in Yavneel's recent memory was Rabbi L, who came to the town during the 1950s. Not one person among the main body of the town residents with whom I spoke uttered so much as a single word of criticism of him, and, indeed, for almost everyone he was seen as the embodiment of the highest values of Jewish faith and a veritable paragon of civic and personal virtue. The Rabbi reminded all, in look and bearing, of their departed forebears—pious, self-effacing, highly learned in religious as well as secular subjects. He was gentle, quiet, and unassuming, and, most importantly, demonstrated a notable inclination to accept almost all behavior that Yavneelim deemed appropriate as expression of *their* religion, willingly sanctifying much while closing an eye to the patently unsanctionable. With Rabbi L it was clear that the community's normative values and behavior were paramount—at least insofar as prudence and a remarkable reluctance to deal with conflict reigned above his own unmistakable Orthodox views and practices.

Rabbi L clearly recognized that in order to function as communal rabbi something more (or less) than adherence to the standard, formal norms of Orthodox Jewish practice was demanded. The kind of Judaism emerging in Yavneel over the years had about it a unique flavor colored by the agricultural involvement of its practitioners. Their lives as farmers demanded not only rhythmic changes in entrenched religious norms, but also recognition of a certain basic organicism, in contrast to the synthetic basis of Diaspora faith whose continuities were temporal rather than spatial. In a small place where knowledge about people is intimate and continually flowing, there emerges a web of loyalties setting the stage for a kind of cultural continuity that Bellah found in Italy to be "not only premodern, but also pre-Christian and even pre-Roman."[10] Yavneelim, unlike their Reform and Conservative brethren in America, did not set out on a prescribed course of religious modernization or change. Yavneelim did not seek change so much as they found themselves responding to the radically changed framework of life as Jewish yeoman farmers, masters of their destiny, sovereign rulers of their independent space for whom the music of faith rather than its dicta resonated.

Yavneelim nonetheless do not want to tamper with the formal structures of faith. While, in Bellah's terms, the "ground bass" might be likened to the "real religion," whereas Orthodox Judaism might be termed the "legal religion,"[11] one does not replace the other so much as encapsulate it. No matter how much compromise there might be with the demands of formal religion, it continues to reflect a legitimacy missing from non-Orthodox expressions such as Reform and Conservative. Yavneelim tend not to distinguish between the two, due to widespread ignorance about them and because they are seen as inauthentic tampering with a historically validated mode of religious expression. "Conservatives try to make goyim of Jews," reported a middle-aged farmer, while another asked, "How can you call someone a rabbi who will marry a Jew to a goy while standing in a church under a cross?" Another villager suggested that these trends in Judaism are in their very nature divisive: "We have to follow our religion. They [Conservative and Reform] want to change our religion. They are not Jews. They go against the Torah. What held us together in the Diaspora was the fact that a Jew was willing to die for his religion." As another old-timer opined, "The Conservative are half-Christian. I am afraid that goyim will penetrate our lives and certainly I want the rabbi to be Orthodox." "The ground-bass religion involves deep loyalties and even a kind of faith,"[12] but in Yavneel as in Italy "habit counts for more than faith." If habit suggests a certain narrowness of conceptualization with respect to the parameters of faith, then it takes clear precedence over religious change. We may not do this or that, but there exists a proper mode of performance. The synagogue I don't pray in is, in fact, the real synagogue. There exists here no ideology supportive of an alternative form of religious Jewishness.

Strangely, standards for the performance of religious tasks are set at a high level, a fact that might serve to enhance the melodic strain of the ground bass. Achieving Orthodoxy requires total dedication to the 613 *mitzvot,* or religious commandments of the tradition, which few can or perhaps choose to observe; and one measures and is measured on a descending scale from full Orthodoxy *(dati)* to traditional *(masorti)* to secular *(hiloni* or *hofshi).* The fit between these categories and the type of behavior that might place a person in a particular slot is different from what one would find in a Diaspora community such as the United States, although not terribly distant from a more broadly-based Israeli conception of the matter. This is especially so with regard to the middle category—the *masorti,* or traditional—where the range seems to meander between what would in other places be called Orthodox to mildly observant or ceremonially oriented, making of it a sort of catch-all for those attempting some sort of inclusion within a religious context. In a rather startling exchange with Mendel, an eighty-three-year-old first-generation farmer—he came to Yavneel from Poland in 1925—the problematic nature of the "traditional" category becomes evident.

*Author:* Was your father religious?

*Mendel:* He was traditional.

*Author:* What does that mean? How do you differentiate between religious and traditional?

*Mendel:* He wasn't fanatic; my mother came from a Hasidic background and my father was a *misnagid* [opponent of Hasidism].

*Author:* But what does it mean in actual fact? You used the Israeli term *masorti* rather than religious and this carries with it a certain meaning, no?

*Mendel:* We kept the Sabbath and ate kosher.

*Author:* Did he travel on the Sabbath?

*Mendel:* No!

*Author:* Did he work on the Sabbath?

*Mendel:* No!

*Author:* Did he pray daily? Did he go to the synagogue?

*Mendel:* Yes, of course. He was a *shaliach tzibur* [prayer leader] and something of a *hazan* [cantor].

*Author:* Did he put on tefillin [phylacteries] every morning?

*Mendel:* Yes, of course.

*Author:* And you say he wasn't religious?

*Mendel:* I don't think that this is religious in today's terminology.

*Author:* In all seriousness?

*Mendel:* Yes, he was traditional, and he loved the Torah—it was all deeply a part of him.

*Author:* He prayed every day, went to synagogue on Shabbat and festivals, fasted on Yom Kippur and Tisha b'Av. Did he also raise a beard?

*Mendel:* Yes, a small one, but he didn't let it grow all the way.

*Author:* Did he always wear a hat, or a *kippah?*

*Mendel:* Yes, always—his head was never bare.

*Author:* Would he, if invited to the home of a non-Jew, partake of any food which might be served him?

*Mendel:* No, perhaps water or maybe tea, but really, no. But then the chances of his being invited to the home of a goy were never very great.

*Masorti* and *dati* are terms that in the Israeli context have assumed powerful political connotations, with *dati* being associated with coercion and disproportionate power, and *masorti* with warmth and memory. Thus Mendel's description of his father's relation to religion and his defining it as traditional can be seen as an act of filial piety as much as a precise definition. For Mendel, a self-defined *hiloni,* to see his father as part of the rejected religious establishment that has captured the term *dati* and asserted exclusive control of its parameters would present a serious obstacle. Assigning his father safely to the catch-all category of *masorti* identifies him as following an Orthodox life-style, but unthreateningly detached from all that this connotes in the Israeli context.

It is also evident that the "traditional" category has about it a certain elasticity, allowing for much expansion and contraction of definition, which makes of it *the* Yavneeli "label of choice." The term performs somewhat like a gyroscope in the sense that it measures one's closeness to an understood but still undefined acceptance of Jewishness, if not Israeliness, by how one relates to the line called tradition, or *masoret*. When asked how he defined himself, in contrast to his father, Mendel said, "I am not religious, I am not traditional, but I honor the tradition." When asked what this meant he assured me, "Everything that is a part of the Jewish people's tradition is honored by me," insisting that "the Bible represents the ancient world, a world of fanaticism which I cannot live by but which I love and respect." Most revealing, Mendel observed that he has stopped reading books altogether, explaining that "I am not interested in speculation. If I read then it is a scientific book or this Bible here [holding a Bible aloft]. See, I have a Bible here."

*Author:* You do read the Bible?

*Mendel:* Yes, yes.

*Author:* Why?

*Mendel:* Because it is the story of the beginning of our nation. What is this? Can I today, from the perspective of thousands of years, say that this is worthless? They believed in this, they were elevated and inspired by this spirit; yes it is the Torah of Mount Sinai, it's the Ten Commandments.

*Author:* Do you accept the Ten Commandments as binding?

*Mendel:* Yes.

*Author:* How?

*Mendel:* I accept them ethically, morally.

*Author:* So you believe in God.

*Mendel:* No, I believe in a supreme force, but I don't know where it is or what it is.

*Author:* Supreme force?

*Mendel:* Yes, maybe it is inside me. Maybe it's processed information, genes, or something.

"I am not religious, I am not traditional," he says; but the music of the religiously-based tradition resonates for Mendel, as it does for so many in the town. The formal religion of Yavneel is Jewish Orthodoxy, but the popular religion which exists alongside the formal one and predominates, serves as much more than merely a vehicle for personal or group redemption. Rather it is "rooted in the basic social structure itself, [it is] the religion embedded in the family, village, work group, and so on,"[13] and functions as both a tie to the past and a bridge to the future. It is, as noted earlier, a religion seeking approval rather than judgment, insight rather than rulings, warmth rather than authority.

Yavneelim do not want to be told how to observe the holy days—they tend to tell one how *they* do it, suggesting that this is the way that *their* tradition has sanctioned. Yavneelim pick and choose and, in Liebman's terms, "transform and transvalue" aspects of religious orthodoxy, which results not so much in a civil religion and certainly not a traditional one but something falling between the two and pointing toward a possible new direction. Civil religion can indeed evolve through "confrontation, dissolution, and reinterpretation,"[14] but in fact these same strategies can support the process by which change in a traditional religious format takes place as well.

Simchat Torah, the festival marking the completion of the yearly cycle of Torah reading in the synagogue, has become one of the most central communal observances in the community or, more correctly, among the core settlers and their descendants. The occasion for many years has been marked by gathering in the main synagogue for *Hakafoth,* when it is the custom to dance holding aloft the Torah scrolls, and participation by men, women and children was widespread. Following the *Hakafoth,* communal singing, dancing, eating, and drinking continued in the synagogue, the streets surrounding the synagogue, and in the more intimate (and less broadly based) confines of various private homes. The festivities lasted on into the early hours of the morning, leaving behind a thoroughly exhausted but, by all reports, happy and uplifted group of participants.

The way in which Yavneelim celebrated the festival is only partially sanctioned by Orthodox practice, and is admittedly closer to the spirit than the letter of the law. Men and women celebrated together, rather than separately as Orthodoxy requires; the singing tended to a mix of traditional religious tunes and rhythms and more recent songs of Eretz Yisrael; and the revelry tended to be more exuberant than what a more staid traditionalism could comfortably countenance. The current community rabbi, who is identified as haredi, or ultra-Orthodox, has succeeded in altering this "festa" in the direction of a more sanctionable Orthodox form, with the result that sullen and often angry townspeople have withdrawn from the celebration. Yavneelim claim that "their" Simchat Torah has been taken from them. Yavneelim were and are convinced that "their" celebration enjoyed the sanction of tradition without being fully aware of the fact that it was largely a tradition of their own making; yet this, in fact, is precisely the way in which religious practices tend to evolve.

Yavneelim were reflecting in this evolution of a "new" tradition "the authority of the eternal yesterday," in Max Weber's felicitous phrasing. They were affirming continuity but also expressing things that had happened in and to their lives as a result of *where* they were and *who* they had become. The formalism expressed in the life of the synagogue was inevitably transposed in the context of a rooted agricultural community from holy day to village festa, from an established to a spontaneous, a legal to an integral celebration. Not only had the lives of the Yavneelim achieved a certain organic wholeness but the changes in the framework of religion, which I would maintain was and is central to their definition of self and worldview, followed a parallel trajectory of unselfconscious, unreflecting and certainly unplanned movement. Yavneelim do not seek the prophetic Judaism of Reform or the halakhic renewal of

Conservative. Their search, if search it be, is in no way cerebral or abstract, ideological or cosmic. It reflects rather a slow, almost imperceptible, expansion and retraction of tradition to meld with their lives while expressing needed and desired linkages to the past, sacred and otherwise.

Yavneelim are at home under the tent of the tradition. Unlike the unmistakable feeling of self-conscious inhibitedness one often feels in the celebrations and prayer of non-Orthodox Diaspora Judaism, one senses in their observance a sense of natural flow, of intimate familiarity going beyond the fact that they speak the same language they pray in. Even on holy days not so widely observed as Simchat Torah, such as the fast of Tisha b'Av marking the destruction of the Temple, this sense of organicism stands out rather palpably.

Only about 100 of approximately 1,000 adult males in the community observe the fast and attend special readings of the Lamentations in the synagogue. Observance here is strictly traditional, but with some evidence of change that will have inevitable repercussions for religion. That is, Tisha b'Av seems to be unfolding not only as an expression of *distant* memory but for the creation of *close* memory. While sitting outside the main synagogue waiting for the beginning of the recitation of Lamentations, a group consisting of Yavneeli core settlers, more recent farmers from the 1930s, and a few of the "newcomers" of Sephardi background who arrived in the 1950s commented on how things were in the community twenty and thirty years ago, noting that we are together again as we were 2,000 years ago—reading the same text commemorating the same event. A direct, relatively unforced attempt was being made to utilize the religious context of continuity as a vehicle for demonstrating and framing an elusive continuity on another level. Events surrounding the destruction of the Temple and the resulting dispersal of the people were talked about on a level of familiarity that suggested an event which occurred yesterday rather than centuries ago; and the evidence of this group's remembering together, diverse though they were in background and history, pointed to victory emerging from devastating defeat.

Is this merely expressive of Israel's "new civil religion" which is "characterized by the penetration of traditional religious symbols into Israeli culture"[15] or rather the slow creation of a neoteric, more rooted religiosity emerging from the changed circumstances of renewed sovereignty and relatedness to place? The very short history of the resettlement of Eretz Yisrael and the creation of the state does not permit anything like a definitive answer at this juncture, but the latter, especially in its "ground bass" formulation, seems a distinct possibility. It is true that the dominant strain in Yavneel's religion emphasizes peoplehood, memory, legitimation, rather than ritual or transcendence. But with the caveat of the rather lessened role given to ritual and rite than is the case in the normative context, the factor of peoplehood and group preservation may be seen as continuing to play their historic role in the people-faith of Israel. The "truism" that "more than the Jewish people have kept the Sabbath, the Sabbath has kept the Jewish people" is, when all is said and done, more than clever word mongering; it has sociological and historical resonance.

While Yavneelim seek in their adherence to a religious framework a blessing, or approval, for that which they find palatable, useful, or good, they are not in this at any great distance from a traditionally religious model though, admittedly, their assumption of autonomy in this regard leads them far afield from orthodoxy. In their insistence, however, that Jewish faith must play a central role in the preservation of Jewish peoplehood, and in underscoring the legitimacy of the renewed tie between people and land, they are well within a historically viable model.

Going beyond this, however, in the majority of discussions held with Yavneelim from the core group as well as some from among the Sephardi "newcomers," something more than affirmation of peoplehood is visible. For this it would have been sufficient to create a civic framework for the preservation and occasional trotting out of certain pieties like the commemoration of the past victories and defeats of the Jews, or the use of traditional blessings on public occasions, or the employment of a rabbi to teach tradition as well as to sanctify events in need of sanctification. All of these functions are, in fact, integrated into the pattern of communal life. When the president of the state of Israel visited the town in April of 1991 in order to kick off the celebration of Yavneel's ninetieth year, he was received in a manner which might be described as "echt" Yavneeli, reflecting a mixture of the modern and the antique, the religious and the secular—one is almost tempted to say, of Esau and Jacob.

## A Yavneel Story

The town spent the day in vivid anticipation of the visit of President Chaim Herzog. Public areas were cleaned and freshened, flower beds were clipped, lawns mowed, and flags displayed in front of all public buildings and hung from lampposts in pairs—one of the town and the other of the state. The one possibly disharmonious note was to be found in the display of the red flag of the "International" in front of the Histadrut labor-council building, a sight that would not have elicited comment in the past but that was seen as somewhat awkward in the conservative Yavneel of the '90s. At six o'clock (and one hour late), the sound of the powerful rotors of the president's helicopter could be heard throughout the valley; within minutes he dropped from the sky onto the sports field, entered the mayor's car, and, flanked by two teenaged Yavneelim looking like young Greek gods who rode on prancing Arabian steeds holding both the Yavneel and state banners, the president drove the approximately five hundred meters from the field to City Hall. There, he was greeted by applause from the adults as well as a lusty rendering of the Israeli welcoming song "Hevenu Shalom Aleichem" by first, second, and third-graders holding small Israeli flags.

On the steps of City Hall the president was met by four men, all representing the formal religious structure. In fact, the only two participants who were beardless and dressed in "modern" fashion were the mayor and the president himself. The other four were the town rabbi, the principal of the local religious state school, the program director of the same school, and "Rav" Binyamin, the unofficial sage and religious leader of the town's Sephardi residents. The president was gently nudged in the direction of a table upon which rested an enormous challah, the braided Sabbath and festival loaf, and a dish of salt. He whipped a skullcap out of his pocket, placed it squarely and decisively on his head, and after saying the traditional blessing dipped a chunk of bread in the salt and obligingly chewed and swallowed. He then bent over so that the diminutive Rav Binyamin could place his hands over his head and bless him, thus bringing to a close this most traditional of Jewish ceremonies for welcoming the great. This in fact constituted the whole of the formal welcome, which was followed by some quite unceremonious events such as dinner with the mayor and a speech to the townspeople later that evening in the community center. (Revealingly, the central theme of his talk was religious tolerance and peace among brethren.)

When asked, townspeople all assured me that this was the way Yavneel always welcomed distinguished visitors. Bread, salt, blessings, and the Rabbi were integral to *the* tradition, and thus were reflected in *our* tradition. They seemed eager to demonstrate how "all right" they are about religion; as one bystander stated, to the strong affirmation of others gathered around, "We don't need religious fanatics to tell or instruct us about our religion."

## An Emerging Religion of Place

Yavneelim are accepting of the role of religion in their personal and collective lives. An important element at work here is the emphasis on religion as the major source of legitimacy for continued national and communal existence. Another factor is the relatively high level of filial piety, leading to reluctance to upset or neglect totally the systems set in place by the founding generation. Ironically, Yavneelim would probably be even more receptive to a greater role for traditional religion if there were greater formal separation between religion and politics, and if they did not feel threatened by what they see as acts of religious coercion on the part of the religious establishment both in Yavneel and in the country as a whole.

Sara, a second-generation descendant of a founding family, says she "would like to see the country run by scientists who know how to organize things" rather than politicians or rabbis, but she adds, "we must be bound to the tradition because this is what has kept us going." When asked if there is too much religion in Israeli society, Avraham counters, "religion, or tradition, is our history. We are the only people for whom religion and nation are one. I don't mind if there is prayer in the school but we must give each child or each family the choice as to whether or not they participate and we must teach the *whole* Bible in every school—religious or not. This situation where religion is the balancing force in politics, however, cannot continue. They are blackmailing us."

Avraham is not Orthodox, but prayer is for him a perfectly comprehensible adjunct to general education. He is not a "perfect believer," but the *whole* Bible (in contrast to selections) must be taught to *all* children. There is a role for religion in public life, but it must choose the high road of volition rather than coercion, which debases it as well as those coerced. To return to Bellah's musical metaphor, it is the "drone bass that continues in spite of all melodic developments in the upper registers." But in something of a departure from Bellah's Italian context, this informal religious "ground bass" does not seem to "drown out" the more formal structure as much as it seeks to retain its more malleable aspects through the addition of an adjustive vibrato. In the course of dozens of interviews and countless conversations with a large proportion of the core population in Yavneel it became clearly evident that while the orthodoxy of the founding generation had declined and in many cases disappeared entirely, the readiness, indeed desire, to include religious observance in both communal and individual lives was nearly universal. In almost every case, there was a decline in orthodoxy, but also adamant refusal to allow for the possibility of total uninvolvement as well as signs of a hesitant, as yet unverbalized, groping for some new religious synthesis. What is emerging is confusing, eclectic, and unsystematic, but no more so, I would venture, than is the case with religious evolution in other contexts.

Hillel, a fourth-generation farmer in his early thirties, reports that "I am not religious at all and don't observe anything." But he qualifies this statement as follows: "On Yom Kippur I fast and eat only kosher on Passover. We don't light candles on Sabbath and I drive my car, but I don't eat pork. The house is kosher, but we don't have separate dishes for meat and dairy. I am less religious than my father who started going to shul again when he retired. I guess it has something to do with age. I am secular. I don't want the religious to push me around or tell me what to do, although I feel that I am quite tolerant with respect to their way of life." When asked if, in view of the above, he would like to see less religion in public life he answered, "No, I would like more. It is, when all is said and done, a good thing."

Erez, a third-generation farmer in his early sixties, reports that he goes to synagogue on holy days, makes *Kiddush,* the blessing over wine, and refuses to identify himself in current coin as either secular or traditional. "I am," he says, "an Israeli Jew who thinks that religion is *the* unifying element of our nation. I respect the tradition, and I think that it is quite beautiful." Erez eats only kosher food, observes the laws of Passover, and tries "not to distance myself too far from the tradition." Ruth, a widow in her late sixties and third-generation, described the very religious pattern of her grandfather, the attenuated one of her father, and, finally, what she herself observes:

> I go to synagogue only for *Yizkor* [prayer for the departed said five times a year in the synagogue], and I fast on Yom Kippur. When my son reached Bar Mitzvah–age I sent him for religious instruction. I "watch" the dairy and meat, and separate them. I have *mezuzot* on my doorposts, but I don't kiss them. For me keeping the tradition means watching over the uniqueness of our people.

"I don't believe in God," she adds, "but when I am in trouble,

I turn to Him—I believe there is something there. I am not traditional, but I have a tradition."

"I am not traditional, but I have a tradition" is another way of saying that the tradition, as passed on, no longer resonates as anything like a complete system. But the almost inchoate patterns now taking root within the community bear the hallmark of a new tradition being formed, reflecting the need, desire, and, most important, the *possibility* of a religion of place—of rootedness. A model seems to be taking form that is not so much an attempt at modernizing or minimalizing religion as it is seeking its natural place within an unbifurcated society—a society, in effect, where the religious tradition, the patterns of work, the sense of place and time, the tones of ceremony, the demands of memory are all of one piece. The religion that one sees in Yavneel is not consciously change-oriented and it is not Orthodox. It is, however, an unsystematic response to changes that have occurred in the society both locally and nationally. Unlike the radical changes introduced by the Reform movement during the nineteenth century and Conservatism, to a much lesser extent, during the twentieth century, Yavneel's religion is not being defensively forged against the backdrop of a dominant non-Jewish environment and culture, but rather against that of a changed *dominantly Jewish* context. Thus, the apparent ease and relative absence of guilt, the basic unselfconsciousness of the matter, its ingenuous nature: "Why do I have *mezuzot* on my doorposts even though I am not religious? For the same reason I had all my four sons circumcised. It's Jewish." There exists here a very natural, unforced conviction that one cannot be an Israeli without being Jewish; and being Jewish means the integration into one's life of a certain core of not only Jewish symbols but of Jewish ritual and belief, tentative as the latter might be.

Yavneelim fast on Yom Kippur; avoid pork; hallow (after a fashion) the Sabbath; celebrate the festivals of Hanukkah, Passover, Sukkot, Purim and Shavuot; mark the Bar Mitzvah of their sons and, increasingly, the Bat Mitzvah of their daughters; do not mix meat and dairy. They bury their dead and mourn their dead according to tradition, ritually circumcise their sons, marry under the *huppah* (canopy), and do not eat leavened food on Passover. In any other context of contemporary Jewry they would be seen as religious, if not overly consistent or punctilious observers of the commandments; but they tend not to define themselves as such, raising the question of why this is so. It is true that the matter of the "Israeli" context plays an important role here: the fact that not much, if any, choice devolves upon the individual with respect to certain of these religious acts. Israelis can *only* marry religiously and bury their dead according to the religious rite over which the Orthodox establishment holds sway. Bakeries—at least in the Jewish sector—do not bake bread over Passover, and Saturday is the country's official day of rest. But no formal prescriptions exist with respect to marking the holy days in one's home, or putting *mezuzot* on one's doorposts, or separating dairy from meat, or even preparing pork in one's kitchen. No rabbinical decree places the Bible in a central position on even the most meager of bookshelves and certainly does not prescribe its almost talismanic reference as a sign and symbol of civic acceptance and full inclusion.

Yavneelim observe what they do, and view the religion of tradition positively because above and beyond any personal reward or fulfillment they may experience, it represents flow, continuity, rootedness. It has about it no less a sense of spontaneity than does the politics, or work, or kin and social networks of the community. Change when it occurs in this context is slow, incremental, unselfconscious, nonideological, rather than defensive, or reactive to essentially external challenges, as is and was the case in the various encounters of Jews with the larger societies within which they lived. Just as changes occurred over time in work patterns, education, lifestyles, and political behavior, for example, so they did in how Yavneelim viewed and lived their religion. This is, of course, anathema to the traditional vision of an unchanging, immutable religious system framing an eternal truth, but this is nevertheless the way it is.

Yavneelim think of themselves as not particularly religious

because they are not religious when measured with the yardstick of Orthodoxy. In a quantifiable sense of how many commandments are observed, how many ignored, how many violated, they stand very much closer to what normative Orthodoxy upholds than do Diaspora communities adhering to one or the other form of alternative Jewish religiosity; but they are fully aware of falling far short of the mark when using the Orthodox standard, which is in fact their measure of choice. The key difference, however, between what is found in Yavneel and, I believe, in Israel generally as opposed to the Diaspora is that Yavneelim see themselves as *violating commandments,* but not *compromising* them. In fact, there is, of course, compromise; but perhaps because of the "natural grace" characteristic of the religious "ground bass," Yavneelim do not see changes as compromises so much as religious expressions rooted in the reality of communal life. It is not so much a case of "we have to know the real rules before we make our own," as a Jewish sociologist from East Germany explained why she wanted Orthodox teachers from Israel to come to that most assimilated of Jewish communities;[16] it is rather that the rules are enmeshed in a wide-ranging web of comfortable familiarity almost inseparable from any other aspect of social life.

## SEPHARDI FOLK RELIGION

What has been said so far about the religion of Yavneel refers largely to the core group of veteran Ashkenazi settlers. In view of the fact that a majority of townspeople are Sephardim (about 55 percent of the population) of relatively recent vintage, this view could not only be skewed but misleading. How does one speak of Yavneel without reference to more than half of the town's citizens? One powerful justification is found in the fact that the tone and atmosphere, the cadences and rhythms of Yavneel life are derived from and still responsive to the pattern developed by the core group. The town's institutions, both formal and informal, as well as its agendas in education, economy, style, and almost all other aspects were established by and continue to be extensively influenced by the core group of settlers and their descendants. In almost every way, Sephardim attempt to emulate Ashkenazim, including, to a certain extent, the matter of religious behavior, although a distinct religious institutional structure is retained for each group.

Notwithstanding, there appears to be a notable difference in levels of religious observance between Sephardim and Ashkenazim, with the former adhering to normative Orthodox standards to a significantly higher degree than the latter. Almost certainly this discrepancy can be explained largely by the fact that the Sephardim (except for the Yemenites) are first- and second-generation Israelis coming from a highly traditional society, which places them closer to the original settlers, in these and other ways, than to the third- and fourth-generation Ashkenazim. Not only in observance, but in the persistence of elements of folk religion—belief in spirits, devils, the intervention of saints—the Sephardim reflect beliefs and customs that have largely disappeared from the religion of the core group.

In an interview carried out with two middle-aged women—Rivka Ovadia of Yemenite descent and Leah Busso, who immigrated from Tunisia—I became increasingly aware of the existence of a worldview different from that of members of the core group of the same age. The fact that both women had no formal education, and were only marginally literate, is another important factor separating them from the core-group Ashkenazim and influencing both the tone and substance of their responses. Because it is so illustrative of a particular way of looking at religion and the world, I have included most of the interview in an effort to highlight not only context but vocabulary and tone as well.

A:     Rivka, you were born here in Yavneel, and your parents?

R:     My parents came here seventy years ago.*

---

*The author (A) interviews Rivka Ovadia (R), born in Yavneel of Yemenite ancestry, and Leah Busso (L), born in Tunisia.

*A:* And your father worked as a farm laborer.

*R:* Yes, my father was a farm laborer.

*A:* Did he eventually get land of his own?

*R:* He had 8 dunams.

*A:* And you grew up here; have you traveled any? Have you lived anywhere else?

*R:* I used to live in Poriah, after I got married.

*A:* But not far from around here, Poriah is a matter of a few kilometers away. So now I'd like to start asking you questions centering upon the subject of religion. The first question is very simple; do you believe in God?

*R:* Yes. Of course I do.

*A:* That is, you have no doubts about it, about the existence of God who created the earth and the sky.

*R:* Yes, God created the earth and the sky, I believe.

*A:* Do you pray?

*R:* No.

*A:* And you don't go to the synagogue?

*R:* No.

*A:* And your father?

*R:* My father does, he's religious, he has two synagogues. He has a big synagogue in Rechovot, and here in Yavneel he also has a synagogue.

*A:* Is he alive?

*R:* No.

*A:* But what does it mean that he had a synagogue in Rechovot and here? Did he walk from here to Rechovot?

*R:* No, that's where my daughters were married, we have

two daughters in Rechovot, and he bought land there and built a synagogue there.

*A:* He built a synagogue?

*R:* Yes, in his name.

*A:* Was he a learned man? Did he not know only how to pray, but to study as well?

*R:* Yes, he was a great scholar.

*A:* Was there enough food for the whole family while you were growing up? Did you suffer?

*R:* Look, in my time, I didn't suffer, but my father and mother told us that times were very hard when they first came to Yavneel. My father used to work a whole day for ten grush [equivalent of ten cents]. He would walk down to Zemach and work there and walk back on Friday. On Sunday he would walk down again.

*A:* How many children were in the family?

*R:* Eleven.

*A:* Eleven?

*R:* Yes, eleven, we received a present from Ben Gurion [in recognition of the large number of children in the family].

*A:* How many brothers and how many sisters?

*R:* Seven sisters and four brothers.

*A:* And they don't all live in Yavneel now?

*R:* No, there are four of us here, two girls and two boys.

*A:* Is the financial situation of those who have stayed better than your father's was?

*R:* You mean now?

*A:* Yes.

R: Yes, now praise God, everyone has money, has everything. The children get a better education, we have everything, thank God.

A: Seeing that you grew up here in a traditional religious Yemenite family, did you believe in holy men? That is, certain people who were holy and could intervene in what is happening down here on earth? Do you know what I'm referring to?

R: No.

A: Like spirits.

R: I believe in that.

A: Where does that originate? Were you taught that by your father, by your mother?

R: My father and mother told us that in Yemen there were spirits. And here in Israel, I also saw it.

A: How do you deal with it when you see it?

R: My father's brother is still living, he lives in Poriah.

A: How old is he?

R: He is eighty-one years old, and he used to talk to the *shed* [devil or malevolent spirit] face to face. But he wouldn't just go up to them. He would approach them with a special book, and he would know how to speak with them. But in Israel there were less, because my father said that Israel is blessed.

A: Leah, you claim that there are spirits abroad but not in Israel.

L: I didn't say, but as she was saying, there's someone in our family who has a book, and they go and talk with them. And not just anyone, people who were given the power by God. Like now there is a *rav* [rabbi] and people who believe in him are blessed by him. Like there was a Rav Abuchatzera. Abuchatzera gives people holy water. I went to see him when he was alive.

A: Now there is Baba Baruch. Is that who you are referring to?

L: No.

A: Baba Sali, Baba Baruch. [Father and son zaddikim, or holy men, from Morocco.]

L: Yes, we believe. My mother, may she rest in peace, she only died three months ago, told me that her father was a rabbi, and my aunt's husband who still lives in B'eer Sheva is a rabbi and a *mohel* [ritual circumciser] and a ritual slaughterer, and how do you say, that is the basis of all my family and my husband's. Our grandparents were all rabbis. My generation did not produce rabbis, but in my mother's generation, they were almost all rabbis. My uncle, who now lives in B'eer Sheva, was taught by my grandfather, my mother's father. By the time he was twenty, he was a *mohel,* a ritual slaughterer, and a *rav.*

A: Nice. But why do you claim that *shedim* are only abroad and not here in Israel?

L: I don't know, but that's what I've heard and I believe it. They say that the land of Israel is holy and that there are no spirits. I don't know why, I didn't ask. When we lived abroad, we were religious and we would never leave the house and when we came to Israel, I began to study. I learned to read and write, which I hadn't learned abroad. My aunt's brother came, the one I told you about, he's now eighty-seven years old, and the synagogue was right next door here, and there I was an only child, and I was a young girl, and usually a girl does not go to a man, even if she is young she is escorted. So I was like his daughter. I was left with him many times, and I would hear how he would teach. Until this day I remember the whole alphabet. When we first came here, we lived in a transit camp for six and a half years and then we moved here, to the *shikun,* about twenty-five years ago, and then volunteers would come to teach us Hebrew.

*A:* Hadn't you learned to pray abroad?

*L:* No, I didn't know anything. I just knew what *A* and *B* were.

*A:* Weren't you even taught the prayers by heart?

*L:* No, we knew blessings, when we eat we bless, when we wash our hands . . . all of the things that were customary in Hebrew.

*A:* I'd like to return to the subject of the *shed* [spirit]. Must the *shed* necessarily be evil or can there be a good *shed?*

*R:* Always evil. He makes people crazy.

*A:* Leah, I see that you disagree, have you had a different experience?

*L:* Yes.

*A:* Can you explain?

*L:* For instance, if someone is sick, going crazy, then he was entered by an evil spirit, he wasn't entered by a *shed.*

*R:* An evil spirit [*ruach ra'a*] *is* a *shed.*

*L:* True, but abroad when there were spirits, and I know that when someone passed by, an evil spirit might enter him and that usually during the day they were asleep and awake during the night.

*R:* The *shedim* are always humans who eat food with no salt. He's exactly like a human being.

*A:* Is that a sign that he's a spirit? If he eats . . .

R:    No, you don't see him. You can hear his voice, but you can't see him.

A:    What's this about his eating without salt?

R:    The spirits usually eat their food without salt.

A:    But you don't see them.

R:    If you give him our food he won't eat it because it has salt.

A:    And were the *shedim* once people or were they not?

R:    No. They are spirits [*ruchot*] that drive you crazy.

A:    Like Satan?

R:    Yes.

L:    Satan is evil.

A:    But not necessarily the *shed?*

L:    No.

R:    The *shed* makes the person sick, what do you mean not evil?

A:    How can you get rid of the *shed?*

L:    We go to a Rav, and he does all kinds of tricks and talks to him. A *shed* is also afraid of fire. And then he does something with a book; [to Rivka] don't tell me it's not so, with us it's like this, with you it's different, I know for a fact, I've seen.

A:    What have you seen?

L:    When I lived in Poriah, there lived a woman who was a big *tzadika* [saintly person]. She did *mitzvot,* she would go from house to house. One day she went by herself to the mikveh [ritual bath], without being escorted, in the evening. With us—I'm not talking about other people like the Yemenites—when a religious woman goes to the mikveh she is not allowed to go alone. She has to go with someone else. Or a woman after giving birth, she is not allowed to be left alone for a month. Someone has to be at home with her, or a bride, when a bride goes to the mikveh, she mustn't go alone. They say that when a woman goes to the mikveh, who is she waiting for? She is waiting for her husband. So along comes a *shed,* and the *shed* takes the shape of a human being, for example, it can come to me in the shape of my husband. He can sleep with me at night and then my husband is forbidden to sleep with me and I must go to the mikveh again.

*A:* But you said you had some experience with this.

*R:* Not I, but my neighbor. She went to the mikveh alone, and when she returned from the mikveh, she was walking with a flashlight, and she passed by my house, which was beside the road, we heard her yell; he simply came to her and put out her flashlight. In those days there was no electricity in Poria, and she felt someone holding her, and so we all ran out of the house, and saw her on the ground full of fear and talking nonsense, and when we Yemenites saw this we immediately knew it was a *shed,* so we went to the rabbi—there was a rabbi in the village—and he opened a book and did all kinds of things and prayed, and he was talking with the *shed,* and he told him to leave this woman or else he would burn him or hurt him. He spoke simply, but there was a special book before him, from which he was reading *Tehilim* [Psalms].

*A:* . . . I'd like to turn to a different subject now. I will ask both of you. For instance, prayer, you don't go to the synagogue, do you?

*R:* No.

*A:* Not at all? Not even on Yom Kippur?

*R:* I go because it's my father's synagogue.

*A:* So on Yom Kippur you do go?

*R:* I go, but not to pray. I go to hear the prayer . . .

*A:* Do you ever pray by yourself? When you are alone, using your own words to talk to God?

*R:* Yes, yes, when I finish eating, as I learned from my mother, I say "praised be God that there is bread to eat and may God be blessed each and every day."

*A:* Do you occasionally ask God to intervene in your life, to help you . . .

*R:* I always say may God protect my children and make them healthy.

*A:* Is that the formula or do you believe?

*R:* I believe. I take care of the synagogue, now that my mother has passed away, I see to the cleaning of the synagogue.

*A:* Is there a minyan there?

*R:* Yes, there is a minyan, thank God.

*A:* In both of the Yemenite synagogues?

*R:* In my father's synagogue there is a minyan. I have five sons who go to pray, so our family alone provides six souls. And then there are some elderly men who know [sic] my father who come to pray at his synagogue.

*A:* Regarding prayer on Shabbat, you don't go to pray every Shabbat?

*R:* No, I don't go every Shabbat.

*A:* Do you go sometimes?

*R:* No, only if there is a memorial service. Then I go prepare plates and cups so that everything will be in order.

*A:* You're like the *shamash* [sexton]?

*R:*     Yes.

*A:*     Regarding household customs, do you light the Sabbath candles?

*R:*     Yes, I light candles every Shabbat, and set a nice table, and we sing Shabbat songs, everyone goes to pray, and I don't light fire on Shabbat.

*A:*     Do all the children go to pray?

*R:*     Yes.

*A:*     Do the boys all wear *kippot* [skullcaps]?

*R:*     Yes.

*A:*     Do you keep kosher at home?

*R:*     Yes, I don't mix milk and meat. I have a grandson three years old who doesn't take his *kippah* off his head.

*A:*     And do you think that's good?

*R:*     Yes, why not? One should feel that it's Shabbat.

*A:*     If one of your children chose to marry a Jew who was totally disassociated with religion, would you oppose?

*R:*     What do you mean by totally disassociated?

*A:*     Very far detached, one who doesn't keep any of the religious traditions or *mitzvot*. One who is a Jew, but doesn't believe in synagogue, who eats on Yom Kippur.

*R:*     I won't force her, you understand? But I know that my daughter is following her mother's footsteps. I followed my mother's and father's way, and my daughters tend towards me.

*A:*     Did your mother go to synagogue?

*R:*     My mother? She looked after the synagogue.

*A:*     She looked after it, but did she go?

R: The synagogue was in my mother's house, she saw to it that it became a synagogue.

A: Did she know how to read and write?

R: No, but she knew the Bible, and knew all the stories. She knew all of the book of Esther. We were eleven children and every Saturday my father would sit us all around the table after prayers, where we would read that week's portion. Each one of us would read one sentence round and round and we would read the Haftorah too. First we would make *Kiddush,* and my father would sit there with some Arak and all kinds of food like a piece of meat and some hard-boiled eggs, and he would listen to our reading. He wouldn't let us out of the house until we finished readng the weekly portion, the *Haftorah* [prophets] and some Rashi. Only then, after noon would he let us go out and play.

A: And with you, Leah, was it the same at home, that is, traditional with regard to the keeping of the Sabbath?

L: Yes, that's right, our household is like her father's household. Their household is not like ours, ours is like her father's. We are now as we were then. I have seven children; five are married, and two girls are not married, they are in America, in New York.

A: Do you come from a small town in Tunisia?

L: We come from Tunis . . .

A: Did you come from the city of Tunis itself?

L: No, from northern Tunis.

A: From a small town?

L: It wasn't so small, but mostly Arabs.

A: Do you know its name?

L: Nafta. Previously it hadn't appeared on the map, but

now it appears on the map, there is a place called Tozar, and after that, Nafta.

*A:* So your household both here and in Tunis was and is traditional, that is, you abide by all the laws, keep kosher, observe the Sabbath?

*L:* Yes. Everything is the same.

*A:* Now, I'd like to ask you a question which might be rather indiscreet for a man to ask. Do you go to the mikveh or have you gone to the mikveh during your married life?

*L:* Yes.

*A:* Sometimes, that is not every month?

*L:* No, I stopped going every month.

*A:* Do you [to Rivka] go to the mikveh?

*R:* Two weeks ago we went to the mikveh, my two daughters who were just married and myself, and they also sleep two weeks in separate beds and two weeks . . .

*A:* And now I'd like to ask Leah something . . .

*R:* No, wait, I'd like to say a few more words. I believe one thing. Whoever wants to be religious has to observe the Sabbath and believe in God, and not to be too much of a . . .

*A:* So you think that's the whole Torah in essence, to observe the Sabbath?

*R:* Yes, to observe the Sabbath, to do *mitzvot,* like it says in the Torah, Thou shalt not steal, thou shalt not commit adultery, thou shalt not murder, thou shalt not bring a false witness, thou shalt not covet they neighbor's wife, ten things. And he didn't require of us, the women, to go and pray. What I must do is praise God each and every day, thank him, that I have bread—like Jacob said, I have bread to eat and clothes to wear, and I will sit peacefully in my father's home.

*A:* You believe in the coming of the Messiah. Where will the Messiah come, to Tiberias or to Yavneel?

*L:* First he will come to the Mount of Olives.

*A:* The Messiah?

*L:* Yes, the Messiah. Why do people prefer to bury their dead in Tiberias rather than in Safad and Jerusalem? Because Tiberias is closer to the way to Jerusalem.

*A:* You mean Yavneel. That Yavneel and Tiberias are closer to Jerusalem and are therefore holier places. . . . So, in the final analysis, you think that the Rabbi here is preparing the road for the coming of the Messiah?

*L:* Yes!

*A:* Do you think that we could have a secular state with no connection to the Jewish religion? Or must there be a connection to the Jewish religion for this to be a Jewish state?

*R:* Look, everybody can do whatever they want in their own home. Whether they are secular or not doesn't matter, I do what I want. I've heard that there are those who are opposed to the listing of your religion on your identity card. This I'm opposed to.

*A:* Why?

*R:* I want to know that I'm a Jew.

*A:* But don't you know that if it isn't written? You know that you're a Jew.

*R:* Listen, when my daughter goes to marry someone, I want it written in his identity card that he is a Jew. . . . I want "Jew" to be listed on the identity card, otherwise she might marry some Arab or some goy.

*A:* So in the end you say that you do want some connection with Judaism and the nation.

*R:* Yes, but if you're not religious, it doesn't disturb me.

*A:* And now my last question, and I will pose it to both of you. What would you view as the ideal situation regarding religion here in Yavneel or in the country as a whole?

*R:* That everyone would observe the Sabbath. Look, I can't force them, but I wouldn't mind if everyone observed the Sabbath because we are Jews, and it should be written in the identity card that we are Jews.

*L:* I would like to see, and I wish this would come true, all of the Jews here and in the Diaspora become more religious than Rav Shick and the penitents, and believe in God and prayer every day. [Rav Shick is the Hasidic leader of the group that has moved to Yavneel].

*R:* Why the Rav Shick? Is he more religious than your father? He's not more religious than my father. You're talking nonsense . . .

*L:* If my father had the money he would do just as the Rav Shick is doing and try to bring everyone back to religion.

*A:* Even though he will bring you to the Ashkenazi method and tradition?

*L:* Why? Don't I know as well as he does?

None of the people I interviewed among the Ashkenazi core group sounded anything like Rivka and Leah with regard to beliefs about spirits, devils, wonder-working saints or the evil eye, although remarkably similar folk beliefs and superstitions were not uncommon among East European shtetl Jews of an earlier generation. And although there exists a vast gap between Ashkenazim and Sephardim in vocabulary and, most important, in religious imagery and worldview, the distance separating the two groups may not be as great as it appears.

Neither group seems overly preoccupied with sin, or remorse, or rumination about the condition of their immortal souls. Reluctantly (and at times testily), they might admit that different paths—rituals, interpretations—may lead to a shared goal. Both groups stress "essence" above practice, so that the Ten Commandments and basic morality take precedence over ritual observance, although the latter still tends to achieve higher emphasis among the Sephardim. While first- and second-generation Sephardim are still more taken with the various aspects of "folk religion" than are the Ashkenazim, this might be more a function of immigrant generation than it is reflective of deeper difference in religious outlook.

My conversation with Leah and Rivka, as well as numerous other discussions with both Sephardim and Ashkenazim in Yavneel, reflects the presence of a rather high degree of filial piety as a key factor in the relationship to religion. "In my father's house" is something of a shared theme for both groups, although the language used and the degree of passion brought to the matter are somewhat different. Rather than totally different themes being emphasized we are witness more to variation on a shared theme. At the center are the key elements of continuity, peoplehood, warmth, approval, and, most important, a sort of stripped-down, basic, rather unsophisticated, unintellectual religious belief. It is a belief that would not pass muster with any religious establishment, Sephardi as well as Ashkenazi, but is part of the warp and woof of the villagers' identity across generations, different traditions, and time of arrival in the community.

## Pork Is Not Tasty, It's Also Not Proper: Religious Beliefs and Practices

American Jewish visitors to Israel are often heard to express surprise, sometimes bordering on shock, when confronted with what appears to be a largely secular society, perceived as being not too different in this respect from their own. It is difficult to imagine just what they had expected to find, but clearly it seems to have more to do with an image of the East European shtetl than with what goes on in the streets of Tel Aviv or Haifa. These expectations are based on widespread ignorance of the Israeli reality, but they also reflect disappointment tempered somewhat by a measure of ambivalence. On the one hand, some American tourists are pleased with the recognizable and the familiar, but on the other, frustrated because of the absence of the presumed virtues of faith and act attributed to the generation of the grandparents and thought to be still alive in Israel. What was cast aside in the Diaspora because of the need to integrate into a largely gentile culture should, it is thought, have found haven and expression in the dominant and sovereign Jewish culture of modern Israel. People are disappointed that there is wife beating, alcoholism, drugs, discotheques, hard rock, crime, and, to top it all, a rather ghettoized community of the very Orthodox who live apart and are perceived as marginal here as in other parts of the Diaspora. The Bible may be taught in the schools but the street behavior of young Israelis seems more closely related to that of youngsters in Baltimore or South Bend than to the Jerusalem and Galilee of imagination.

For many there is the sense that an agreement has been violated. The agreement has never been vocalized, never formally arrived at, but it would seem that a sort of silent division of labor—as between the tribes of Zevulun and Issachar—was preached wherein the Israelis would live lives of deep continuity with the Jewish, essentially religious, past of this people, while the Diaspora would cheer and support this development with its resources—financial, political, and emotional. When confronted by this notion, Israelis tend to find it amusing and generally attribute it to the naiveté of Americans, or in the worst case, to invincible ignorance.

Whereas many Israelis find this attitude to be odd, curiously, however, they largely share this perception of how things should be. Insofar as there is a future for Judaism and for the Jewish people, it is widely felt that Israel will act as the spearhead of creative survival and in effect will be responsible for maintaining the authentic tradition, which is first and foremost the religious tradition of the pre-Holocaust generation. The broad Israeli response to what they understand constitutes Reform and Conservative Jewry is that these are inauthentic perversions of the tradition and that however onerous the demands of Orthodoxy, it is in fact the legitimate framework for the expression of their religious outlook.[17] However, this aura of legitimacy that has been passed down to Orthodoxy does not carry with it a devotion to a comprehensive or systematic body of belief or ritual or ceremonial practice so much as it does a sense of *propriety* with respect to what is done and not done. Some things are just not done if one wishes to include oneself within the corpus of Jewish peoplehood, and Israelis seem to define the matter somewhat more vigorously and narrowly than does, let us say, American Jewry.[18]

American Jews in this Diaspora context tend to look over their shoulders at what members of comparable social groups in the broader culture are doing or saying, including in the matter of religion. It is not accidental that ceremonies, rites of passage, patterns of prayer, and congregational organizations in the United States tend to be consonant with the dominant upper-middle-class mold, rather than those hallowed by tradition. Sometimes they mesh, and mesh well, with the tradition, and at other times one sees at work factors evocative of a new dispensation such as the extraordinary emphasis placed on confirmation ceremonies, or Hanukkah as an anodyne for Christmas, or the rabbi as a pastoral rather than religiously authoritative figure.

Israelis also look over their shoulders, but here more often than not they tend to measure behavior and standards against what is viewed as an authentic reflection of Jewish praxis and a Jewish universe. Here one assumes that the gentiles will not approve, but nobody thinks to ask. The question, often the silent question, posed together with the backward glance, is "how close to the original, to the true pattern of Orthodoxy is this or that act or position?" The president, I would surmise, did not bring a skullcap to Yavneel because of the nature of the occasion being celebrated: he *always* has one on hand. Why?

Because the leader of the Jewish state might find himself at any time called upon to participate in some act having religious overtones, and it would *never* do to trim tradition through neglect, denial, or even unpreparedness. The president is not only the head of state but the leading Jewish citizen of the state; and as such his referent is the Orthodox tradition rather than any personal belief or bias that he as an individual might harbor. His public religious behavior is expected and approved, and the fact that he is a yachtsman, tennis player, and aristocratically inclined cosmopolitan who feels quite at home in Gstaad or a Parisian salon must be and is eclipsed in his representational role. (The single president in Israel's history who was not able to perform in this fashion, the internationally renowned scientist Ephraim Katzir, was also, it should be noted, Israel's least popular and thus least successful holder of the office who concluded his service after only one term.)

Politicians, public servants, leaders of the Army, educators all tend to "look over their shoulders" to check the propriety of this or that act, or policy, or response against the backdrop of the Orthodox tradition. To a marked extent this is related to the peculiar and rather unique polity of Israel where religiously orthodox political parties can make or break governments and where, in fact, they hold in their hands the balance of political power. But beyond this factor, whose importance cannot be underestimated, there exists a wider social consensus that approves the inclusion of religious acts and ceremonials in the public and private life of the country and its citizens. Although Israelis grumble about rabbinic interference into private lives ranging from how (and if) one marries or gets divorced, the manner in which one is buried, and whether or not one is permitted a cornea transplant and much more, there exists no anticlerical movement in the country, nor has there been much in the way of either spontaneous or organized protest on the part of the non-Orthodox. One can only conclude that either religious tradition as defined by the Orthodox establishment largely reflects the desires of great numbers of Israelis, or that Orthodoxy fills some key role on the psychopolitical map of the country. Most likely, it is a complex combination of factors, making precise analysis difficult as well as highly tentative.

Tentativeness is enhanced rather than lessened when turning to the results of surveys and polls carried out in the country at large, as well as the particular survey carried out in Yavneel in 1988. In the national samples, Israelis defined themselves such that about 20 percent are Orthodox *(dati)*, 45 percent secular *(hiloni)*, and 35 percent traditional *(masorti)*.[19] The Orthodox are those whose lives are guided and marked by observance of the commandments and by their granting full authority to the Orthodox rabbinical leadership to interpret and oversee observance; secular Israelis are those who do not structure their lives in relation to the observance of the commandments and do not seek or accept religious sanction for their acts; whereas the quite amorphous traditional category is comprised of those who value religion, observe partially and idiosyncratically, and waffle with respect to the amount of authority willingly granted to the established religious leadership.

Orthodoxy does not present any insurmountable problem of definition (at least not for those outside this camp), and in view of the fact that contemporary secularism in Israel is more behavioral than ideological in nature, it, too, is a fairly straightforward category to define.[20] The traditional category, however, does present problems because of its amorphous and catch-all nature. Behaviorally it might run the gamut from absolutely minimal and rather symbolic observance, such as the lighting of Hanukkah candles (with or without a blessing) to attendance at occasional Sabbath morning services, the religious confirmation of youngsters, or even a fairly high degree of kashruth observance and more. It might reflect a desire for continuity, a mode for expanding and anchoring a sense of "Israeliness," or merely a reluctance to be labeled a secularist.

My sense of the matter is that the traditional camp in Israel is far larger—given the loose categorization—than the surveys suggest, and that by most standards Israel is to a marked degree a religious society. While *observance* might be circumscribed by commitment to the Orthodox pattern, *celebration* is not, so that if 23 percent of the population *observes* the Sabbath by attending synagogue and refraining from travel or other forbidden activities, a far higher proportion of the population *celebrates* the Sabbath in ways not sanctioned by Orthodoxy but nevertheless clearly delimited. Can this large segment of the population be defined as secular even if they classify themselves as such? There is a secular segment of the Israeli population who are clearly so on grounds of both ideology and behavior. My sense, however, is that this secular group constitutes considerably less than the 45 percent of the population according to the various polls and surveys and that, in fact, we must view the traditional group as by far the largest and most salient in the society.

When survey data for the country as a whole tells us that 99 percent of the Jewish population attend a seder on Passover and 88 percent light Hanukkah candles, it might very well still be possible to square this with a generally secular commitment or outlook.[21] Clearly, if 88 percent of American non-Jews have Christmas trees in their homes, it tells us very little about religious orientation other than in the most formal affiliatory sense, if that. The same absence of a clear message can be garnered from the proportions of Israelis who attend a seder or light Hanukkah candles.

But what are we to make of figures telling us that 79 percent buy only kosher meat, 74 percent fast on Yom Kippur, and 44 percent separate meat and dairy dishes?[22] The Yavneel survey elicited very similar figures of 76 percent, 71 percent, and 50 percent for the above, as well as demonstrating some other strong inclinations toward an embrace of Jewish tradition in the community. For example, fully 73 percent of Yavneel respondents (188 households out of the approximately 400 in the community) reported that they refrained from eating leavened food products during Passover, and 50 percent performed the ceremony of burning leaven prior to the festival. On the other hand, 49 percent did not concern themselves with the provision of special kosher-for-Passover dishes, using instead their ordinary implements during the festival. Similarly high levels of adherence to tradition were reported for Sukkot, with 75 percent of Yavneel respondents claiming to build a *sukkah,* the traditional booth, and, most remarkably, 25 percent claiming to take all or most of their meals in the sukkah during the week, and 32 percent asserting that they ate some of their meals there.[23]

With respect to certain behavior that might almost be termed reflexive in nature, such as *mezuzot* on the doorposts of homes, Bar Mitzvah ceremonies for boys, participation in the Passover seder, or the lighting of Hanukkah candles, participation is nearly total. Simply stated, these are elements of the "bass religion" of the community, which are observed instinctively and have about them a naturalness utterly lacking in artifice or reflection. It would appear that Yavneel residents would no more reject or ignore these communal pieties than they would choose to chant psalms on street corners or publicly embrace Buddhism.

Much more problematic for the observer, however, are data dealing with matters of belief and practice that are not reflexive or universal, but still widespread. What, for example, does one make of the fact that 69 percent of Yavneelim assert their belief in God's giving the Torah to the Jewish people at Mount Sinai, while only 37 percent of them believe in reward and punishment associated with the Law? About one-half of respondents believe in the continuity of the soul after death, but 61 percent reject the idea of resurrection. Forty-three percent believe in the coming of the Messiah and 55 percent that a "higher force" guides Israel, while fully 67 percent believe that the Jews are "chosen." Seventy-two percent claim belief in God, although an insignificant proportion of the remaining respondents did not assert some kind of belief in a "higher power," bringing Yavneel very close to or beyond the remarkable 93 percent of Americans who claim to believe in God.

In the Yavneel survey, only 16 percent of the respondents define themselves as not in any way traditional, while 13 percent claim to be completely observant, with an additional 6 percent asserting "almost" complete observance. An additional 28 percent say that they observe the tradition, and 36 percent lay claim to a little observance. Notwithstanding, 42 percent define themselves as not religious, while an additional 30 percent say of themselves that they are not "particularly religious." In other words, we are witness here to a fairly high level of religious observance within a population that does not see itself as being religious.

It is clear that a high proportion of Yavneelim feel attached to tradition, recognize the essential legitimacy of its orthodox interpretation, and judge their behavior using Orthodoxy as a measure, thus placing themselves in the category of the nonreligious. Yavneelim think of themselves as nonreligious because they measure themselves against the backdrop of the normative tradition rather than that of the pervasive "ground-bass" that by nature is not susceptible to quantification—so much observance, so much nonobservance. Traditional religion prescribes 613 commandments, providing a rather precise measure of compliance and noncompliance; but the pervasive religious atmosphere of Yavneel rejects what might be called divine accountancy at the same time that it rather sheepishly accepts its legitimacy—historical if not always temporal.

Quite without conscious thought about the matter, Yavneelim have evolved a kind of religious web within which their Judaism is being spun out and embellished. We don't believe in God, but in Him who has chosen the Jewish people and commanded them to follow a certain destiny. We don't carefully observe the rule of kashruth, but pork is not tasty and it certainly is not nice. The Passover is family but more—much more. We were slaves in the land of Egypt, and perhaps even more tellingly a people was shaped and formed from a rabble. We don't carefully observe the Sabbath of tradition, but we celebrate it as a deep tie to the past and a bridge to the future. The concept of reward and punishment is a misty one, applicable to the emergent phase of Judaism, but an internalized gyroscopic pointer guides us to apprehend its meaning intuitively.

Thus, with only the rarest of exceptions almost all Yavneelim abstain from pork and shellfish. Some state outright that these foods revolt them; others say they are not really tasty. All or almost all agree that eating them is *lo yafeh,* not nice, or to elevate the response, "unaesthetic." In only one case of militant rejection did a respondent gleefully and rather provocatively revel in the violation of this central taboo: a man mischievously described bowing to his sons' desire for a traditional Bar Mitzvah ceremony to which he was clearly opposed, but partially "corrected" his acquiescence with a follow-up lunch of shrimp. In other cases where the forbidden foods were eaten it tended to be outside the home, and admission of the fact was reluctant, usually bearing the stamp of at least a bit of guilt. Again we are witness to the projection of a sense of *propriety* with respect to the tradition. It is not that God forbade this or that, or that the rabbis did, but rather that there are acceptable and unacceptable modes of Jewish behavior; that they tend to parallel rather closely the normative religious patterns is neither accidental nor without significance.

The cumulative impression gained from questionnaires, conversations, and interviews in the community points to an overarching propensity to accept the Orthodox pattern of Judaism as the legitimate point of departure in both religious behavior and ideology. Yavneelim really don't have a serious argument with upholders, formal and informal, of the traditional Orthodox religious structure. They are not anticlerical in principle, although there exists a widely shared view of what the limits of rabbinical authority should be. They are not in the majority opposed to the basic patterns of Jewish ritual and certainly not to what is understood of the moral underpinnings and demands of Jewish faith. Both synagogue and home-based ritual are seen as appealing and highly functional on both an individual and communal basis. They are, in short, rather comfortable with their religion, and if one of the central functions of higher religion is to dispel this sort of comfort within one's spiritual skin—introducing instead an element of "holy agitation"—then this pattern must be sought elsewhere. As in Bellah's Italy, so in Yavneel the "average" citizen accepts that the religious context within which he lives is "true," and then proceeds to cut the cloth—within bounds—to fit the suit.

The significant change witnessed in Yavneel to what had been the pattern of Diaspora Judaism for millennia concerns the kind of rooted comfort or ease with which Judaism is perceived. Although some 35 percent thought Judaism the only true religion, and an additional 46 percent thought it true but no more so than other religions, one is struck by the way in which religion has been integrated visibly into the lives of the town's residents. Rarely, in the years in which I observed life in the village, did I engage in what might be described as a religious or theological discussion, with, of course, the exception of Black Asa, a few others, and the newly arrived Hasidim. Discussion about the role of the religious establishment, about rabbis and politics, about how it was and how it is—yes; but never about truth or falsity, a caring God or a hidden God, the school of Hillel or the school of Shammai, good or evil, Reform or Conservatism. These were either all in the nature of givens or, probably more likely, were not deemed sufficiently important in the lives of the residents.

Yet, neither is the role of religion in the lives of the villagers marginal or without importance. Contrary to the Diaspora format marked as it tended to be by great intensity concerning the relations between God and men, Jews and non-Jews, this world and the next, sin and punishment, or, following the emancipation, a movement away from the religious imperative entirely, Yavneel is pointing to a new direction where religion provides a sort of defining background buzz. It does not constitute a central concern, nor does it define the parameters of daily existence. Whereas defining oneself as Jewish or being so defined by others often provided the core or kernel of one's identity in the Diaspora, Yavneelim see their Jewishness as playing an essentially integrative role in their selfhood, but certainly laying no claim to centrality. Its hallmark is a certain ease, a sense of wholeness, a feeling of comfort—religion as context rather than destiny.

With the exception of two or three residents, even the confirmed atheists and agnostics find something good or positive to say about religion, and even see some curious role for themselves under its spreading wings. Affirming Judaism whether or not one considers oneself a believer is not psychologically taxing, much as affirming Catholicism is not in Bellah's Italian context. It is simply "there" as part of the personal and communal self-definition. But for Jews and Judaism this is a departure. To be a Jew has carried with it a complex web of affirmations, defenses, choices. It was and remains a veritable cauldron of choices. The Diaspora Jew who chose atheism necessarily rejected ritual observance and all that it implied. In Yavneel, however, most of the community's professed atheists and agnostics (not to speak of those who choose to understate this proclivity) refrain from pork, fast on Yom Kippur, ritually circumcise their sons, celebrate in a fairly traditional manner Hanukkah, Purim, Sukkot, and Passover, place *mezuzot* on their doorposts, and more. These observances and celebrations have become part and parcel of the rhythm of their lives, and not necessarily by default. It is not because no choice exists, but rather because no choice was demanded; and religious practices that elsewhere and at other times require an active and reflective affirmation are here slipped into like a comfortable pair of slippers.

## ATHEISTS AND BELIEVERS: TOGETHER AND APART

Religious belief and behavior in the village run the full gamut from atheistic rejection to what detractors might call a deep fundamentalist embrace of Orthodoxy. Most Yavneelim accept a role for religion in their lives, and the phenomenon of militant atheism or undeviating secularism is almost completely absent. Most of those who define themselves as secular, or nonbelievers, when pressed seem to arrive at some mild deist position justified either on the grounds of a shadow of personal doubt or, more likely, the need of men and women generally to embrace something beyond the "everyday." There is also widespread agreement that religion—Jewish religion—fulfills a legitimating function vis-à-vis the state that no other force seems adequate to fulfill. Finally, the level of what I have called "filial piety," or respect for the memory of parents and a desire to ensure continuity, seems to translate inevitably into a readiness to lock into the ancient religious tradition rather than other possibilities that for most appear to be inadequate as potential vehicles for either group memory or communal survival.

Will Herberg, attempting to explain the basis for the post–World War II religious revival in the United States, invoked "Hansen's Law," which concludes about the immigrant population of America that what the sons chose to forget the grandsons chose to remember.[24] In speaking of the immigrant trauma, it is claimed that the sons and daughters of immigrants rejected the cultural baggage of the parental generation in an attempt to become wholly American, whereas the grandchildren, not having to prove their credentials in this respect, busily sought out factors of cultural distinctiveness that they could embrace as their personal cultural inheritance *and* contribution to the communality of America. Clearly, it could not be language, dress, or a variety of other elements that would set them outside the broad cultural consensus. But given the pluralistic religious structure of America this distinction could legitimately be expressed in an embrace of the religious confession of one's forebears, which was viewed not only as not lessening one's sense of Americanness but, indeed, as enhancing it.

The differences between the migrations to Palestine at the end of the nineteenth century and to the New World are too extensive to enumerate here, but at least one must be noted. For many, Jews and non-Jews alike, what was being sought in going to America was a break with the past rather than its repair. Most of the Jewish immigrants arriving at the turn of the century from the villages and towns of Eastern Europe did not seek to shuck off their Jewishness or reject their faith, but neither did they expect to fulfill themselves religiously at a higher level than was possible at home. If anything, they feared (correctly) that the opposite would be the case. Very few thought that a new dimension could be added to Judaism as a result of the move; and, indeed, among the traditional religious leadership, opposition to immigration persisted until the outbreak of World War II on the deeply held assumption that America represented a threat to Jewish continuity. Among this traditional leadership there was opposition to the move to Zion as well, but at least in the early stages of return this tended to be based on fears of the growth of false messianism or misguided attempts at hurrying the Messiah rather than on fear of assimilation or the weakening of religious commitment.

The majority of the founding settlers of Yavneel were Orthodox in belief and practice, and they largely succeeded in transferring this pattern to the new landscape. It was not their religion that they sought to change, or to repair, as much as it was the context of alienation, the status of stranger, that they sought to abrogate and that decidedly had constituted their fate in the various exiles from which they came. The move to Zion represented a change in the direction of a newly organic, unbifurcated mode of living in which an easy flow between religion, work, family, and other aspects of life would flourish. This aim, in effect, must be seen as constituting a revolution in Jewish life no less significant in its long-term implications than the embrace of Zionism or the promise of emancipation.

Changes in all areas of life clearly occurred over time, and just as the agricultural methods, personal life-styles, patterns of education, political behavior, and more, were influenced by events and surroundings, so too was the religion of the community. Primarily the changes in Yavneel were of a behavioral kind, which might be summed up as "less" religious observance, but also an ideational shift in which the binding dimension of religious authority was attenuated and weakened. More and more, through free choice, picking and choosing, easing of that which might be considered burdensome or onerous, Yavneelim have softened traditional practices, and in the process introduced a certain level of permissiveness. In this Yavneelim have followed the broad avenues previously paved in other societies as well as in the Holy Land itself.

What is singular here, one might even say remarkable, is to be found in the deep penetration and continuing salience of the religious factor in the lives of the great majority of the village's citizens. Not only has the "religion of the fathers" not been rejected, but no overriding sense of a need for reform or correction on a formal level has been expressed or presumably experienced. Changes have occurred and been introduced, but when it is suggested that perhaps conservative or liberal Judaism would be more suitable, the idea is rejected by almost all. As the African-American historian Eric Lincoln once observed: "When you see a Black who isn't a Baptist somebody has been fooling around with his religion." Similarly, something is awry with a Yavneeli who rejects the religious tradition to the point of seeing absolutely no role for it in his or the community's existence, or expresses a desire for systematic institutional and ideational change. When a Yavneeli rejects religion, or denies God, his argument tends not to be based on strict rationalism or an alternative vision but rather Sinai and the Ten Commandments. For example, Yehuda, a retired engineer, explains his agnosticism in this way:

> I'm a free person but I don't know—there is some belief deep in the heart as they say. After all, we witness natural phenomena which cannot be explained. And just as no one can prove that God exists, no one, as yet, can prove that he does not exist. There is some force, perhaps it is called nature or something else; there is some force which intervenes in nature. When I press down on a table with the pressure of one kilogram, the table presses back with the same force. If it couldn't press back, it would break. And so, there is something . . . it cannot be denied. But all of these rituals say nothing to me. For me the essence of religion lies in the Ten Commandments. Thus a man who lives by the Ten Commandments is viewed by God, if he exists, as an excellent person. It says, "Thou shalt not steal, thou shalt not covet"; these are all good things.

"But," I asked, "do you accept the commandment to believe in God?"

> No, of course not. But I can seek some sort of explanation as to what happened there [at Sinai]. After all, we were slaves for so many years, a nation of slaves. And Moses, due to his being

abandoned and then adopted into Pharaoh's household, received a good education and then later when he found out that he was a Jew, he wanted to liberate his people. And *what* a people this was! A nation of slaves who were illiterate, and he had to give them some sort of constitution or something. So what was he to do? Could he say, I am giving you these laws? So he said God gave them to him and he went to the top of the mountain and sat there for a week and came down and said, "Here, God gave them to me."

Setting aside what one may call an exercise in pop theology, and a seemingly ineffable Jewish affirmation of the benefits to be had from a "good education" from whatever source, Yehuda is expressing a guarded rejection of the source of Revelation, but not of its content. Yehuda, though an avowed "non-religionist," hopes to dispense somehow with the god of Revelation (although not with "some force") while maintaining the "essence" of the matter. Yehuda cannot imagine Israel without the *faith* of Israel, however liberally or flexibly it is defined: "I am not religious," he says, "but I tell you I respect those who wear the knitted skull caps who both fulfill *mitzvot*, believe in God—which doesn't bother me, you understand—and do their duty. They serve in the Army, they believe in the nation and, in the final analysis, it is a Jewish state we have deemed to establish here and thus it should have a certain Jewish character." "Do you mean to say a religious character?," I ask him. "Yes, a little—but not overdone."

"Little" being a relative term, one cannot fail to observe the pervasiveness of a religious backdrop in the life of the village. Rather remarkable, however, is that with the exception of those falling on the very orthodox end of the scale whose commitment is manifest in everything from dress to social relationship to work, there is little to distinguish between those who define themselves as secular and those who see themselves as traditional. One would be hard-pressed to determine positions on religious observance from visible public behavior with the important exception, of course, of regular synagogue attendance. Social relationships seem unhindered by one's religious stance, with an easy flow of contact between traditionalists and secularists. Political behavior, on the whole, and with the exception of those at the radical extremes, tends to be conservative/centrist whether or not a person sees himself as religious, traditional, or secular. Similarly with attitudes to work, ties to place, and broad conceptions of morality—public or private. There seems to be a communal consensus on the limits, parameters, and observances that signal inclusion in the mainstream or relegate a person to marginal status. Even among the most outspoken secularists there is a readiness to inclusivity with regard to the tradition, and a recognition that its absence or denial would detract from the authenticity of their lives, or at the very least their claims on full inclusion in the community. The most extreme position that I heard put forth for complete secularism was presented to me by Amos, a forty-year-old professional and third-generation Yavneeli:

> Are you asking if I believe? I believe, I am a great believer in man's conscience, and in ethics. I believe in sacrifice, I believe in the nation, I believe in good faith and a willingness to contribute—I believe in anything you want. What I don't believe in is a superior being who sits on some cloud somewhere and manages account books dealing with the earthlings. In this I do not believe. I consider this rather primitive. And that is how I educate my children. In any case, I am tolerant and understanding toward any man, whatever his beliefs, which means I can also except a Jew who believes in the God of Abraham, Isaac, and Jacob as well as one who believes in Jesus Christ. On principle I am opposed to any kind of ritual, but from time to time—and when I feel like it, you understand—I light candles on Friday night: just for the atmosphere and to give us a nice feeling. I don't consider it a religious act, and I do it at eight o'clock when we have dinner rather than when the sun sets.

> Yes, on Hanukkah I light candles, because it is a historical holiday for me, and, yes, on Passover I have a seder. I think of it as a holiday of spring, and not as something representing our exit from Egypt. It symbolizes the spring, on the one hand, and

> a sort of passing from slavery to freedom for our nation, on the other. In my own Haggadah there are more elements of Zionism with passages depicting the War of Independence and other things connected with the nation's return to its land, and not Rabbi X said this and Rabbi Y said that, as it is written in the traditional Haggadah. We eat matzot a week or ten days before Passover begins, because we like eating them after a whole year of doing without. After a few days, we lose interest, so we take some bread out of the freezer and enjoy living the way we want to. We are total nonbelievers.

From my many conversations with him, I know that his secularism is deeply felt. There is no contesting Amos's claim to being a "total nonbeliever"; he is not a "secret" believer nor is he an "unconscious" believer. But despite his rejection of belief and tempering of holiday observance, what might be called his "symbolic life" derives from and draws upon the religious tradition.

No matter what he believes or does not believe there is little that separates Amos from Rafi, a municipal worker of Tunisian origin of about the same age who also claims to be a lifelong nonobserver, but who does admit to a belief in God. "I never ate unkosher, I don't eat leaven on Passover, I fast on Yom Kippur," Rafi remarked, "but you can't observe just this and that and call yourself religious." Both Rafi and Amos see themselves as nonreligious, yet observe selectively and idiosyncratically, and although one sees his behavior as a failing and the other as an achievement, in practical terms the differences are surface and minimal. Aside from aspects of class and origin there is not much—in terms of religious behavior—separating the two. Even in the matter of his son's Bar Mitzvah, which Amos refused to allow to take place in the town synagogue, he express a kind of sub-rosa traditionalism that keeps him firmly within the communal consensus and perhaps more than that.

> I persuaded him to have his Bar Mitzvah at the Western Wall in Jerusalem, and indeed it was quite moving. I must admit it. I contacted the Rabbi of the Wall, and he gave us a

date, and as it turned out it was exactly the date it should have been [the date coinciding with the Hebrew calendar day of his birth]. We got the name of a rabbi who would wait for us there, and the whole family turned out. The rabbi was waiting for us; he showed us in and we went through the whole little ceremony. It took about half an hour for Yoram to read the Torah portion. Before this he learned how to put on tefillin (phylacteries) in Yavneel, taught to him by a religious old-timer who likes to do this sort of thing. It was very moving. It was a very moving act at the Western Wall, which has such glorious symbolic meaning in Israel's history, which I don't want to go into, but I was very touched.

I should emphasize that Amos together with old Shimon are considered, by themselves as well as others, the town's most outspoken and militant secularists. Both lay claim to having no religious beliefs and to holding no religious sentiments. Their lack of belief is not in question, but what is equally unquestionable is the fact that the natural, enveloping rhythm of Yavneel's folk religion is an integral and, indeed, accepted part of their life history, making for a kind of coherent worldview that has not generally characterized the Judaism of exile. It is a Judaism of easy flow between memory, choice, and act. Although Amos sought to convince his son that instead of being called to the Torah he follow the kibbutz tradition of the Bar Mitzvah by taking upon himself the completion of thirteen *mitzvot,* defined as good or at least challenging deeds, the ceremony marking the occasion accepted the traditional Jewish age for confirmation (thirteen) and its goal (the assumption of adult responsibility hallowed by tradition). Though Amos is a confirmed atheist, he was nonetheless by his own admission "touched" and "moved" by the religious ceremony, contrary though it might have been to his stated ideology. Instead of a sense of betrayal of deeply held principles, or a feeling of having succumbed to coercive outside forces, he experienced feelings of joy and pride.

In Yavneel, religion has a good name and the carrying out of acts associated with the "bass" religion are *de rigueur.* Young and old, veterans and newcomers, farmers and nonfarmers—

all appear to embrace what might be termed a "lowest-common-denominator" traditionalism, which in other contexts would place them at least among the semi-observant. The head of the local *Chevrah Kadishah,* the burial society, is not a Sabbath observer, but sees his task in the society as a holy undertaking. The former head of the farmers' union "usually" doesn't work on the Sabbath, and drives his car, but would not conceive of not celebrating the holidays "as my grandfather did," although he defines himself as "not religious." An old farmer started to go to synagogue when his father died in order to say *Kaddish* (the Jewish daily prayer for the dead), and found out that he "liked it." So he puts on phylacteries every day, prays regularly, but works on the Sabbath when he feels he must. "I like religion," he says, and "I'm all for it. A man has to be afraid of something, but I am against coercion. Nobody is going to tell me how to behave." A young fourth-generation farmer who also sees himself as "far from religious" doesn't mix meat and dairy (as the laws of kashruth prescribe), doesn't eat leaven on Passover, "absolutely" doesn't eat pork, and, as for God, observes that "maybe in my subconscious I do believe in Him."

In the town one might be privy to criticism, indeed vicious and biting criticism of the town rabbi, or of the Hasidim, or the "unholy" mix of religion and politics that characterizes the Israeli scene; but the broader category of Judaism as the faith of the Jewish people remains unscathed and indeed continues to enjoy a high degree of credit for truth, probity, and other virtues. This is an attitude seemingly shared by believers and unbelievers alike, and appears almost unshakable—almost, but not completely. There exists in Yavneel, as in Israel generally, a broad reservoir of credit for religion and those who are deemed to represent it that seems at times boundless. Corruption surrounding the institution of kashruth, cruel neglect of women's rights in matters of divorce and custody, political machinations by the religious parties which would bring a blush to the cheeks of an old Tammany Hall functionary, acts of violence perpetrated for this or that holy end blessed by either approval or silence on the part of religious leadership, seem to make the front page of every daily newspaper. But most Israelis react to this with an insouciance that defies rational explanation, and tend to think of these acts as perhaps unfortunate, certainly unaesthetic, but clearly far from the criminal culpability that would be leveled were they to derive from other sources. Opposing in an active fashion what is deemed religion is—like the consumption of pork—not nice! It is seen as, in effect, soiling one's own nest, defiling the memory of the ancestors, and, not unimportantly, weakening the basis of legitimacy that the society so sorely seeks.

Nonetheless, one suspects that there is a limit to the tolerance for behavior not consistent with the values of the broader community. The religious scene of Yavneel is, in this regard, perhaps a bellwether of what awaits the society as a whole: a willingness to embrace and integrate Jewish religion into everyday life on all levels, together with a growing sense that a hiatus between Orthodoxy and the *real* religion of the country is developing. There exists the beginnings of a crisis of religious authority brought about by the inability of the Orthodox establishment to recognize the victory that *is or was already theirs.* As we find in Yavneel, putative secularists as well, of course, as those defining themselves as religious, shared and share much more than they don't in terms of how they relate to the tradition. But if we are able to see the first stirrings of a failure of communitas, it is in the insistence of the established religious leadership and the ultra-Orthodox, or haredi, sector to raise the level of coercive demands for Orthodox behavior in a society increasingly evolving a kind of folk Judaism with an authenticity of its own. This folk or "bass" religion is parallel to, rather than in place of, the normative pattern; and rather than constituting a threat, it would appear to promise a context of deep continuity with the Orthodox pattern if allowed to do so.

What appears to separate believers and nonbelievers in Yavneel is found in a growing fear among the latter of being engulfed in a web of Orthodoxy that is viewed as foreign and certainly imposed rather than evolved. In place of the comfort that marks the integrated bass religion, there is a perceived sense that the agitation of the *Galut* Judaism of the grandfathers' generation, a Judaism of iron *mitzvot* and formal observance, is being insinuated into their lives. The reactions thus far to this perceived threat tend to be tinged with sadness and a sense of regret rather than embedded hostility, although anger is growing among some people; and, indeed, Yavneel is perhaps the first settlement in the country where an active movement to keep ultra-Orthodox Jews from settling in their midst has emerged.

Menashe, one of the leaders of this opposition group who is also one of the most respected scions of an original settler family, plaintively recounted what he perceives as the Yavneel reality today as against what it was in years past.

> My father was a free thinker, what they called a "radical," but my grandfather was Orthodox, and when one of his sons who lived in Beit Alpha would visit him on Saturday, he would tell him to come along to the synagogue with him. He knew he traveled by train and wagon, so he said to neighbors who commented that the mitzvah of settling the land made up for other transgressions, and might even be more important. But not everybody was as tolerant as he was. Old man Kuznitz who lived next door to the shul used to stand outside during prayer, and if anybody approached on horseback or wagon he would grab the reins and forbid them to proceed. Nobody would dare to stop him. What? Would anybody strike an old man? So, in effect, old Yavneel was closed down on Shabbat. If anybody wanted to work or ride a horse we took great pains to take the long way around through the fields, avoiding the main street and showing respect for the religious.
>
> We didn't look for a fight with the religious and they, on the whole, didn't look for a fight with us. Yavneel was probably the first place in the country which tried to create a harmonious life-style between the religious and the secular. It was the first place in the country to reach an agreement that there would be a teacher of religion in the public school, and that the headmaster would be observant. Every once in a while there was some kind of argument about religion, but we argued much more about farming and land and water than we did about religion. Yavneel knew how to keep the peace.

But now they are trying to change us, to impose by force their way of life on us, and we won't let them. I will do whatever is necessary to preserve our way of life, so that my grandchildren can live here. My grandchildren—the oldest is fourteen—have already turned "anti" haredi, and they will soon become antireligious. These people have turned what was good into an unlivable hell.

Most of the Sephardi citizens of Yavneel fit comfortably into the religious framework of the community, observing a respect for tradition and fluid celebration of key events in the shared religious calendar, while also fearful of coerced changes in their modes of observance. But, for reasons to be explained later, they are, on the whole, uninvolved in organized efforts to prevent large-scale haredi settlement in the community. Conventional Israeli wisdom avers that Sephardim who are religious or traditional tend to be more tolerant of nonobservance or attenuated observance than are the Ashkenazi religious, and indeed that does seem to be sustained by the reactions of Sephardi townspeople. Not only were relationships between religious and self-defined nonreligious Sephardim open and seemingly without conflict, but within families there exists an easygoing acceptance of different levels of observance. In a number of families one can see religiously Orthodox grandparents, traditional children of a "bass" orientation, and their own children, some of whom might sport skullcaps and others not. Kobi, a hired worker on a Jordan Valley kibbutz, was born in Tunisia but brought up in Yavneel. His life history is quite typical of his generation, and his religious stance might be termed that of a "fading traditionalist": not letting go of what was, a threatened pride in his Sephardi heritage, a deep regard for religion combined with a rather unusual mix of observance and nonobservance.

I am a *ba'al tefila* [prayer leader] in our synagogue, and in this I am following my father who was a *hazan* [cantor]. I sent my children to the religious school here, but when they grew up they stopped being religious. What can you do? When they grow up you no longer have any control over them. We have to keep the religious way and so I am against Reform Jews. Even though I respect religion, the Hasidim here don't consider me kosher. One of them came to my son and started asking him questions about my observing or not observing Shabbat. Do I turn on the TV? Do I turn on lights? After prayer one Friday night I confronted him and warned him not to start fights in good families with their rumors. We, I said, are willing to respect you, and you must treat us the same. When I was young I played football on Shabbat—so does this make me unkosher? This was the way we were able to get closer to the Ashkenazim, and we never had any problem until they [the Hasidim] came. We get along, although I still prefer to pray the Sephardic way. It is warmer than the prayer style of the Ashkenazim. We have our religious tradition and it is no less than theirs. They will have trouble if they don't respect us.

The use of "respect" with regard to the religious tradition has assumed some of the trappings of a communal mantra. The reference to religion almost invariably has attached to it the term *kavod* (honor or respect) or the affirmation that *"ani mechabed"* (I respect).

## A Yavneel Story

As you know, I am not a religious man and neither was my father before me, nor are my children after me. But I respect people who live in an honest fashion. I admire honest people. I'll tell you something. A soldier under my command in the War of Independence was killed—he was only seventeen. One of the most difficult tasks given the officers was visiting the families of soldiers who fell. I went to this soldier's house—it was on Hakranot Street in Haifa . . . . I even remember the number, 24. We went in and found the father, an old man who appeared to be about sixty-five or seventy. We told him what happened, and he looked at us and said "God gave, God took, God be blessed." But he said it in such a way that you could tell that here was a man who really believes. The mother started to cry, so he said to her, "This is a matter for men; go to the other room." And he told us the story of his life. This son was born almost twenty years after they were married and was an only child. His name was David, and his son's name was Solomon (Shloymek), and with Solomon the book was closed, the story brought to an end. "God gives, God takes." He believed! He truly believed, and I respect this *and* the faith which sustained him.

Whether Sephardi "newcomer" or veteran settler, the willingness to credit faith, to honor the tradition, still acts as a bulwark against any serious outbreak of anticlericalism, and when criticism is leveled it tends to express sadness and regret rather than true hostility. The veteran settler who recounted this story is himself a bereaved parent who lost a son in one of Israel's wars. And although he is a militant secularist he recognizes that the institution of religion is not only a powerful sustaining force personally for those who "truly" believe, but a no less pivotal force in buttressing group continuity. Indeed, one cannot deny the influence of this latter factor in the evolving of this framework of respect for a tradition so variably embraced and for a group identity in which believer and scoffer appear to share so many values.

## WE ARE HERE ONLY BECAUSE WE ARE JEWS: RELIGION AS A LEGITIMATING FORCE

For the founders as well as for their grandchildren and great-grandchildren almost one hundred years later a sense of complete "ease in Zion" remains elusive. Perhaps it could not be otherwise. Roots, a deep sense of place, the absence of a need to justify or explain why one is here rather than elsewhere requires, above all, time—a great deal of time—where generation follows generation and shared memory need no longer be constructed, pieced together, as it were, in a conscious effort to establish the legitimacy of one's existence. When roots are deep, surrender rather than volition determines identity. You are who you are. One's sense of self, at least with regard to place, washes over one and there is no need to strain in the creation of a desired destiny; it is simply as much a part of a person as his or her name or parentage, or physiognomy. Time has provided *the* Jewish definitional context, whereas space, a sense of space and ease with the *idea* and the *reality* of space, has proved difficult to achieve. Yavneelim have, I believe, come closer than any other community in the country to this "natural" relatedness to place, needing no explanation, no excuse, no apology; but even here the process retains a certain air of fragility. The success enjoyed by Yavneel in its reach for a natural relatedness to place is, while impressive, still far from complete. The national or space memory of Jews has been, other than in an ontological sense, underexercised for millennia; and a simple desire for its existence is insufficient for its anchored and natural creation. One or two generations in place are not sufficient; and based on the Yavneel experience it would appear that three or four generations are *still* not sufficient. Perhaps to have expected otherwise, as have so many, was self-deceptive, reflecting a curious insensitivity to historical and sociological process.

Israelis generally, including Yavneelim, have never quite been able to credit the Palestinian refugees' insistence that they be allowed to return to their old villages and towns, answering their seemingly perverse demand with the assertion that they can be resettled just as easily in Syria and Jordan. This position was maintained not only because Israeli national needs might require it, but also because of an inability to truly fathom this kind of deep tie to place. Hundreds of years in place have crated a web of "in-placeness" for the Palestinian that even the yeoman farmer of Yavneel could not really absorb in the deepest sense. Clearly the movement toward the reaffirmation of space as a natural ingredient in Jewish experience and practice is progressing—witness the difference between the yeomen of Yavneel and those with only one or two generations of Israeli identity behind them—but the process, as noted, is not yet complete. Thus, there exists a continuing felt need to seek justification, to create common memory, to anchor continuity, and the chosen device (or perhaps the only logical one) is sought in the one dimension of Jewishness that is most deeply woven into the fabric of Jewish experience—the religion of Israel.

Political Zionism sought, and succeeded remarkably in providing, an alternative or parallel vision to the religious one; but with the passage of time its effectiveness, in this regard as in others, has been eroded. The secularist position that was for decades an accompanying and, some would aver, integral aspect of Zionism has declined since the creation of the state and can no longer provide an alternative vision. When all is said and done, the secularist stance of a Jewish nation *sans* Jewish religion has shown itself to be shallow if not, indeed, empty. It cannot pull, it cannot preserve, it cannot anchor, and it certainly cannot legitimate. For many, if not most, Israelis, there exists a deep-seated fear that their presence here lacks legitimacy. The biblical or religious argument over and above "inevitable necessity" is sensed as being their only really adequate legitimating cloak. The return to the promised land was carried out with the deed in hand—The Holy Book that assigns title and has the weight of being accepted as such by at least that part of the world of the "other" that matters most. Herzl and Brenner are no match for Moses and Isaiah, and the evidence for this becomes more and more manifest with the passage of time and the continuing crisis of legitimacy.

It is not without significance that 68 percent of Israelis think that religious values should be strengthened, or even more remarkably, that 46 percent think that the return movement of "born-again Jews" has a positive effect on Israeli society.[25] What sense could these astounding figures make in the context of an overwhelmingly non-Orthodox society without taking into consideration the arguments I have just touched upon? These points are especially striking when we realize that both "religion" in its ultra-Orthodox manifestation and the "return" movement that is invariably a part of it reject basic elements of the national consensus such as Army service, a commitment to productive labor, liberalism, and pluralism. There is no lack of awareness among the general public of these positions of the ultra-Orthodox community—and yet there exists this apparently unshakable willingness to see positive, indeed necessary, functions for religion in national life. What adds to the power of this embrace of tradition is its naturalness, its unforced nature. In Yavneel, for example, one is constantly impressed with the ease and readiness with which quotes from the Bible or even the Mishnah spring so readily to the lips of traditionalist and secularist alike. Rather than being a device, it is normal, natural, and deeply a part of personal experience. Black Asa resorts to religious sources no more frequently than does Shimon, or Amos, or Yehuda, or Kobi, or numerous other citizens of the town who see themselves as secularists or nonbelievers; and in this they are doing first and foremost what comes naturally, and because there exists an almost visceral understanding among them that here lies ultimate justification for their renewed national existence.

Ferdynand Zweig, in a seminal book on Israel published more than twenty years ago and before the partial collapse of the Zionist secular vision, observed that Israeli society was one informed throughout by a structure of myth almost completely tied to religious imagery and to a religious base.[26] Undergirding the society there flourishes a system of myths which he identified as the myths of the Holy Book, the Holy Land, redemption, continuity, return, fulfillment, and exile, among others. The myth of the pioneer hero, which has played a key role in the unfolding drama of Israel's rebirth, has weakened and retreated as a sustaining strut in the dynamic, at the same time that the traditional religious myth structure has reinsinuated itself to a position of prominence where it had been dormant but clearly alive.

It would be incorrect, however, to suggest that battle has been joined between the two undergirding conceptions of Israel's rebirth—secular Zionism and religious traditionalism—with the latter victorious and the former leaving the stage in defeat. Matters are, as one might expect, infinitely more complex than would appear to be the case on the surface. Although the need and desire for a role for Jewish religion is manifest both in Yavneel and the country at large, and there exists a great well of positive feeling for religion, the potential for serious conflict between two highly diverse worldviews is palpable. The inclination to use religious symbols and sacred history to buttress the national enterprise has grown significantly in Israel since 1967, which results in the payment of a sort of licensing fee to the perceived keepers of the tradition through the provision of disproportionate funding to Orthodox institutions and the acceptance of behavior and ideas going counter to the national consensus. The conflicting worldviews coexist, but the potential for dissolution of the delicate symbiosis exists as well.

This is graphically demonstrated in the ceremony which takes place at the Western Wall, known as the *kotel*, the only remaining part of the temple of Herod that has become since its liberation in 1967 the most symbolically important physical site in the sacred geography of the country. A quiet struggle has been joined between the Orthodox and the rest of the population with respect to the nature of the site. Is it simply a religiously significant ruin, which, it should be noted, is not sanctioned or programmed into the formal Orthodox lexicon? Or is it a national symbol of return and rebirth on the very ashes of defeat and dispersal almost two thousand years before? The ceremony involving the swearing in of paratroopers at the Western Wall is a fixed event that demonstrates some of the implications of this dilemma.

## An Israeli Story

During the Days of Awe hundreds of young men were being sworn into the paratroops at the Western Wall. They were given two items—a rifle and a Bible—and at a given point after the mass administering of the oath they raised both into the night sky shouting, each and every one, "I swear, I swear, I swear." The unit's rabbi addressed them speaking of the meaning of the Days of Awe, of the need to reflect and change. There were drums, and bugles, and flags, and muscle.

Two hundred meters away and against the Wall itself hundreds of other young men, also uniformed after a fashion, albeit in black from head to toe, were also dealing with the Days of Awe, shouting *their* shouts and *their* oaths to the heavens. Here there were no flags, no drums, and very little visible muscle. One could not escape the conclusion that what was being viewed here were not acts emanating from two branches of the same tree, but those of utterly distinct, separate, and hostile elements. The black-clad haredim hurried—some ran—by the assembled paratroopers and their families, averting their gaze, some actually covering their eyes, allowing for no doubt that for them the existence of the celebrants was of no more significance than rain or wind. The non-Orthodox were the "other" no less than the rest of the tainted world of the goyim, the nations; and their fate, lives, and celebrations concerned them as little as if they did not exist at all.

The ceremony, with its decided pagan overtones and alien muscularity, is a near perfect example, many times repeated, of how the national framework attempts to use the legitimating potential of traditional religion toward the aim of solidifying what is perceived as a still incomplete or fragile national self-conception. The armored corps is sworn in at Masada; the paratroops and other units at the Western Wall. Independence Day is marked by special prayers; a portion from the Bible closes the evening offerings on television, and the sonorous repetition of the *Shma Yisroel,* the "Hear O Israel" creed, starts the day's broadcasting on radio. Popular songs based on the themes of the birth pangs of the Messiah, or the six days of creation, or Elijah the prophet, occupy a not inconsiderable portion of the popular song repertoire, and all religious holy days enjoy prime-time coverage on radio, TV, and other media. Israeli society is still striving for a national identity, which is seen as elusive or not fully adequate, making for a special role for the skein of continuity provided by the religious context,[27] but the process carries within it the seed of an evolving deep-seated conflict with those for whom religious faith is the standard of truth rather than a malleable device for what are understood to be profane ends.

In Yavneel, in this small place in Galilee, the drama enveloping the larger canvas can be viewed in a more modest, yet quite heightened dimension. Despite the much deeper sense of rootedness that characterizes the veteran population of the town, there is, nevertheless, a quite pervasive sense that something more is needed to buttress continuity. Menashe, the veteran settler, is, in every respect, a true son of Yavneel—soldier, farmer, and fierce upholder of Zionist verities. One cannot imagine him in any place *but* Yavneel, or in any role but those that he so naturally embodies. He is tough, combative, committed, and unswerving in his loyalties, as well as in his powerful prejudices. In Menashe's world there are comrades for whom no undertaking on his part is too great, and opponents who will be fought relentlessly and with no quarter given. Yavneel is his inheritance, the promised land that he devotedly hopes will remain the possession of his children and of their children after them. It is his anchor, his small but essential place in the chain of history reaching back to the far past, as well as the shelter from which he launches himself into the larger canvas of a reborn Israel. It is the model that he had hoped would provide the outline, if not the substance, of a new or renewed Jewish relatedness to place.

The religion of Israel does not speak to Menashe in any personal sense, but he is deeply aware of what it has meant and continues to mean in having preserved and shaped the Jewish people. For him the central concepts are "continuity," "roots," and "place," rather than "God," "His Law," and the highly delimited life-style established by tradition as the framework of Jewish belief. He is suspicious of and rejects the context of faith, and especially is this the case when, as he understands it, this faith is bent on undermining what he and the pioneering revolutionary generations preceding him had struggled to achieve. When, for example, he speaks of the Hasidim who have in the past few years chosen Yavneel as their home, his anger and rage at what he sees as behavior destructive of all that he and others had sought to put in place makes it difficult for the otherwise phlegmatic farmer to discourse rationally. The feeling of the yeoman Jewish farmer may well be likened to the retort of John Updike to the religious young protagonist in his novel *Roger's Version:* When the young man asserts that "the devil is doubt," Updike answers, "Doubt may give your dinner a funny taste, but it's faith that goes out and kills."[28]

But Menashe is conflicted. Like others in the village, he knows that "the devil is the absence of doubt," but he also knows that the denuding of tradition, which is essentially the normative faith of Israel, strikes at the very underpinnings of the enterprise to which he has devoted his life. This dilemma may result in a terribly confused, somewhat illogical response in which a belief in the Jewish religion is affirmed, although it is a religion in which Zionism replaces God.

> If I bring up my children to be Zionists, Jews but not necessarily religious Jews, we are acting correctly. Even though we don't keep tradition or pray in the synagogue or believe in God, we are Jews and we are Zionists, and we want to build our state and live in our land and provide them with roots. This creates an attachment to the Jewish religion: not through God, but through Zionism and the return to the homeland.

Menashe is reluctant, indeed unable, to completely disconnect. Rather than say we have replaced Jewish religion, Jewish faith, with a new dispensation there is persistent recourse to a sanctified fiction in which roots and an attachment to the homeland are the equivalent, if not the reality, of Jewish religiosity itself. Almost no one in the village is willing to say, "Enough, the religion of the past is dead and is to be properly buried so that we can go on." Somehow, the villagers recognize that the burial will inter more than the God-belief of the fathers and will in some way sunder the inheritance of the children. As Menashe explains:

> Young people ask, "What right do I have to live in this country?" The question is a legitimate one. Everyone, especially in an agricultural settlement, wants to see his children continue his way, his path, in the most prosaic sense of keeping the farm, the land. There is an Arab saying which has it that if the animal that ploughs is the offspring of your cow, and the man who ploughs is the son of your wife—the success of your ploughing

is assured. You see—there must be continuity if there are to be roots. This tie to the land was not born yesterday. Herzl failed when he sought a solution somewhere else than in Palestine because this is the only place where we have historical rights. It was promised to us. We came here because of a historical link to the place, and the Zionist leadership soon learned that the Jews would not be attracted to any place which lacked this tie. So when young people ask what right we have I point to the Book where it was promised to us.

Baruch, another settler who defines himself as a skeptic, also sees the link between a religious tradition to which he says he does not subscribe and his presence in Yavneel:

> Do I think that I have a valid claim to this country without the religious aspect? This is a very difficult question. I don't have a clear conscience on this subject. I believe that without the longing for Zion which has always been expressed by the Jewish people we never would have returned and would not have survived. And now, once here and after having declared a state, and with a population of over four million, perhaps it would be natural for the whole thing [religion] to weaken. But as a foundation—that is what brought us back here. And I see another factor—that if not for religion we would be prepared to make a great many compromises, and this will weaken us and prevent our getting a bit of security and some reasonable living space. Any small shock among our neighbors could erase us from the map. And I see that it is those who have a greater belief in our history and our religious right to be here and those who are willing to go to places of great hardships and take upon themselves the responsibility of settlement just like the pioneers who first settled the country. I don't agree with the politics of Gush Emunim but they, with their faith and courage, are the real pioneers of our day.

Comments such as this one affirm a religion that encapsulates, enhances, and justifies Zionist claims and ideals. For Baruch as well as for others who see themselves as skeptics, or secular, or nonbelievers, there is a reaching out to those who embody in their acts and ideology a combination of Zionist pioneering virtue and the credentials of legitimacy embedded in the Jewish historical context of faith.

For Yavneelim who stand on the margins of faith, or even by their own assertion, outside its framework, there persists a reluctance to follow a "logical" path of full rejection. Somehow the consumption of pork is always "not nice," or the Passover seder is national and communal—even universal—in its meaning, and fasting on Yom Kippur is "good for you." Ultimately, the refusal to unravel flows back to the assertion of Jewishness and the justification for being *here* rather than elsewhere. "If you ask me what is the difference between me and a gentile who also accepts the Ten Commandments, I will tell you that in human terms there is no difference. But my people has a history. I was born to Jews and I am a Jew. My people has a history and I respect this history—but all these rituals do not speak to me; they simply say nothing to me." Within thirty seconds of having made this straightforward assertion, Amnon rather sheepishly added:

> I do fast on Yom Kippur, but there were many times in my life when I did not fast. I do so most of all for health reasons. It is very healthy to let the stomach rest for one day a year or even for more than one day a year. But I don't feel any sense of holiness when I enter the synagogue where for those few who *really* believe and are *really* praying I have the greatest respect. But there are people sitting there talking and chattering about their business dealings, and what's happening in the fields, and there is no feeling of holiness. Whatever you want to hear about you can hear in the synagogue on this supposedly holy day.
>
> Prayers don't speak to me in any way. I cannot repeat that "God is such and such" twenty times. Isn't once enough? I think that if I say *Baruch Hashem* [Blessed is the name] after a good meal, or if I was spared, saved from some difficult situation, then I have done everything. What more need I say—*Rebono shel Olam* [Master of the Universe]?
>
> I don't believe in God. I don't believe that anyone really spoke with God. Either it's self-delusion or it's a conscious intellectual tool used by a superior man who wants to lead a people. It's a good idea and that's all. But I do feel, I don't know

... sometimes I do feel a feeling of gratitude toward someone to something and I say "Thank God." But this is a habit, a convention. But most of all I see these observances as a national debt for which I am responsible; *keeping the tradition is the unifying element which has held us all together* (italics mine).

Again, it does not lie within my power to judge whether or not Amnon, or any other respondent, is "telling the truth" when he defines himself one way or another. Like so many other Yavneelim, and Israelis, Amnon claims he is a nonbeliever who sees value in the continuity of certain traditional behaviors. Clearly, the element of continuity, both of a personal and communal nature, plays a heightened role in his sometimes rather serpentine path to retention of a large dose of not only tradition, but sheer ritualism. For so many Yavneelim, as, I would maintain, for so many Israelis generally, there continues to exist a two-pronged problem of legitimacy: How does one still claim to be a Jew in the absence of Jewish faith or, at the very least, Jewish tradition, which is seen as an outgrowth of faith? And how does one justify a painful, often tragic return to a homeland from which we have been essentially absent for two millennia and which was, in the meantime, occupied by others who have been displaced as a result of this return? While few among the villagers spend much measurable time in breast-beating about the plight of the native Arab population—those who have remained and those who have fled— and while most would assert that we have no problem because justice is so clearly on our side, I nonetheless claim that there exists a gnawing sensitivity to the issue that demands closure. There is a decided nervousness in the air, a heavy need to explain ourselves—sometimes on the basis of greater need, sometimes on that of greater legitimate title, and sometimes on the basis of greater love for the stones and soil of Zion. Few are the conversations with Yavneelim where, somehow or other, the title deed to the land is not justified along one or all of these lines. The idea of religious legitimation is insinuated in myriad conversations in homes, by the wayside, in cafes—

wherever there is some opportunity to answer the unasked but lingering question of justification. "Intellect," says Berko, "is against religion—but why do we fight for Israel? Because our fathers were given this land and this is our excuse . . ."

Even for those like old Meriskey, a son of one of the founding families who has returned to stricter observance of the tradition, there is faith but beyond faith the assertion that "the existence of the people as such depends on the observance of the *mitzvot.*" For Emma, "keeping the religious tradition is a way to preserve the uniqueness of our people." Furthermore, she adds, "it says in the Bible that you shall come and work the land. I see ourselves here as a continuation of the Israelites from the Bible who have lived here from the time of Yehoshua Bin Nun [Joshua]." Riva, a young woman of Yemenite extraction who does not define herself as secular, but personally is not observant, asks, "What—if not religion, the Bible, and our tradition—would justify our living here in this country? I know that God gave us the land of Israel, and that we are the chosen people, and *that's* what gives us the right to be here. It's been handed down from generation to generation: so we were taught and that's the way it is. We know that we are the people of Israel and that we are in the land of Israel and that's all."

One senses in many of these responses a measure of combativeness with regard to the claim. Many of the statements were indeed spoken through tightened lips and with a forward-thrusting jaw. There is a sense that the speaker is digging in, and something like a final defense line is being prepared against the pressing forces from without: "A Jew is someone who cares about this country," asserts Pinye, a grandson of founders, and he adds, "being a Jew forces you to appreciate this country."

More, it would seem, than the Jewish people exist to live the life of Torah, the Torah exists to assure the existence of the Jewish people. Carl Mayer was correct when, searching for a sociological explanation for the persistence of the Jews, he observed that it is the Jewish religion that lies at the heart of what otherwise must be viewed as this inexplicable survival.[29] Carl Mayer is unknown among the villagers; but his theory is embraced in almost uncanny fashion in the recognitions that chosenness, ritual, the God of Sinai, and redemption form the underpinning of Jewish existence and, by derivation, the claim to this land.

A recurrent theme voiced by the villagers is that they are Jews and that this Jewish identity presupposes a bond with the faith of Israel. Even if belief is tenuous, if faith is weak, if doubts predominate, we cannot poison the well from which we drink. God—the God we may or may not believe in with a perfect faith—gave us this land as an inheritance. But beyond this clear need to justify, to lay legitimate claim to the inheritance, there exists an almost inchoate, atavistic grip on *religion* as inseparable from Jewish selfhood, no matter how varied the epiphany—for example, in this conversation with a Yavneeli:

*Author:* Are you religious? Are you a religious man?

*Yavneeli:* My heart is religious, not I.

*Author:* You don't go to synagogue?

*Yavneeli:* I used to go, but I don't now.

*Author:* Was your father religious?

*Yavneeli:* No.

*Author:* Nor your mother?

*Yavneeli:* No, I used to go to synagogue because I had studied at the Talmud Torah.

*Author:* So you were religious as a child. Until what age were you religious?

*Yavneeli:* I am religious now as well.

*Author:* So you claim that you are still religious, but that you no longer go to synagogue?

*Yavneeli:* Correct.

*Author:* That is to say that you believe in God?

| | |
|---|---|
| *Yavneeli:* | So and so. |
| *Author:* | What do you mean by "so and so"? |
| *Yavneeli:* | I believe and I don't believe. |
| *Author:* | You mean that you believe but you have doubts? |
| *Yavneeli:* | Yes, I have doubts. |

It would be misleading to conclude that the tie to tradition is an instrumental device for justifying the Jewish presence in Eretz Yisrael. That it performs this function is obvious, but it is also clear that a struggle is afoot on the deeper level where a connection between national self-definition and relatedness to the tradition, to the faith of Israel, is being formed. The Yavneeli who responded to these questions could have justifiably described himself as *not* religious, but unconfirmed in his position. Revealingly, however, he chose to emphasize the "religious positive," as it were, when he said, "I am religious now as well." I believe and I don't believe, but I am religious. I have doubts, but I am religious. In our Zionism is our religion. In our Israeliness is our Jewishness.

The strength of religion as a legitimating buttress to national existence derives from the fact that it is *not* exclusively or even primarily instrumental. The Jewish religion is a powerful support in the struggle for national self-definition because it was and remains a pivotal force in Jewish identity. It is an irritant, a gadfly, a stimulus, a basis for certainty and a context for doubt. It is infinitely flexible because, contrary to assertions concerning its demise, it retains a high degree of vibrancy and a tensile strength that surprises and, at times, confounds. It lives because it touches lives where it counts—bestowing comfort in bereavement, family continuity, collective memory, the structuring of self, as well as linking the returnee to the misty dream, anchoring it in the here-and-now, and providing the ultimate defense against its enemies. This view of religion is expressed by Shuki, a third-generation farmer:

As a kid we were completely nonreligious. My father used to be religious, but this was because *his* father was the informal rabbi of Yavneel in the early years. Recently, my father "returned" to religion, and now he sort of acts the same role that his father had, teaching kids for their Bar Mitzvah, and so on. His return was not sudden, but neither was his departure. We always kept kosher, but now he won't drive on Shabbat and he always wears a hat. I guess what caused the process of return to pick up was my brother's death in the war, and later the fact that I married a girl from a religious kibbutz. About myself, I really don't know how to define myself religiously. I am sort of sorry that my wife tends to be less observant than when we were married. I don't know if I believe in God but I tend to think that there is some superior power out there. I fast on Yom Kippur, but not really because of religious reasons. I do it in order to preserve the framework of the home—to pass on to my kids what I got in my father's and grandfather's house. I regard it more a reflection of national uniqueness than anything else.

I try to sing *Kiddush* [blessing of the Sabbath wine] on Friday night, and while I used to eat pork, I don't anymore. It just isn't tasty anymore! I go to synagogue on the holidays not because I believe so much but because I am a Jew and I feel my Jewishness. I don't know if it is possible to be an Israeli without being Jewish. I have a problem with fighting and dying in war. Do we do it because this is a Jewish land or because we are Israelis? To be honest with you I think my Israeliness is more important to me than my Jewishness, but I don't think we can sustain this country without the Jewish dimension. You make it difficult for me when you ask me if our claim to the country is tied to our Jewishness. I have a problem with that. When my son asks me what right do we have to this country that the Arabs don't have, I have no answer. What I believe is that this is the *only* place we have *some* kind of right to and after what happened to us in history we have to fight and keep it even though we may not be completely in the right. The world is not a just place and perhaps we are not 100 percent just ourselves. With regard to how we should shape our religious life here, I am not sure. It is difficult for me to say with surety. On the face of it I would prefer separation between religion and state, but if this brings about a split in the Jewish people it would bother me a lot. Funny—even though I am not Orthodox,

I would like all Jews to be Orthodox. I hope my children will find their place here.

It is not at all clear what Shuki intends when he says that he "would like all Jews to be Orthodox." From the tone and tenor of his remarks it could be surmised that rather than Orthodoxy per se he wishes for a more assured status for religious tradition—for continuity in his own and the community's life, for greater direction and more precise guidelines in his everyday existence. He is aware of something having been lost, and in assuming changed patterns in his personal life— abstention from pork, saying *Kiddush,* fasting on Yom Kippur, occasional attendance at religious services—he is attempting to refill the depleted vessel of a defining tradition. He is well aware of the fact that his modest level of observance does not define him as Orthodox, and it is highly doubtful that what he "wishes for" bears any relationship to the accepted norms of Orthodoxy in Israel—or elsewhere. When both the haredi newcomers in Yavneel and Shuki, a clearly non-Orthodox descendant of one of the community's founding families, declare that they "would like all Jews to be Orthodox," they are envisioning divergent, or at least dissimilar, goals.

Shuki wishes that his "children will find their place here," and by "here" he means both Israel and Yavneel. He recognizes the centrality of the religious tradition in the formation and sustenance of both a Jewish *and* Israeli identity, but it is clear from both his life-style and his rhetoric that the evolving "bass religion" of the village and the country is being embraced, rather than a return to the Orthodox religion of his forebears.

Whether or not his "children will find their place here" depends on a number of factors, such as the economic future of the village, the seemingly ineluctable pull of the city, as well as purely personal inclinations. Superimposed on these factors, however, there looms a no less weighty question concerning the possibility of a differing ethos coming to dominate the community.

The steady infiltration into Yavneel since 1986 of haredi believers, followers of the rigorous and demanding Orthodoxy of Bratslav, has raised questions about present and future directions, bearing on both the private and public domains, such as the nature of public religious observance, personal freedom, political control, educational direction, the civic aesthetic, work, defense, status, power, and more. In short, just about every detail of communal existence—when, taken together, forming the outlines of its culture—is perceived by the non-haredi villagers as threatened by the growing number of Bratslav Hasidim in their midst, even to the extent that many are questioning whether or not they "will find their place here."

# 3

# A City of Bratslav: The Hasidic Invasion

FOR A REASON STILL MURKY and unclear to most residents of the town, Yavneel was chosen as a place of settlement for an offshoot of the Bratslav Hasidim led by the Admor, Eliezer Shick of Brooklyn.[1] The appearance in the town of the Rebbe and an initial settlement group of twelve families in 1986 created shock waves that continue to reverberate throughout the community, bringing to the surface tensions, conflicts, doubts, and questioning that, prior to this jolting event, were either dormant or, in some cases, nonexistent. As if catapulted from another world, a group of Hasidic men and women rather suddenly appeared on the streets of the town, superimposing the sights, tempo, and outlook generally associated with the forebears of the original settlers upon the bucolic canvas of little Yavneel. This initial wave of haredi settlers rented quarters wherever in town they could be found—in Smadar, Shikun, Mishmar Hashlosha, as well as old Yavneel itself. All were young, most were married, and they tended to be drawn almost exclusively from the ranks of the *ba'alei t'shuvah,* newly observant returnees to faith of both Sephardi and Ashkenazi background, including three who were either born or raised on kibbutzim.

Yavneel, which has always seen itself as representing the new Jew—the fighting, laboring, landed Jew of Zionist fulfillment—was precipitously confronted by these representatives of a rejected past, who by their very presence seemed to raise doubt as to whether victory or retrogressive defeat was to be their lot. For many, it was as if a visitation of dead souls from a buried past had occurred in their midst, calling into question all that four generations of Yavneelim had fought and struggled to establish as hallmarks of the new Jew in reborn Zion. Suddenly, the familiar street sounds of tractor and cart were intermingled with those of dilapidated automobiles ferrying intense-looking bearded men to meet with the Rebbe; venturing forth to surrounding communities (and further afield) in order to spread the Rebbe's message and transporting troops of children to nurseries and schools. Superimposed upon the hum of motors one heard the enveloping lilt, the singsong, of Talmudic study and the sound of intense prayer such as Yavneel had not witnessed in its past. Young Hasidim garbed in black gabardine, bearded and with earlocks, mixed with Yavneel farmers in their rough work garb, and on Sabbath the contrast was even more pronounced as the Hasidim walked to synagogue in long *kapotes,* many wearing fur-trimmed hats (the *shtrayml*), and a good few with white knee-socks into which their pants were tucked. Hasidic women in wigs and long dresses, with many children in tow, shopped together with town women in tight jeans or shorts, and not a few in tank tops and other revealing styles. Seemingly endless numbers of small children—boys with yarmulkes and earlocks, girls wearing long stockings and sleeves covering their arms past the elbow—played together in the streets, contrasting with the other children in how they looked and behaved.

The foreignness of these newcomers was emphasized not only in the surface manifestation of highly dissimilar dress but also in the rhythm and tempo of their lives, which were almost entirely shaped by their religious commitment. While Yavneel worked, the Hasidim prayed or studied. While Yavneel slept, many of the Hasidim wandered about in the fields or on the hillsides in an exercise of *hitbodedut,* isolation for holy contemplation. While Yavneel followed a calendar framed by the demands of the agricultural cycle, or a shared context of communal and national holidays, the Hasidim were guided by the traditional religious schedule of feast and fast, along with the Rebbe's visits to town from America (where he spends most of the year) when all regular events went into abeyance and everything focused on the zaddik's presence. While Yavneel strove mightily to create the new Zion, the Hasidim attempted to replicate Bratslav as it was during the closing years of the eighteenth century in Poland.

It would be difficult to imagine an equally contradictory conflation as that which has emerged since the arrival of the Bratslav Hasidim. There exists scarcely an area of thought or action where one is not conscious of the presence of two highly divergent worldviews framing the lives of both the veteran residents and the newcomers. Yavneelim—whether descended from the original settlers or the more recently arrived Sephardim—are committed to a modern, secular vision of individual and communal life, in which the presence of an informed religious "ground bass" allows for diverse interpretation and expression. The Hasidim, in contrast, are enveloped in a traditional web of belief and action in which religion, the faith of the fathers, is not merely central, but everything. For them, questions of individual interpretation of the tradition do not exist. For them, religious law, as elaborated in the tradition and interpreted by the zaddik, is incontrovertible and binding.

The appearance of the Hasidim in the town, and the response of the townspeople to their coming, did not occur in a vacuum or in a context of openmindedness. Yavneel is very much a place in modern Israel, and the Hasidim are clearly representative of a life-style that opposes the "descent" into modernity. The Zionist perspective is not unknown to the one ultra-Orthodox group, nor is the programmatic commitment to ultra-Orthodox dominance unknown to the other. Yavneelim, like most other citizens of Israel who do not live in certain sections of Jerusalem, or B'nai B'rak, or a few other haredi enclaves in the country, were for some time aware of tensions between the haredi segment of the population and those who defined themselves or were defined by the ultra-Orthodox as secular or nonobservant. All citizens of Israel are aware of the major role assumed by an Orthodox religious establishment in matters of personal status, as well as the fact that the political system in the country allows for disproportionate political power to be concentrated in this decidedly minority segment of the population.

But to know or to be aware of something in somewhat abstract terms is quite different from being in direct contact with a possibly threatening or, at least undesired involvement. Yavneelim, like other Israelis, maintain a wide variety of views with respect to Orthodoxy's role in the society, including, among those who are not Orthodox, serious reservations about their high profile and aggressive assertion of a minority perspective on society at large. Since the rise to power of the Likud in 1977, there has occurred a parallel growth in the power and influence of Orthodox and ultra-Orthodox groups in both government and quasi-governmental structures. Accompanying their growth of power are growing signs of hostility, and at least on the part of the non-Orthodox, serious concern that their daily lives will be constrained, if not controlled, by religious demands very much *not* of their own choosing. Rumblings about "religious coercion," or "rabbinical rule," or "theocracy," or even "ayattolism," have been heard among non-Orthodox groups representing all shades of the political spectrum.

Although few in number, some violent encounters have occurred in Jerusalem and B'nai B'rak—usually over the Orthodox insistence that certain roads be closed to traffic on the

Sabbath and holy days, and counter demands on the part of the non-Orthodox that these arteries remain open at all times. In the main, however, serious encounters between different segments of the public over issues of religious observance have been few in number. Given the volatile and emotional nature of these disputes, one highly probable reason for the relatively benign nature of the religious encounters stems from the general segregation of Orthodox and non-Orthodox groups as to neighborhoods, schools, and institutions, as well as regarding claims upon and control of local resources. Thus the encounter between these disparate worldviews has tended to be played out largely in the media and the national political arena, with little in the way of actual physical challenge or confrontation. Few neighborhoods have been targeted for a process of invasion and succession on the part of either camp. In most instances "turf" has been, if not inviolate, then at least largely respected; although with the pressure of large families and the resulting demands for space among the haredim, "incursions" are becoming more frequent and will likely increase in certain areas of Jerusalem, Ramat Gan, and Safed. Confrontation, where it does occur, is invariably characterized by the move of haredim into previously non-haredi areas, rather than the opposite. But, again, where this has occurred it has tended to be incremental, slow-moving, and unprecipitous, providing an air of normal change to what could, at a faster pace, have been considered provocative.

It is against this backdrop that the arrival in Yavneel, in 1986, of the Hasidic followers of Rav Eliezer Shick must be viewed: an overwhelmingly non-Orthodox and certainly non-haredi community, not abutting on any concentration of Orthodox residents and not representing any historical patina of holiness, being chosen as a place of concentrated settlement on the part of ultra-Orthodox believers led by a charismatic zaddik. Though in its own self-definition, as well as in its appraisal by others, a center of Zionist pioneering values, Yavneel is suddenly chosen as home by the very people who have been heard about, or perhaps seen on TV, as most forceful opponents of this vision. Yavneel, which resented the "intrusion" of even the town rabbi in the way in which it celebrated Simchat Torah or other religious occasions, finds itself slated to become the focus of large numbers of true believers who are guided in their every move by the iron grip of fixed tradition.

Yavneel seems to be the first community in Israel that is clearly and unselfconsciously non-Orthodox to have experienced a significant, highly organized, and pointedly planned influx of haredi believers who appear intent on becoming the dominant element in the town. In simple terms, Yavneel seems to have been marked for a takeover by an "invading" group of ideologically motivated outsiders; and this program has aided in moving a relatively abstract or benign struggle between disparate worldviews to a new plane of actualization and conflict, with repercussions stretching beyond Yavneel itself. What had previously been rather nervously "watched" by the wider population with regard to haredi positions, acts, and demands was now, and in Yavneel, being *confronted* in an active way. If seemingly offhanded comments were exchanged between friends and neighbors about how "the Orthodox are taking over," or how "the blacks (ultra-Orthodox) were seeking dominance," these formerly distant, rhetorical concerns suddenly became very near and actual. What had been thought of as *potential* threat was transformed into the *actual* threat of being displaced or overwhelmed by an essentially unassimilable way of living and belief. What had previously been condemned as inordinate political power in the hands of a minority that led to skewed funding for their institutions and religious legislation was now seen as a confrontation with a disciplined bloc that had voting power and, most important, a program, elusive though it might be. Early on it became clear that placing the haredi newcomers on the local town council and the local religious council could have radical day-to-day repercussions. The Hasidim were not so much interested in raising the level of religious observance, or elevating facilities for religious education, as they were in the total transformation of Yavneel into

Bratslav, and of Israel into a Pale of Settlement that awaited the imminent coming of the Messiah. And Yavneel was frightened!

## The Whole World Is a Very Narrow Bridge: Goals of the Hasidim

"The fire which I have kindled will burn until the coming of the Messiah," said Rabbi Nahman of Bratslav, the founder and still central figure of this most curious of Hasidic groups. Bratslav Hasidim are singular in a number of respects, the most striking of which is their continued veneration of their founder, who died in 1810 and was never replaced by a successor.[2] The place of charismatic leadership in Hasidism is well known, and the fact that Bratslav has contrived to exist for over 180 years in the absence of a living wielder of charisma is remarkable. Indeed, the fire "which I have kindled" does seem to burn with, if anything, heightened luminescence; and to this day Bratslav can claim the loyalties of two to three thousand Hasidim in Israel and abroad, no doubt greater in number than when Rabbi Nahman was alive. The Bratslav Hasidim are often referred to as the "dead Hasidim" in a somewhat snide reference to the fact that their departed leader has never been replaced.

Nahman was born in Medzibozh on the fourth of April, 1772. His mother was Feige, daughter of Udel, who was the only daughter of the Baal Shem Tov (the Besht), the founder of Hasidism. As the great-grandson of the movement's founder, Nahman spent his earliest years in the charged environment that his great forebears' legacy had stimulated. Legend has it that from an early age Nahman demonstrated great powers of intellect combined with a superlative spirituality embedded in a mystic core, which together with his esteemed pedigree most assuredly pointed to a promising future of leadership. It was predicted of him when he turned thirteen (the year in which he also married) that he would become "the greatest of all the zaddikim."[3]

He became a kabbalist, engaging in a variety of ascetic exercises such as prolonged fasts and icy plunges into the ritual bath on freezing winter mornings. He tended to wander alone in fields and forests where he engaged in meditation and contemplation. He seemed to have missed few opportunities to afflict his body in an effort to "soar" beyond, to achieve true holiness, which one suspects he hoped would exceed the achievement of his holy ancestor—the Besht himself.[4]

Nahman was an extremely complex individual whose deepest character remains elusive. Much has been written about both the man and the movement, but still the inner figure slips away as sand through one's fingers. He preached joy, but was clearly depressed for most if not all of his short life. He preached purity, but was clearly, if not obsessed, then very much in the grip of a pattern of deep sexual confusion. He was profoundly serious, but played the fool. He called for love but invited, even reveled in, conflict. He sought community but frequently fled its embrace to disappear from view or go on extended unexplained journeys. He practiced at a refined level of rationality but extolled the irrational. He was a philosopher who hated philosophy and philosophers, even going so far as to condemn the great Maimonides as a perverter of souls. He suffered from deep fears of personal inadequacy but was at the same time convinced that his greatness was nonpareil, that in fact he was the precursor of the Messiah if not the Messiah himself.[5]

Nahman became a rebbe at the age of eighteen, and proceeded to make his mark as one of the most remarkable zaddikim to be produced by the Hasidic movement. Starting in the small community of Medvedevka, he moved on to Bratslav, and finally during the last two years of his life to Uman, where he died of tuberculosis and is buried. Nahman's "torah," his teachings, have come down to us essentially through the works of his disciple and scribe Rabbi Nathan Sternhanz of Nemirov, who carefully noted down Nahman's discourses, aphorisms, stories, and indeed, on many occasions, his silences. It is through these volumes—essentially *Likkutey Moharan* and *Likkutey Moharam Tinjana,* the first published in 1806 and the second after Nahman's death in 1811—that we are able to evaluate the teachings of this highly paradoxical and intriguing figure. Other works—*Likkutey Tefillot, Likkutey Halakhot, Sefer Hamodot*—were also edited and transcribed by Nathan, and together form the primary corpus of Nahman's (and Nathan's) work.

Essentially, the message of Bratslav is one of faith above all. Nahman extols faith to the point where holy belief is preferable to knowledgeable skepticism; poverty in a context of faith is preferred to materialism and wealth that undermine faith; joy in place of somberness; discipline interpreted and applied by the zaddik rather than arrived at individually or worse through heresies like the Enlightenment. Holiness is the ultimate aim of every Jew, and the function of the zaddik is to point the way. The believer cannot achieve it alone. The individual has a part to play, tasks to fulfill, a discipline to uphold, but the zaddik is an essential part of the plan. The believer should confess *(vidui)* his sins to the zaddik, and the zaddik in turn will help in seeking correction. The believer should isolate himself *(hitbodedut)* for a period of time each day and speak directly to God in the language he knows best and in his own words. The believer should eschew all artificial and potentially dangerous paths to joy or false communion such as tobacco or alcohol. The believer should live every moment of every day as if it were to be his last and, above all, must banish despair from his life, for as the zaddik tells us, "Man's path through life is over an exceedingly narrow bridge. Be strong and believe that God's mercies fill the Universe."[6]

Aspects of the Bratslav "Torah" can be found in other offshoots of the Hasidic movement, but the personality of Nahman gives it a highly specific patina. Nahman looms over the movement with a presence that brooks no shrinkage in the role of the distant founding figure. He lives through his fables and his comforts and, perhaps most of all, through his tortured life on earth with which every Hasid can measure his own portion of pain. He lives through his uncontested assertion that he represents a force of faith and a closeness to the Almighty, certainly unparalleled in his own generation, and perhaps in all the generations of man. He lives through the painful hegira of his symbolically rich journey to the Holy Land, which clearly was so much more than a pilgrimage and disappointingly so much less than a passageway to redemption.

The journey to the Holy Land, which took place when Nahman was twenty-six years old, helps in illuminating the relationship to Yavneel and in unraveling (or perhaps further obscuring) the figure of Nahman himself, as well as those who have embraced his teachings. Although it is probable that both veteran Yavneelim and Bratslav Hasidim will reject the observation, I would nevertheless assert that Nahman's "episode" in Palestine can be viewed as a general metaphor for the relationship of the Jewish people to the Holy Land and perhaps to the very concept of redemption as well.[7] The story of Nahman's journey has resonance and meaning going beyond the narrow confines of the Bratslav movement, or Hasidism, or the haredi *standpunkt,* addressing the broader issue of the Jews' ambivalent relationship to space and, more specifically, to the holy space of Zion.

Nahman, at the age of twenty-six, and following the Passover liturgy where the phrase "Next year in Jerusalem" ends the service, announces that he will put flesh on this pious hope and journey to the Holy Land. Preparations begin and one gains the unmistakable impression that they tend to be largely of a mystical, symbolic, and even other-worldly nature. He goes to visit his parents who still live in Medzibozh, where his great-grandfather is buried. He has an apparition of the Besht from which he learns that he must visit the city of Kamieniec, and stays the night alone there, although it is forbidden for Jews to stay in the city after dark. No one is told why or what he does during this night; but it is akin to a night in the belly of the whale, or a precursor to the contamination and cleansing of the land. The decision to go is firmed, and notwithstanding the pleas of his wife and the fears of his disciples before the dangerous journey, he sets out.

Martin Buber observes that the journey is a constant test for the overcoming of obstacles. As Nahman says, "At every step of the journey I have risked my soul."[8] Risk, holy risk, and the smashing of obstacles connected with reaching the Holy Land consume Nahman; and his victory will determine his worthiness to enter the land, and more. At Odessa he boards ship for Istanbul, even though warned that the sea route is most dangerous. A storm breaks out, the ship is threatened, but in the end the ship arrives safely. In Istanbul Nahman appears to have suffered a breakdown and behaved strangely. He is humiliated and abused, but sees it as a test of his character and his ability to rise heavenward from the lowest depths of rejection and despair. He leaves Istanbul—again by ship—and again a great storm wells up. His fellow passengers are weeping and praying but he, Nahman, remains calm and at peace. Other difficulties beset the traveler, but finally the ship arrives at Jaffa where rough seas prevent its anchoring. It proceeds to Haifa, where Nahman debarks opposite the cave of the Prophet Elijah on Mount Carmel.

He is overcome with the joy of arrival, but this is soon followed by a deep melancholy and the wish to return immediately to Poland. Nahman refuses invitations to Safed and Tiberias, forgets about going to Jerusalem, and remains for some weeks in Haifa where he forms a strange relationship to a young Arab. The young Arab seems to have conceived a great affection for him, speaking to him at length in a language that, of course, Nahman does not understand. Not only does he not understand Arabic, but clearly enough the zaddik cannot know that the Arab is offering him a horse and a donkey for his journey, welcoming him, as it were, to the land. In his ignorance of what is being offered, Nahman remains mute, and the enraged Arab wants to fight him, leading to Nahman's flight. Ultimately the matter is "cleared up," and the Arab continues to admire the holy man, although Nahman is reported to have observed that "he suffered more from the Arab's love than from his anger."[9]

Nahman finally bestirs himself and travels to Tiberias, on the shore of the Sea of Galilee, where he visits the tombs of mystics and holy men. He then proceeds to make arrangements for his return to Poland without ever reaching, or trying to go to, Jerusalem.

Nahman is reported to have commented that after walking four ells (steps) in the Holy Land he had accomplished what he set out to do and was ready to return to Poland. *Yerushalayim shel ma'ala,* the heavenly Jerusalem, rather than *Yerushalayim shel ma'ta,* the earthly Jerusalem, assumes centrality in his thought and in his action. He is reported to have said on innumerable occasions that his trip to Palestine was the most important action he had taken, although the meaning of this statement is hard to truly discern. Did the concrete reality of the land convince him that a life of holiness can be lived in any clime? Did the overwhelming sense of spirituality that emanated from its soil and was reflected in its sky have an immediate effect upon those who trod its ground or breathed its air, making it unnecessary to linger? Was it the land's perfection, or its imperfection, which proved too much for him?

Nahman rhapsodized about the powers of the land to heal, to elevate, to create. He sings of its propensity to set aside anger in the human breast, to dispel cruelty, to establish justice. But, he admonishes, the Jews cannot get back to the land—not because of those who have replaced them and now inhabit the holy place, but because of the imperfection and haughtiness that now overpowers the Jewish soul.[10] Yet, there is still hope that its powers might set things right for the Jews and for the world:

> The land is a small, humiliated land—yet the hope of the world is contained within it. Whoever settles in it in truth, so that he has intercourse with the holiness of the land and helps it to prepare the way for the redemption of the world, into his apparently poverty-stricken life there streams the glory of the higher spheres, yearning for union with the lower.[11]

A tall order, an overwhelming summons, a frightening charge. Nahman was, like so many before and after him, locked into a deeply ambivalent relationship with the land of Israel: at one and the same time attracted and repelled, hating and loving, wanting and not wanting. The excruciating intensity of its concreteness places too much of a burden on its children, which in the end results in their sullying the dream or fleeing its heavy responsibility. Indeed, when all is said and done, it is the heavenly Jerusalem rather than the corrupted earthly city that is possible to bear in constant anticipation and with holy patience, bringing with it, as it does, a considerably smaller measure of pain. It is, finally, escape from pain and disappointment rather than rhapsodic joy and pleasure that is sought—even by the holiest among us.

In today's Yavneel, it is readily apparent that insofar as Nahman's contemporary followers have absorbed his outlook and his "way," the basis for deep conflict with the earlier settlers proves unavoidable. But conflict does not arise because one group loves and is committed to the land, while the other owes fealty to a higher value. Both the Hasidim and the settlers place the land in a central position in their distinct visions of Zion, so that rather than it being important to one and marginal to the other, it is central to both, but in so profoundly different ways as to, in and of itself, constitute a ground for conflict.

In Nahman's torah, the land is the framework and stimulus for the release of spirituality at the highest and purest level. It is the seedbed of revelation that heals people and strengthens them. It is the foundation stone of creation, and the basis for the world to come.[12] It is, in short, the physical point of departure from which the Jew will soar to the highest levels of what was promised in the covenant between people and God—to become a perfected instrument, a nation of priests and a holy people. For Yavneel's founders and sons, as well as for those who followed the Zionist vision in whatever manifestation, the land was seen in quite different terms. Here, too, the land of Israel was to provide the ground for a departure. But rather than heavenward, the direction of the journey was decidedly toward what was viewed as a re-entry into history: the history of the peoples and nations of the world where space as well as time designate; where the rhythm of life would be in harmony with nature rather than the heavens; where plow and scythe balance pen and text. For both groups the town represents an arena of return to wholeness, but the content of this wholeness is, for the one, spiritual and, for the other, temporal. Thus, the relatedness of the two groups to the land signifies not so much a polar opposition but rather the turning inside-out of a single conception that colors and complicates the encounter between the two.

Although Martin Buber's observation, that "some day it will be impossible to see and understand the best of what has arisen and is arising now in the way of new human life in the Jewish settlement of Palestine *without connecting it with Hasidism*,"[13] might go further than subsequent events would justify, the obvious, albeit skewed, link between Hasidism and pioneering Zionism requires exploration. The idea of some sort of eschatological fulfillment is prominent in both movements, and it is probably no accident that so many of the early idealists, dreamers, and activists of the early settler movement can trace immediate roots to the Hasidic maelstrom of the Pale and Podolia. Interestingly, in moving among the Hasidim who now constitute, according to their numbers, some sixty families and more than three hundred individuals including children, there is a decided impression of "group" emerging. They project a feeling of young people in the advanced organizational stages of a youth movement, or perhaps the beginning stages of a kibbutz, or some other utopian undertaking. They signal to and smile at one another. They hit each other's outstretched palms in a less graceful adaptation of black folk greeting and seemingly enfold one another by eye when passing in the street. They are enthusiastic, they radiate optimism and a sense of new beginnings, as the following anecdote illustrates.

## A Yavneel Story

*Hasid:* Do you observe the *ot*?

*Author:* No, not really.

*Hasid:* Do you believe in God?

*Author:* I have my strong doubts.

*Hasid:* Are you at least happy that you were born a Jew?

*Author:* Yes!

## A City of Bratslav

At this point the interlocutor grabbed me by the shoulders, called to two or three others who were studying holy texts nearby, and danced a dance of joy, going round and round in a circle until I begged for release. All the while the Hasid shouted "he is glad he was born a Jew," to the evident pleasure and knowing acceptance of his fellows. It is doubtful, had I identified myself as a Zionist to any of the group of core settlers, that anything remotely resembling this ecstatic enthusiasm would have been displayed at the revelation.

Suddenly, little Yavneel, which had begun to show signs of an indolent comfort with its space and its various structures, which had more than begun the descent from the heights of a deep ideological commitment to a kind of "taken for granted" tinting of their surroundings with accepted but understated pieties, was confronted by a wave of deeply believing, deeply committed enthusiasts bearing discipline and leadership. Almost instantaneously, the broad suspicion of ultra-Orthodox aims with respect to the non-Orthodox society moved from the pages of the national press to appear boldly in the streets of Yavneel, giving rise to two related queries: Why the appearance of Hasidim in the midst of a clearly non-Orthodox farming community, a paragon of Zionist virtue far from the sustaining sources of the Orthodox centers? And, why (specifically) Yavneel rather than dozens of other towns? What were the goals of the Hasidim? Would they suddenly develop tolerance for other life-styles, which had not been demonstrated previously in conflicts with their non-Orthodox neighbors? Would they proselytize among the children and other "vulnerable" people in the town? Would they take over politically? Would they fragment the town with political alliances and deals with *haves* and *have nots, ins* and *outs,* veterans and newcomers, Ashkenazim and Sephardim? Would "our" town become "their" town?

With respect to "Why Yavneel?," the townspeople arrived at a variety of explanations, some aided by flattery on the part of the Rebbe and his followers, although others hinted at dark motives. The Rebbe and his supporters suggested that Yavneel was selected because the Rebbe fell in love with this beautiful place. "Can you explain," asked the Rebbe, "why you married your wife?" Sometimes Hasidim would add a more mystical turn to the effect that the Mishnah speaks of the Messiah first appearing in Galilee; and thus Yavneel, this *echt* Galilee town, was a natural if not singular choice for a place in which to await his coming. Some suggested even more precisely that the Messiah would first appear on the mountain at the foot of which Yavneel is built.[14] The Rebbe himself resorts to all of the above, and even gave as a reason my suggestion that Yavneel in sociological-demographic terms was almost a microcosm of Israeli society, thus offering him (the Rebbe) a viable arena in which to work or begin his work.

Those who are not Hasidim tend to see the matter in more somber terms hinting at sinister motivation or hidden agendas. It is sometimes suggested that the Rebbe appeared at the instigation and invitation of the town rabbi, who wanted to turn Yavneel into a haredi enclave. Another assumption is that the town was chosen because one of the Rebbe's closest Hasidim had earlier moved here and found it "ripe" for the picking. Some held to the view that the town's weakened economic base was proving attractive because it would be cheaper to buy up depressed properties. And a few thought the Rebbe needed distance from haredi centers for protection from the wrath of his competitors and enemies. Still others, noting the Rebbe's strength among people of Sephardic background, were of the opinion that an isolated Galilee community with a large Sephardi population would prove a natural base for expansion.

Though untidy and decidedly uneconomical, it is quite possible that all or most of these explanations are, in some ways, correct. It does not seem possible to obtain hard-and-fast answers from the Rebbe or the Hasidim, who are, after all, the initiators in the matter, and this for perhaps two reasons. First, as with most small, sectlike religious groupings who are or feel that they are beleaguered, there is a marked reluctance to be pinned down. Ambiguity is felt to provide a measure of protection, where specificity might call forth focused opposition, especially from enemies. Second, just as Nahman didn't really know why he journeyed to Eretz Yisrael, only after the fact endowing the move with rich symbolic weight, so his current followers, and, I suspect, their leader are not fully clear as to why Yavneel. From the point of view of the Hasidim, the reason for the particular choice of Yavneel is not a terribly serious concern. Just as Nahman by going to Bratslav created a holy space by virtue of his choice and presence, so did Yavneel take on a highly elevated significance by virtue of Rav Shick's decision to locate there. It could, I suggest, have just as easily been a neighboring or, for that matter, distant community whose significance derives not from any intrinsic quality other than the presence of the zaddik.

But if the choice of Yavneel might have been idiosyncratic—an almost aggressive assertion of the Rebbe's power to turn the profane into the sacred, the impure into the pure—the choice is a quasi-conscious effort to replicate Nahman's past and to create holiness where it did not exist before, and against significant odds. The fact that Bratslav Hasidim believe in reincarnation no doubt adds to the heightening of a perception that replication and return is a law of existence, and that perhaps the Rebbe is Nahman, or his redactor Nathan, in present guise. This possibility, that a guiding principle of action for the Rebbe and his followers is based on a belief in both the possibility and desirability of replicating the founding impulse of the movement, does in fact go a long way toward explaining acts that are otherwise difficult to fathom.

The main objective of the Hasidim is to turn Yavneel into Bratslav, and in the process of doing so, to provide a testing and yet protective crucible for the creation and sustenance of a community of believers. "Why," ask non-Hasidic residents, "pick Yavneel when there are so many Orthodox communities in the country?" The answer is multifaceted, but among other things, has to do with moving into the jaws of the lion, where the faint-hearted will either be strengthened or winnowed out. It provides, additionally, the possibility of turning the profane into the holy. The Rebbe has observed that "if we succeed in turning Yavneel into a holy city, it will save the world."[15] Just as Nahman was opposed by many, including some important figures among the Hasidic leadership of his day, and nevertheless triumphed, so will Eliezer Shick. Just as Nahman predicted that bitter defeat for himself and his ideas would be followed by ultimate victory, so it will be with Yavneel's Bratslaver. Conflict with the forces of evil rather than easygoing mutuality is the mark of the true Bratslaver, as is so clearly demonstrated in their changed relationships to the rabbi of Yavneel.

After two years of cooperation between the town rabbi and the Rebbe and his followers, there suddenly appeared in print and orally within the Bratslav group a series of brutal attacks on the Rabbi, accusing him of the most heinous doings to the point of calling for his near expungence from the book of life. He was charged with thievery, venality, lack of religious punctiliousness, and made to appear quite the satanic figure. Nobody in town could quite fathom the cause for this sudden turn from friendly cooperation, even possibly conspiratorial union, to high antipathy. Why did the Rebbe and his followers turn, in a venomous fashion, on the one more or less established figure in town who welcomed and nurtured them, making of a trusted friend a rather befuddled enemy? Could it be that a well-known comment of Nahman's upon his return from the journey to Palestine casts light on the matter? "I have brought my followers a present," he wrote, "and this present is called controversy."

> I can foresee that many of my teachings will be disputed, even amongst religious Jews. Satan himself will wage a tireless battle against my adherents and against me. He will succeed in influencing some zaddikim who will turn the masses against my teaching. A time will come when there will be only five of my followers left. But by strengthening their hearts and clinging to my advice they will ultimately cause others to recognize the truth of my teachings. The fire which I have kindled will burn until the coming of the Messiah.[16]

There is little doubt that the Rebbe does feel a deep sense of connection to the sainted zaddik of Bratslav, and that he has programmed much of the history of the Bratslaver movement into his current agenda. Among these continuities, the choice of Galilee rather than Jerusalem is, I think, derived both from practical considerations and the startling and unexplained failure of Nahman to go up to Jerusalem.[17] Rav Shick's frequent appearances and removals from Yavneel, while bearing little of the mystery surrounding Nahman's journeys and disappearances, nonetheless does repeat the pattern of presence and withdrawal. Nahman's penchant for fraternizing with fallen types like scoffers or secular Jews has been copied by Shick, who has been seen knocking on the doors of town atheists, offering to say Kaddish for the greatest among them, Shimon—who is childless—when he dies.* Finally the "need" to be reviled and beset by opponents, and to be brought low so that he could rise up, is being acted out with vigor on all fronts. It is a matter of *yerida l'tzorach aliyah,* the fall that must precede the rise.

Clearly the Rebbe aims to re-enact the life of Nahman and to re-create Bratslav in Yavneel, but with a significant difference. Nahman, insofar as the historical record speaks, did not intend to "take over" Bratslav, or Uman, or any other place in which he lived. Nahman drew a figurative circle around himself and his followers, and *there* was the holy space; everything surrounding this space was a matter of profound indifference to him. Rav Shick and his followers, however, are intent upon transforming the entire community of Yavneel into one where the Torah of Rav Nahman will hold sway. The Hasidim focus on buying property wherever and whenever it becomes available. In four years they have grown from the initial nine or twelve families to sixty families, and they maintain that the only barrier to a much greater increase is the unavailability of housing. With already more than 10 percent of the voting power (probably double that in actual terms because of group discipline) they will shortly hold the balance of power on both the town council and the religious council. There is nothing

---

*Although Shimon was about eighty at the time, he asked Rav Shick how he was so certain that the situation would not be reversed, making it necessary for Shimon to say Kaddish for the Rebbe. The Rebbe apologized.

in the recent history of relations between secular and ultra-Orthodox groups in Israel that might indicate haredi reluctance to impose religious legislation involving many aspects of communal life; and indeed a failure to do so when they have the power to decide religious issues would place them in violation of a powerful norm. In a personal conversation with me, the Rebbe remarked that he intends to bring two hundred families to Yavneel, and even allowing for a degree of hyperbole, or enthusiasm, it is clear that this intention is perceived in the dominant presence of Bratslav Hasidim in the community. If he succeeds in bringing half that number to Yavneel, a total transformation of the community will result.

Is there a broader agenda underlying the desire to transform the town than that which appears on the surface? I suspect that at the outset nothing more than a convenient and comfortable base for the nurturance of a sense of "group" was the aim; but with the growth of local opposition and the widespread publicity enjoyed by the clashes that have occurred between blocs of locals and the Hasidic newcomers, some new possibilities have presented themselves. With opposition, the Rebbe has been put on the map, and the more he is opposed the greater his celebrity and attractiveness to certain segments of the population. Opposition has the practical effect of granting publicity, and the more elevated effect of permitting imitation of Nahman's path. Additionally, the fact that the town is divided along "ethnic" lines has served to whet the Rebbe's appetite for becoming the patron of downtrodden Sephardim and presenting himself in this guise at all turns. If victory is achieved and a previously secular community is transformed into a haredi community—in the face, it should be added, of vigorous opposition—it might provide not only a pattern for future action but a powerful *stimulus* for undertakings of this kind. And because of the Rebbe's visible and militant stance, the same town that has been described as being among the first to try to establish a "harmonious life-style including both Orthodox and non-Orthodox Jews" may become the first town in Israel to attempt to prevent Jews of deep religious commitment from swelling their ranks.

The Rebbe has demonstrated a notable taste for conflict as well as a refined tactical sense. He first appeared before the town council in 1986 asking to be awarded a block of land for building his court *(hatzer),* which would have included a yeshiva and synagogue as well as his home. The town mayor first encouraged him and, then, sensing either trouble or political hay to be made with the veteran settlers among whom he could not be counted, withdrew this support. The veteran settlers opposed the Hasidic presence, sensing that the Rebbe held larger ambitions for the town than could be safely assimilated by the core group. But, announcing that "the more you fight me the stronger I will become," the Rebbe proceeded to privately buy a piece of choice property at the southeastern tip of the town's original main street. He knocked down the old stone structure and outbuildings, and built a substantial modern villa that included a *mikveh,* or ritual bath, and a combination Bet Midrash (study hall) and synagogue, which could accommodate up to seventy worshipers.

Rather than continue to poke his finger in the eye of his opponents, however, he spread the word that he was a liberal who could live with Sabbath violators and non-Orthodox Jews of all stripes. He spread the story of his regard for a neighbor in Brooklyn, a nonobservant Russian immigrant, and how he did not interfere with his driving on Shabbat. He walked about the town extending greetings to residents, and especially sought out active opponents such as members of a committee formed to fight the Hasidic "takeover," in order to speak with them and convince them that he was "a regular fellow." He hired a jeep and local guide to take in the sights, and went bounding over the surrounding hills and the "Messiah's" mountain apparently enjoying himself. At the same time, however, he very much busied himself with the politics of the community, trying to form all manner of alliances. For example, he tried to ingratiate himself with the head of the local committee opposing his presence in the town, even appearing at his door to ask the atheist (for so he described himself) if he would be interested in running for mayor with the Rebbe's blessing and backing. The opposition leader declined and did not become a supporter, but the Rebbe willy-nilly did become somewhat less of an enemy. He also attempted a reconciliation with the current mayor, who had first welcomed and then opposed him. Seeking to mine the rich vein of ethnic hostility, the Rebbe presented himself as a voice for the downtrodden Sephardim from whom he expected massive support. And here was to be found fertile ground, albeit with far from guaranteed fruits.

## The Hasidim and the "Ethnics"

It is not only with respect to a bold pattern of invasion and succession into what had previously been non-haredi communities that we are witness to a possibly significant new development in relationships between the secular and ultra-Orthodox segments of Israel society. We see in Yavneel a first attempt to range far afield with a flanking thrust deep into "enemy country" rather than, as in the past, a pattern of creeping expansionism brought about by demographic rather than ideological pressures—and also a conscious appeal to ethnic "sensitivities" as a weapon in the struggle. Outreach to Sephardim is not exactly a new phenomenon in Israel, especially given the high degree of politicization of religion that exists in the society. Haredi groups have included Sephardi youngsters in their educational institutions and yeshivas, and here and there Sephardic families have associated themselves with the essentially Ashkenazi ultra-Orthodox camp, and continue to do so, even though a specifically Sephardi Orthodox framework—political, social, and educational—has been in existence for the past decade or so.[18]

Rare, however, is the configuration of the Bratslav Hasidim in Yavneel, where approximately three-fourths of the believers are Sephardi, with all signs pointing to a continuation of this trend.[19] This is rare, and on the surface quite strange, given that Hasidism is an East European movement, and Bratslav in particular, with its ascetic practices, quite foreign to the Sephardic tradition. Nonetheless, there is already in place a skeleton, and more than a skeleton, of cooperation and understanding between a number of the town's Sephardim and the Bratslav Hasidim of Eliezer Shick. A few marriages have taken place between male followers of the Rebbe and Sephardic women from Shikun; some local Sephardic young men have an association with the group, and it is clear that local recruitment, if it is to take off, will be among the Sephardim rather than the veteran settlers.

The reasons for this assumption are fairly straightforward. The Sephardim are by now the numerical majority in the town as well as in the country and their sheer weight of numbers cannot be ignored. But, more important, the Sephardim are still largely bound by a dominant traditionalism, which largely forecloses active opposition to religion and religious authority as represented by rabbis and holy men. The Sephardim represent, in large measure, a segment of the population bearing resentment toward the establishment. In Yavneel this resentment is understood to derive from the instrumental interest shown in them by the Ashkenazi veterans who were desirous of their labor, or political alliances with them, but who were otherwise monumentally uninterested in their souls or their culture. The Rebbe (and the Rabbi), on the other hand, are intensely interested in their souls, which is viewed as a form of affirmation unavailable through their Ashkenazi connections. Furthermore, the propensity of people who see their own condition as one of oppression to identify their plight with similarly afflicted groups places the sympathy of the *edot*, as the Sephardic ethnic communities are known, with the Hasidim, who are seen as being under attack by the very establishment who have, they maintain, caused them grief and hardship! As is so often stated in the Middle East, the enemy of my enemy is my friend. Not least in importance is the clear and visible fact that so high a proportion of the Rebbe's followers are of Sephardic origin, including his two local leaders, which, together with the rather conscious syncretisms practiced with respect to integration of both Sephardic and Ashkenazi religious patterns in prayer and song, provide an emotional environment not generally available among other Orthodox groups. Additionally, the Hasidim, with their enthralling enthusiasm and emotionalism, are bound to appeal to the Sephardim from Morocco or Tunisia more than does the cold, rational (it is said) Ashkenazi version of religious practice. Even the figure of the zaddik resonates familiarly with the North African pattern of holy men such as the Baba Sali, who, in effect, served very much as Sephardic rebbes.[20]

The veteran settlers see the possibility—indeed the probability—of a natural tie between the Hasidim and the *edot* because of their shared negatives. For many among the core group, the Rebbe represents a primitive residue of Diaspora culture that enjoys an excellent fit with what they regard as the "primitiveness" of the Sephardim. The veneration and respect shown the Rebbe is akin to that shown the Baba Sali and his ne'er-do-well son and successor, the Baba Baruch, and in each case it is defined as "idol worship": "They lose their individuality when they tie themselves to a zaddik who tells them when and how to do everything. This isn't Judaism—this is idol worship," comments a leader among the veteran settlers. Like others in his group, he is disturbed by what he sees as the influence of both the "throwback" values of the Bratslav and the "primitiveness" never quite exorcised by the Sephardim.

Here, it should be noted once again that Yavneel, like the larger society of which it is a part, is far from a homogeneous society. It is almost exclusively Jewish (exclusively if one includes, as Yavneelim themselves do, two families who describe themselves as Hebrew Christians), but beyond the single religious identification it is a complex weave of differing ethnic and cultural hues. The major division in the town's population before the arrival of the Hasidim was, of course, between the veteran group of core settlers and the "newcomers" who arrived after the creation of the state in 1948 and were overwhelmingly of North African origin. There is also the small Yemenite community that came in 1911 and 1914; and while enjoying "veteran" status in a chronological sense and a sort of patronizing acceptance on the part of the core group, it nonetheless sees itself as not much less deprived or aggrieved than are the "newcomers."

A vast body of literature exists that examines the problem

of what has variously been called the "two Israels," the problem of the Oriental Jews' second-class status, the Sephardi-Ashkenazi conflict, or the lack of integration of the *edot hamizrach*, "eastern" communities.[21] This issue generally has been analyzed in terms of three conceptual approaches: the question of culture, which focuses on differences in culture and mentality between groups; the question of class, which focuses on the competition for resources, highlighting exploitation and economic dominance; and the question of pluralism, which views the segmentation of society into culturally differentiated groups as a structural feature of most modern societies. An examination of this literature, or a critique of these various issues cannot occupy us here, but an attempt to map the demographic reality of the village according to the subjective framework of the residents themselves is essential.

More than half the current population of Yavneel are Sephardi newcomers from North Africa who see themselves in large measure as being deprived psychologically, economically, and in terms of "power." This is symbolized to them, and to some outside observers, by the fact that of all the five sections comprising Yavneel there is only one that has no name—referred to as Shikun or, simply, housing project. This is the part of town with the major concentration of "newcomers" from the 1950s immigration wave, and it is located in the section that used to house the immigrant transit camp. It is here that most of the town's "social problems," such as truancy, domestic violence, minor crime, and welfare cases, tend to be concentrated. The place gives off an aura of depression, with both houses and surroundings in a state of advanced seediness and, in some cases, disrepair. The houses themselves are ticky-tacky structures that are hot in the summer and cold in the winter, in addition to being cramped and architecturally without distinction. They were put up by the government in the 1970s to replace the original transit-camp structures, and while some families have expanded and improved their homes, the buildings are generally unattractive and of poor design and even lesser quality. However, one quickly senses that the differences observed in this neighborhood are not simply of a physical nature, and that the people who live here are not quite the "same" as those in Bet Gan or Old Yavneel.

Homes tend to be poorly appointed, with some nearly empty of furniture other than the barest essentials and others furnished with clearly inexpensive and low-quality "suites." Many homes suggest a flavor of temporariness, as if the residents were packed and ready for a move—or perhaps flight. In a goodly proportion of homes, the television is on as long as a station—any station—can be received. During one visit I noticed most homes tuned to METV (Middle East Television), which broadcasts in English and is totally undecipherable to most of the elderly or housebound who were within earshot of the set at the time. The television programs seem to function as a sort of dead accompaniment to the loneliness and apartness that seems to play a heightened role—at least among the older residents of Shikun.

Shikun is a neighborhood with a grudge. It is a place where the residents speak of *us* and *them* as elsewhere; but here "us" are clearly *dafukim,* screwed, whereas "them" always get the brass ring. "They" have land; "we" have children. "They" have big houses; "we" get these little boxes. "They" have money; "we" have an overdraft. "They" have recourse to seats of power such as the National Land Authority, the Knesset, the police, the higher reaches of the Army, the universities, science and industry, while "we" do the dirty work and stay poor and ignorant. "They" are white; "we" are "schvartzers."

The story of Alon Azulai might not be typical—for whose story can be so described—but his condemnation of what he sees as the Ashkenazi establishment is widely shared among the town's Sephardim. Here is his story:

> I came to Israel with my family when I was seven years old. We came from Tunis and were sent at first to Safed and then to Yavneel. We were housed in the *ma'abara* [transit camp] and my father, like everybody else, went to work in the Jordan Valley kibbutzim and was paid next to nothing. Not only was he paid starvation wages, but his honor, his self-respect, was taken from him. For those who worked in the factories or packing

houses of the kibbutzim, the bus would come to Yavneel at 4 A.M. and get them to work before 5 because the buses were needed to go to Haifa at that hour. So they waited outside the gates, in winter in rain and often cold, for the kibbutzim to let them in for work at 6 A.M. Why did they do that? To treat people like dust so that others wouldn't be inconvenienced? But did they complain? Did they riot? No, they came from the outside into a new world, and they thought that it was only temporary; things would change, things would get better. But the opposite happened—things got worse. Our parents were primitive just like the Ashkenazim say they were. They did not understand; after all, they were only Jews from an Arab country and this, they thought, was Zionism. But now they are going to have to deal with me and my sons; they will have a problem with the sons of Alon Azulai.

Since we came here we have been considered different, and we have been treated different. They [the Ashkenazim] are the owners [*ba'alim*] here and though I never told my kids what they did to us, it penetrates through what they see and hear. They see that we don't mix; that they stay there and we are stuck here. And that's how extremism goes from one generation to another—slowly, without effort, even not wanting it to happen but it does. They separated us so that we wouldn't mix, and this was their mistake. My daughter will refuse the possibility of marriage with one of them: she hates them and doesn't even want to let them in our house. Even school, which could have closed the gap between us, was instead a tool for widening it. The teachers always gave more to the Ashkenazi kids—more time, more encouragement, more means. The Ashkenazi kids had parents who understood the system, who spoke a common language with the teachers, while our parents didn't know what world they were in. They [the teachers] told my mother that I did not understand, and that I had a low IQ, so I was moved to another school in Smadar in the fourth grade. True—I didn't know how to calculate or how to write because when I refused to study, as kids do, they let me be and didn't insist that I "join the class." With the Ashkenazi kids, though, they insisted on learning. I say all this with pain in my heart. They only tried to make us ignorant, to keep us low.

So I say to you—what does it matter to me if the Rebbe comes to Yavneel or if the Rabbi tries to impose religion. I told both the Hasidim and Rabbi F that I can be counted among their supporters. There is room for both of them, and not just the farmers who don't want to see the place develop. They are against building factories in Yavneel because then they won't have anybody to clean their houses. They are afraid that the Hasidim will become a majority here, and they are afraid that the Sephardim back them and in this way will come into their own. They are afraid that I will take my revenge for welcoming *their* sons who returned from the Army back to the farm while *I* came back to a servant's house. I bless the Rebbe and the Hasidim for coming and maybe they will bring blessings to us, too. You know, I feel bitter—I never made it. The Arabs around here advanced more than we did. We have no task other than to raise kids for the Army. The state doesn't give a damn for us. It's a good thing we have wars here every ten years or so because we are busy with that rather than killing each other. Actually we have more in common with the Arabs than we do with the Ashkenazim, and if there were peace our relationships with the Arabs would be stronger *and* warmer than with the Ashkenazim. What did you say? Where would I find Arabs around here? Not to worry—the Ashkenazim have them in their fields.

Although his level of rhetoric is perhaps more bitter, almost all of the sentiments expressed by Alon Azulai have been voiced by dozens of other Sephardim. None of those with whom I spoke during the years I spent in the town suggested that the reality of discrimination against them was without basis. Every one of the Sephardic residents had his or her story of egregious insult, of being denied either a sense of full participation or a fair share of the community's resources. There is a deep conviction among many, if not all, of the town's eastern "newcomers" that the core settlers, the Ashkenazi establishment, had an important stake in holding them back, in not encouraging, indeed, not permitting, Sephardim to advance.

Both Yemenites and the more recently arrived Sephardi groups claim overwhelmingly that the Ashkenazim would not countenance them becoming landholding farmers. As a matter of fact, part of the town folklore revolves about how one interprets the story of the allotment of land to the Yemenites, with clear lines of demarcation separating the "haves" and "have nots" in the recounting. The Yemenites were, in 1936, awarded either six, eight, or ten dunams of land per family (no one can agree on the exact number), but it did not turn out well. Most sold the land to the earlier settlers after a few years; that much is agreed upon. But the Ashkenazim say the Yemenites failed because they were heirs to the mentality of the hired hand, who has somebody behind him to take the risks and make the hard decisions. They failed because they really did not want to succeed. The Yemenites claim that they failed because the land was no good, or too remote, or too parcelized, for them to make it, as it was designed to be by those who didn't want to lose good dependable farm laborers to an errant wave of independence. Similarly, many among the 1950s immigrants claim that as a result of Lands Authority mechanisms, they were cheated of the possibility to have land allocated and to farm. Core settlers claim that when agriculture was bad until the late 1960s nobody was that interested in land, and that only with agricultural prosperity in the 1970s and early 1980s did the cry of "discrimination" suddenly arise.

Whatever the "truth" of the matter, the arresting result of the conflict is the sense of having been mistreated that persists among the *edot*—even, it would appear, among those who have, as it were, made it. On more than one occasion I remember hearing a devastating critique of the Ashkenazi establishment in surroundings which belied at least some of the serious allegations that were leveled. In one instance, a farmer of Tunisian background, sitting with me and an Orthodox Ashkenazi farmer from a nearby community, complained piteously about having been "screwed" by the Ashkenazim who gave his group nothing. He asserted that even when Sephardim "rose," as when becoming mayor on at least two occasions, they were quickly co-opted by the Ashkenazi establishment: they sold out and put the squeeze on their own. "Why did they charge 200 shekel for a family subscription to the pool? How come my wife used to work as a maid? How come those close to the dish get fed and those far away get nothing?" Having reached a peak of chagrin he announced that he would leave this place [Israel] if he could and was sorry it could not be. One might have imagined that an unbridgeable chasm of bitterness was here being expressed, that could only end with broken crockery or perhaps a punch thrown at the hapless Ashkenazi farmer sitting beside him. Life was clearly seen to be unbearable: yet, within a minute or two of his *cri de coeur*, the farmer was speaking of his video recording machine and the fact that he was eating better than the Ashkenazi farmers before the boom of the late 1960s. Then, with his arm around the shoulder of his stricken Ashkenazi neighbor, he walked out and rode away in his one-year-old Japanese sedan.

Clearly, relationships between Sephardim and Ashkenazim in actuality differ from the way in which they are often represented. Expressively, free reign is given to the voicing of a deep sense of deprivation among Sephardim, of having been mistreated by the dominant Ashkenazim. Hearing some of these complaints expressed, as often as not, in terms of wrenching pain, at times of despair and hopelessness, one is led to wonder how the society manages to avoid bloody combat between the two "ethnic" blocs. From the Sephardi side, one hears of discrimination in education, jobs, promotions, the Army—in short, at all levels of Israeli society including the religious. "Why did they want us to fail?" "Why did they keep us (or, as it was said, 'make us') ignorant?" "Why did they insult and try to destroy our culture?" And so on! From the Ashkenazi side one hears of disdain for the alleged "primitiveness" of the *edot*, for their lack of ambition, for their skewed values, for their neglect of education, for their innate violence, and, perhaps most hurtful, the questions, "What are 'they' complaining about? We have given them everything and in an eminently fair manner."

But there is not, and has not been, bloody combat in the streets of Yavneel or anywhere else. Aside from a riot in Haifa in the 1950s, and the Black Panther phenomenon* in the 1970s, the ethnic "lid" has been kept very much on. On the behavioral level, Ashkenazim and Sephardim mix and meet. Intermarriage is at about 27 percent, and when class is controlled for, integration in jobs, neighborhoods, schools, and elsewhere is unproblematic. Friendships between the groups occur in a variety of frameworks. There exists a shared universe of experience on any number of levels, ranging from a shared sense of oneness regarding the Arab-Israeli conflict to a common sense of origin, history, and, to an extent, memory. Thus, rather than a collision between two separate, hostile, and antagonistic blocs playing out a zero-sum scenario, which rhetoric often leads us to embrace, there exists a rather more benign encounter bobbing under, but near to, the surface.

Rather than the model of blacks and whites in America or of Arabs and Jews in Israel, the historical parallels that might more closely illuminate the situation in Israel could be, to a lesser extent, the Litvak-Galitzianer breach in Eastern Europe, or more appropriate, the past conflict between German Jews and East European Jewish immigrants in the United States. Other than in retrospect little about these clashes was cute or bathed in warmth; real pain and hostility was experienced. Tragedy was no doubt an accompaniment of prejudiced decisions not to allow intergroup marriages or to discourage other forms of intimacy and social intercourse. The clash between the German Jews and the East European immigrants in America following the turn of the century is an especially relevant model, influenced as it was by factors of class difference and "chronological arrival" in the new country. Although those American Jews who are aware of the hostile reality of intragroup relationships at the end of the nineteenth century down through the 1930s would tend to smile about it today, the

---

*The Black Panthers was a militant organization of young people of Moroccan origin, founded in Jerusalem after the Six Day War with the aim of empowering the poor *edot*. It fizzled and dissolved within a few years of appearing.

conflict was real enough in its time and real enough in its implications. But it did go away!

Similarly, the pain experienced and expressed by the less powerful group in the Israeli encounter is real enough, although, I would maintain, exaggerated in rhetoric. The reasons for the exaggeration of the conflict are, to some extent, both cultural and instrumental. I would agree with Harvey Goldberg's assertion that "the focus on ethnic boundaries" may persist because "they mark and help perpetuate boundaries between social groups which are useful for these groups to maintain for economic, political, or other reasons." They tend to create, says Goldberg, "an illusion of distinctiveness . . . so that what they have in common (but care not to admit) is the presupposition of the newly developed emblems of their particularity."[22] In short, the possibility that Jews from North Africa and Jews from Europe might share more than they do not, while shocking to ethnic warriors in both camps—those fearful of Levantinizing propensities borne by the *edot* and those who abhor the cultural imperialism of the Ashkenazim—must be seriously appraised. This might go a long way toward explaining the seeming gulf between rhetoric and behavior, between the cries of bitterness and mutual warmth, which seem so jolting and inexplicable.

This might also explain how it has come to pass that fully three-fourths of the Bratslav Hasidim in Yavneel are of Middle Eastern and North African background. Perhaps in the religious context, where memory shared and created points to a unity in the collective past, we see the usefulness of the framework as a potential bridging device more effective and less fraught with parochial baggage than channels such as the political or ideological. Perhaps because the religious framework, especially that guided by charismatic forms of leadership, is more receptive to syncretism, to the integration of different rhythms and practices, than are other cultural structures, it is a canvas more fit for cultural integration and the lowering of ethnic barriers to which both sides are committed. The real enough anger expressed by many Sephardim cannot be accommodated so effectively by structures anxious to defend their dominance and at the same time open their gates to outsiders. But a structure that can change many of its patterns under charismatic guidance (by fiat as it were), and is desirous of widening its membership by reaching out to a shared legitimacy rather than focusing on "temporal" differences, can deal with the anger *and* channel as well as dampen it.

How, it might be asked, did Persian, Moroccan, Libyan, and Iraqi Jews find it so "easy" to become Bratslav Hasidim? Partly it is because some key aspects of the religious tradition are shared by all traditional streams of Judaism, or at least are "cross-adaptable" with relatively minor and yet highly functional tuning. This "tuning" allows for a judicious mix of elements from both traditions—the Ashkenazi and the Sephardi—such as songs and *niggunim,* the traditional wordless songs that are hummed by the Hasidim; and it is functional in the sense that the singers feel a sense of mutual participation as well as their own cultural input, even though the religious practice might be largely drawn from one tradition. This cannot be said about the Zionist ideological underpinnings typical of the dominant core groups. My own observations, taken from field notes, of the celebration of Hanukkah in Shikun illustrate this process.

> Tonight Shikun celebrated Hanukkah, and did so in a way that should have been foreign to them and probably was in some ways, but which in sum enjoyed a remarakble fit. About sixty children and twenty-five adults (almost all male) were gathered in the main Sephardi synagogue awaiting the arrival of the Habad Mitzvah Tank and some Habad Hasidim who somehow or other were given charge of the event.[23]
>
> The evening was in essence an event run by Ashkenazim for Sephardim, and thus could have been an irritant but again, somehow, was not. When the Mitzvah Tank finally arrived, blasting away with Hasidic tunes from its loudspeakers, it was greeted with genuine joy and attempts to hum along—at least on the part of the adults. Later, in the synagogue in somewhat

belated recognition that these songs were not part of the eastern tradition, some tapes of eastern music were played, but the crowd did not appear to be any more or less taken by this than by the "European" offerings. All was seen, I think, as part of the authentic shared religious tradition, albeit with differing signatures.

When the evening got under way it featured talks from two Ashkenazim and one Sephardi—all however representing the haredi viewpoint. The town rabbi provided a condescending little talk whose message was—we fought the Hellenists once and beat them and we can do it again and win. We don't need all this emphasis on the body, and sports, and other foreign elements. What we need, he said, was a return to the eternal verities of Jewish spirituality. He then introduced a representative of Habad who told the bored assembly about the two months he recently spent at the court of the Lubavitcher Rebbe in Brooklyn replete with examples of wonders performed by the rebbe, and ended by taking a bottle of vodka out of his jacket pocket, which, he announced, was given to him by the rebbe, who asked that he share it with them. (At this point the town drunk yelled *y'allah,* the Arabic equivalent of "right on"). Following this the crowd went out to light the giant eight-foot menorah which was placed on a trailer behind the Mitzvah Tank.

Finally, the Lubavitch representative introduced Rabbi S, who was described as a well-known former infantry officer and ex-kibbutz member who became a *ba'al t'shuvah,* or returnee to faith, and a follower of Rav Shick and the Bratslav way. It should be noted that a great suspension of belief was required to imagine the slight, bearded, earlocked figure dressed in a black *kapote* in any of the previous roles attributed to him, but in fact and at least in broad strokes the attributions were accurate. Rabbi S, who shares with Rabbi A the position of leading local assistant to the Rebbe, talked about the great spiritual merit he earned while visiting not only his own spiritual mentor in Brooklyn (Shick) but the Lubavitcher Rebbe as well. That is, he recounted the "wonder" (he called it a miracle) that befell him when his plane could *not* take off from New York because of engine trouble. This he understood to be a message from the Lubavitch, whom he had vowed to visit but had neglected to do. He promptly left the plane, went to visit the Lubavitcher Rebbe and received great spiritual merit as a result.

The evening ended with a raffle won by a local Sephardi youngster awarding him two weeks at the court of the Lubavitcher Rebbe in Brooklyn. His crestfallen acceptance suggested a buried wish that it had been Disneyland rather than the court of the great rabbi.

Very little in this description of the holiday celebration could not have been replicated in an Ashkenazi mold at an earlier time. The lack of order, or to put it more positively, the familial atmosphere of the synagogue, could have described a shtetl prayer hall, with its cross-section of types gathered together for a shared common purpose. Also notable is the recounting of wonders crafted by holy figures who are both personal and communal role models or yardsticks against which we can measure our own moral and spiritual condition.

The fact that Rabbi S, the ex-soldier and ex-kibbutznik, was of Persian background was highly important and irrelevant at one and the same time. It is important in demonstrating the possibility of establishing common ground between the various subgroups and communal histories that comprise *Klal Yisrael,* the entire Jewish community, and it is irrelevant because the act of return to faith that characterizes so large a proportion of the Bratslav Hasidim has, to some extent, canceled or transformed prior differences. When a young man from a kibbutz, or a poor neighborhood, or low-status ethnic group, or for that matter, as a result of purely personal disorientation such as a failing marriage, becomes a *ba'al t'shuvah,* or returnee, and takes on the role of disciple under the Rebbe, he is able to start life over again; the rules change for him, in effect, even though he may remain in the same place.[24] Being Persian, or Russian, or an ex-con, recedes in importance, as do all aspects of one's past identity and loyalties.

Paradoxically, although it is Zionist ideology that has elevated the concept of *mizug galuyot,* the unity and fusion of the exiles, to a high principle, and the haredim who continue to entertain grave doubts about the legitimacy of Sephardi religious practice, the ultra-Orthodox religious context tends to be more open and flexible in this regard. The secular context seems to demand something akin to total assimilation, while the haredi framework sifts and sorts between essentials and those matters seen as peripheral. Thus, it is acceptable, among haredim, for the Sephardi to sing the songs of his father and grandfather, to utilize the prayer rhythm of his youth, to elevate his familiar saints and holy men, entering them in the pantheon of the believer, even to add a modest twist or two of traditional clothing to the standard garb. No matter what the prior history or personal background of the disciple, the unifying element of belief in the power of the zaddik to bridge all differences creates a filtering mechanism which acknowledges the legitimacy of distinctiveness at the same time that it encourages an overwhelming sameness which ultimately negates the importance of these differences.

## Two Hasidim

Ariel and Simon are two disciples of Rav Shick who are products of utterly dissimilar backgrounds, but—at least on the surface—appear cast from the same mold. This caveat—at least on the surface—is important and should not be ignored. Although an act of conversion bears with it the dimension of death to the old self and rebirth in a new self, the matter, while not allegorical, is also not literally "true." Clearly, matters of personal history, even when perhaps transformed, are not canceled. Being born to a Persian rug merchant in Jerusalem or an American businessman in New England bears certain marks that distinguish and separate, no matter what the nature of the shared new love or loyalty. Yet the remarkable element here is not what remains separate and distinctive but the degree to which prior chasms can be bridged and almost overcome in the new context.

### Simon

My name is Simon and I was born in Massachusetts, grew up in New England where I attended a private high school—

the Putney School. I went to private school because I didn't like the surroundings in the school located in the town in which we lived. [Simon does not further explain.] I am a third-generation American—My grandparents came to America when very young at the end of the nineteenth century, and I grew up in a very secular house. We observed nothing or almost nothing. About the only thing Jewish that we did was light Hanukkah candles—and then only sporadically. No Sabbath candles were lit, no going to shul, and no keeping kosher. Yes, we even had pork in the house—everything.

After high school I went off to college and there was a Habad house there which started me on the road to *t'shuvah* [return to faith]. I went on Shabbos, and more often than that, and I began to experience a conflict between what I was learning in school and what I learned at Habad House. I was becoming religious and learning once again that God created the world in six days and I decided I wanted to go this way rather than with the philosophy of the college professor. I dropped out and went all over America looking for something, and in the end I came to a small communal farm in New York which was all Jewish. They were trying to build some kind of Jewish existence, and a lot of people there came out of Habad, but soon left. They came in strong and left strong—with a bang.

They left observance completely, although they still attempted Sabbath observance and making *Kiddush*—things like that. I guess you could say that everybody has their strong points, their good points. They *did* say *Kiddush,* and for me even that was a step up. I was lost, I was in darkness, you understand? At least I was making some stab at Jewish identity. While there, I saw a television program on the Holocaust and I started to think, you know—what is the difference between me and them? Why? Why did they suffer so? There had to be some reason. It is not a coincidence, not an accident. Anybody with even limited faith in God must realize that things are not coincidence. They have to see that there is something over all and that what happens in the world is not an accident, and realizing this I really started to identify with my Jewish existence.

Things, how do you say, evolved and I met a girl, got married, went back to college with the support of her father, but things didn't work out. She was a girl with a lot of problems, and in the end she committed suicide after eight months of marriage. I was in shock, and everybody had a suggestion for what I should do. I went to work as a house painter, and there in Stamford an old man who I met told me I have to get my act together and I should go to a yeshiva. I did, and one thing led to another and from the yeshiva I decided to come to Israel to continue to learn which I did. Here I went to Safed and after a year of learning [study in a yeshiva] they made a *shiduch* [match] for me with my present wife. In the yeshiva some fellow students told me about Rav Shick, and when he visited a few years back I went to hear him, and that was that.

You ask me if I believe in reincarnation and the answer is of course, it is one of the basics of our faith. You really want to ask me if I believe that Rav Shick is a reincarnation of Rabenu [Nahman], and about this I have no opinion. Rav Shick wrote me a letter—I have a whole stack of letters here, personal letters from the Rebbe and in one letter, which I will show you he wrote something and marked it with a yellow magic marker. He said I should *mefarsem* [publicize] the fact that nobody has any permission to say anything in his name except what is written on paper. Now the only place I ever saw written on paper that Rav Shick is a reincarnation of Rabbi Nahman is in a newspaper. I don't believe what is written in newspapers because this can be simple gossip. What I did see on paper is that before the Rebbe started to publish he had a great deal of doubt as to whether or not to write. He didn't feel that he could take the responsibility of writing letters to people answering their most anguished problems in an official format, so he prayed a lot to *Hashem* [God] asking what he should do. He had a dream and Rabbi Nahman came to him in the dream. Rabbi Nahman was walking together with Rabbi Natan, his student. Natan was very close to Nahman's face as if he were listening very closely to every word being said and they were walking in a field. So Rav Shick dreamt that he approached Rabbi Nahman to ask him what to do and at this point Rabbi Natan was angered by the interruption. But Nahman took Rav Shick by the shoulders and said *"Shrayb, mein kind, shrayb"* [write, my child, write]. "I am with you, I will help you." In the same dream, after they had departed, Rav Natan came running back and said to Rav Shick, "I'm sorry—I didn't know who you were. I'm sorry I was so impatient about your interrupting us," and he said "You should write, you should write." So Rav Shick writes that at this point the *neshama* [soul] of Rav Natan became a part of him. Aside from this, I have seen nothing else.

As for me—I hope that soon the Messiah will come and faith will become the main focus of the Jewish people. Everyone will start searching after faith, how to know God and His ways and how to keep His law. I have learned that every Jew should have *nechama* [comfort] and *simcha* [joy] in his life. That's the important thing to me. That's what I really feel.

## Ariel

You started this interview by asking me how long I have lived here in Bratslav and then apologized for your mistake. It's not a mistake at all. On the flyleaf of all our publications it now says Yavneel, a city of Bratslav. So I have lived here in the city of Bratslav for six years. As to why we call this place the city of Bratslav, there is a simple explanation. It is written that the whole body is where the head is, and so, if with God's help, our head who is our leader Rav Shick will come here to live, then all of his followers will come here, and that means tens or hundreds of families. It is as with Nahman who said that because of his presence in Bratslav it was as if he was in Jerusalem, and because of Rav Shick's presence it would be as Bratslav.

I have been a Hasid for ten years, and before that it is better that you not ask. I was born in Jerusalem to a Persian family which was very religious. Not just religious—but haredi. My father was a great zaddik and many Ashkenazim—figures big in Torah—would come to him for his blessings. He was a holy man, though not a rabbi. Actually, he earned his living by buying and selling rugs, with a bit of real-estate on the side. In all his dealings he upheld the highest standards of morality and had the respect of all. We were nine children and some are religious and some are not.

You ask me how I, a Sephardi, have come to be a follower

of Rav Shick? I'm still a Sephardi, and joining Bratslav has not changed my origins. It's simply that the way of Bratslav brings a man closer to our father in heaven. I pray in the Sephardic way, and everything has stayed the same. I don't know Yiddish, and it is unnecessary that I know Yiddish. The Bible is written in Hebrew after all. I came to Rav Shick and Bratslav through books, the Rav's book. I read them slowly and I wanted to know who the writer was, who was this man? So about seven or eight years ago I went to Brooklyn and stayed with the Rav for three months. You know, nothing happens by chance. The Holy Ba'al Shem Tov said that the Jew doesn't go—he is taken. Since you [the author] are Jewish you didn't come here by chance. It wasn't chance which brought you to Israel. Each step that you take is not taken by you but by heaven. You are directed where to go and when. . . . You say you agree with me? Well, I'm not surprised because every Jew agrees with such a thing.

We are here in Yavneel to study, to perfect ourselves. This is our whole purpose because, as you know, Rabenu said "The whole world is a very narrow bridge," and we haven't the time in this world to seek unimportant things. We have come to this bridge, and one has to know how to cross it, and we have to cross it in peace. It is the peace of Yavneel which will give us the right atmosphere for the search. The Ashkenazim here are worried that we will disturb their peace: that we will tell them how to live, what they are permitted to do and what not. It's a natural fear; they have a right to it, but it's our right to do the things we must do. The future of Yavneel is a future as a religious community. It is definite. As I told you—if the head is here then the whole body will be here.

The Sephardim are more open to us. Rav Shick explained it as having to do with the fact that the Sephardim don't always have someone to go to in order to unburden their hearts. The Ashkenazim have a whole host of admorim and zaddikim to whom to go, but the Sephardim don't. There are figures among the Sephardim too, but a man like Rav Shick touches all hearts, every Jewish heart and not only the hearts of this or that *eda* [singular of *edot*, or communities]. What is a Hasid? What is the simple meaning of Hasid? The Hasid is a person who has a problem and bears his heart before his admor. Hasid does not merely mean side curls and beard. A Hasid is a person who has another person with whom he can discuss his problems. A Hasid can be a Sephardi or an Ashkenazi and there are Sephardim who follow other rebbes. But with Bratslav it is simply that if you know the literature and get close to Rav Shick you cannot help but see the truth here, the clear truth. If one doesn't want to deceive oneself, to live a counterfeit life, you come here and see the genuine truth.

My religious life is different from that of my father. My father was nervous [sic] and I, in accordance with Bratslav, am forbidden to be nervous. I also used to be very nervous. I am a completely different person now from what I was. Rabbi Nahman said that "mikveh" and "anger" are the same in *gematria:* they are both 151. Whoever goes to mikveh—and I go every day—rids himself of a bit of anger each time.

I have no problem with being Sephardi and a follower of Rav Shick, who is an Ashkenazi. The Rebbe has taught us never to fight or disrespect our parents: not only our real parents but the parental tradition, the roots from which we came. With us there is no issue between Ashkenazim and Sephardim. There is something, but it's not that—it's between farmers and Sephardim. The farmers consider themselves to be landed gentry here, just as the Germans termed themselves the red-blooded race and the rest of the world yellow-blooded people [sic]. Before it was the farmers' fear that the Sephardim would take their land, and now they are afraid that Rav Shick will win the Sephardim.

In background and personal history Simon and Ariel represent two very different worlds. And prior to their association with Bratslav and Rav Shick they would have had much difficulty in finding common ground—one from a privileged background in America with a family far along the road to assimilation; the other from a traditional Sephardi family that had made its home in Jerusalem. Simon was protected, pampered, indulged, and essentially left to find his own way; Ariel, a rebel who served a lengthy prison term for an unknown offense, first rejected the religion of his father and then clawed his way back, although not quite to the father he left behind, but to one bearing a strange new message that nevertheless found resonance with his past. Both were suffering from a sense of being adrift in the world without guidance, without direction—fearing that if they continued in their old paths they would face personal disaster. Unlike Shimon and Black Asa, who shared a common past only to diverge along the fault-line of faith, Simon and Ariel, coming from radically differing worlds, were joined together at this very same juncture. Simon and Ariel are two Hasidim, while Shimon and Black Asa are two Yavneelim. The significant difference is that one identity is ascriptive and one achieved. In the one there are shared memories and worldviews clouded by differences over religious belief; in the other, it is the shared religious loyalty that overcomes the prior worldviews and experiences. The "American" Simon and the "Persian" Ariel can come together with a certain ease that would elude the Sephardic "newcomer" and Ashkenazi settler who presumably share the broad Zionist vision of a unified Jewish people.

Can one therefore assume that the future promise of an integrated Yavneel and perhaps the country as a whole will be better assured in movements and trends represented by religious orthodoxy? Will Sephardim in large number embrace the Hasidic or haredi way, giving rise to a new constellation of forces here such that in place of Ashkenazim versus Sephardim, we will see *religious* Ashkenazim and Sephardim as against nonreligious Ashkenazim and Sephardim? Notwithstanding that the Hasidim are able to bridge the gap created by the sense among Sephardim that their culture and history are held in contempt by the dominant Ashkenazim, it is not at all clear that it will result in any new constellation of forces. Very few Yavneelim of Sephardic background have thus far joined the Bratslav other than through marriage. Even though Friday night at the Rebbe's might be the most integrated time and place in town, the Hasidim and other ultra-Orthodox groups are not the wave of the future here or elsewhere in the country.

The significance of their appearance in Yavneel, and the

various responses of different segments of the population to them, lies in how ascendant and descendant worldviews might meet—in a wavelike fashion of ups, downs, and curves that nevertheless demonstrates clear direction. The Hasidim in Yavneel are of interest because, among other reasons, they have gone against the grain. That is, a sectlike group that usually seeks protective isolation, or the company of the likeminded, decided instead to confront head-on the dominant ethos of the community, seeking to breach the wall of indifference and hostility by a conscious outreach to a subordinate group in the population. The Hasidim acted as if the future belonged to them; and, as one Yavneeli veteran phrased it, "This place has become a test case: thus far and no further."

## Worldviews in Conflict

The Bratslav phenomenon in Yavneel has placed in bold relief not only a specific challenge to a small town in Galilee, but one that affects the society at large. Bratslav in Yavneel has succeeded in raising key issues affecting the society, which demand active response of the day-to-day, ordinary, and practical kind rather than the distant political maneuverings and high tones that have generally characterized the encounter between the camps of religious ultra-Orthodoxy and the non-Orthodox majority; and it has allowed for the verbalizing of tensions between ethnic groupings at the grass roots rather than in politicized contexts. In Yavneel ultra-Orthodox believers have come into direct contact *and* conflict with a competing worldview that they seek to replace. The central values of the community, such as Zionism, labor, and defense, are seen in a thoroughly different light by the two groups, and their meeting has served to underscore and highlight the distance between them.

Zionism, for the haredim, has nothing to do with the political, cultural and ideological structures that have emerged over the past century. The Hasidim are not interested in evolving a new Jewish self-conception, but rather in recapturing what they perceive to be the unchanging, eternal Jew of deep faith and total commitment to the commandments. Bratslav is not interested in *mizug galuyot*—fusion of the exiles—in the sense of weaving a new tapestry of Jewishness, but in acting as an absorbing filter through which differences are winnowed out in the assumption of a common discipline. Different traditions are respected insofar as they strengthen a sense of a common core, but in the end both Simon and Ariel are expected to merge their individual identities and pasts so that a new communal identity, sanctified in a very specific way, will emerge. In a community dedicated to labor and, indeed, to the pioneering idiom of reclaiming the land, the sight of dozens of young men who devote themselves to study, or missionizing, or odd jobs, living essentially on public or donated funds, has elicited resentment and even furious anger, which had not been the case when Yavneel residents merely *heard* about this community in Jerusalem or B'nai B'rak. Similarly, with respect to Army service, which, in a society such as Israel's, has become a symbol for full participation as opposed to lingering on the fringes of society, the daily sight of healthy young men who have opted out provokes deep negative reactions.

The move of the Bratslav Hasidim into Yavneel has become a consciously verbalized metaphor for both camps of the struggle over the present and future shape of Israeli society. Yavneelim sensed this from the very inception of the Hasidic move into town, when they organized—or, rather, some leading figures among them organized—a committee to fight the intrusion. The committee met informally at the homes of various members in order to organize opinions and take steps against what they viewed as a Hasidic invasion. Overwhelmingly the committee was comprised of Ashkenazim and veteran settlers, and they were not unaware of this imbalance. They frankly attributed it to the desire or inclination of many Sephardim to relish any discomfort experienced by the establishment "even though they themselves would be among the first to suffer from haredi coercion." Shortly thereafter, a countercommittee was organized, largely Sephardi and religious, though not haredi, called "The Committee for Peace," which attempted to blunt the efforts of the opposition. This latter group argued the impossibility of Jews opposing the settlement in their midst of other Jews, no matter the strength or tone of their religious commitment. In a sense this theme could be read as both a critique and correction of the perceived unacceptance of the Sephardim over the years, although clearly just as Jewish as the core settlers.

This charge of anti-Zionist behavior (in the sense of being against the ingathering of *all* Jews) has in fact struck a chord among many residents of both the Ashkenazi and Sephardi groups. A sense of guilt over imposing, or trying to impose, restrictions on the inclusion of Jews who might be highly Orthodox and thus perhaps more, not less, Jewish has caused considerable discomfort. As two and then three years of haredi settlement passed, and it became clear that no radical change in the face of the community had occurred, the active settler oppositionists tended to back away from confrontation, to believe that perhaps the phenomenon could be lived with. With the exception of a very few, led by Old Shimon, who continued to confront the haredim through myriad devices, including anti-Hasidic graffiti, scribbled on tin and placed in front of his workshop, most of the active oppositionists retreated, if not into silence, than at least to a stance of watchful waiting.[25] Perhaps Yavneel would, in the end, be able to absorb this group, as they had absorbed other not so "appropriate" groups in the past. The Hasidim, when all is said and done, did turn out to be, on the whole, likeable enough people with whom it was perhaps possible to coexist. The idea that these were indeed two very different worlds slipped more and more from view.

Yavneel, in most essential ways, is part of the liberal world, which holds that if one extends to one's neighbors the freedom to live life in a certain way this freedom will be reciprocated. The Hasidim are true believers and do not share this outlook. Tolerance, for true believers of any kind, is a one-way street. When in the minority they will, as they must, demand tolerance for the minority point of view; but when in the majority they will refuse to accord to error the same rights that accrue to truth. Because the Hasidim are decent people who speak softly and generally live lives beyond reproach one can be easily lulled into thinking of them as fellow liberals who perhaps dress funny. But they are not! Their faith and their discipline and their single-mindedness will bring them to narrow the environment in which they live to fit their own singular dimensions. They *cannot* allow violation of the Sabbath when it is in their power to prevent it. They *cannot* allow *treyf* (unkosher) to gain a foothold in the house of Israel when they can act against it.

These "truths" began to take hold when the Hasidim of Yavneel went on the attack on all fronts during their fourth year in the town. With shocking precipitousness the former alliance with the town rabbi, whom many Yavneelim had accused of being behind the settlement of Hasidim in town, was sundered amid accusations of malfeasance and worse. The Rabbi was accused of pocketing money earmarked from the Ministry of Religion for repair and renewal of the local mikveh. He was accused of using his influence to prevent a local Hasid who is a ritual slaughterer from opening an abattoir and butchery in town. The local religious council was pilloried as a den of corruption bent on slandering the Bratslav community in an effort to hide their own incompetence from the town's citizens. These accusations were leveled in a new publication called *Light of Yavneel,* which began to appear in 1990, first sixteen pages on rough newsprint, and after a few months about thirty-six pages on expensive glossy paper with a cover sheet in color. The local rabbi was referred to as "the boss," and his religious council members as thugs and hooligans. Items in the journal recounted in great detail how the Rebbe and the Hasidim were welcomed by the town—indeed sought after in the case of the Rebbe for advice and guidance—only to be libeled by "the boss" and his minions. The paper was distributed free on a weekly or biweekly basis to every household in town, and the claim was soon made that the village could barely wait for the appearance of subsequent issues. The Rebbe contributed a regular column where he called upon his followers to "improve" the image of true Judaism among those who have slipped from the God-fearing ways of the founding generation.

Rather than attempting to convince the community that they constituted no threat, this new haredi strategy involved a demonstration of self-confidence and the flexing of muscle. The strategic switch was the decision to bypass (and undermine) the local religious establishment and especially its head—the Rabbi—and to provide a clear alternative in the haredi way. The Hasidim, it seems, believed their message, and themselves, to be eagerly awaited by the majority of the town, a not uncommon reaction among sectarians of all kinds who tend to read tolerance as acceptance, civility as commitment, and indecision as acquiescence. Thus, their tactics involved a concerted and highly audible attempt to undermine the existing religious establishment through outright defamation and to present themselves as the eagerly awaited replacement. At the same time that they attempted to destabilize the current religious establishment, a great deal of space and attention was given to calls for coexistence, mutual understanding, and internal peace. They projected a view of Yavneel as a potential model for the country at large of a community where people of different backgrounds could live together in mutual respect and, above all, in peace. Courses and workshops on religious themes were offered to town dwellers combined with warnings that attending courses offered by the town rabbi or under the auspices of the religious council would "lead both young and old astray." Within this context, it is not absolutely clear if the haredi attack on the town rabbi represents a misreading of the situation based on the rooted subjectivity which sees immobility or passive acceptance as, at the very least, a step below conviction; or if it represents a tactic with internal aims and ramifications, such as a felt need to focus on a threatening enemy (real or fabricated) in order to firm up the ranks and perhaps control internal divisions.

The town rabbi is, as it happens, a perfect target for a number of reasons. He is generally unpopular among the settler groups, and although more acceptable to the Sephardim he cannot be said to be a central figure in their lives. While identifying with the haredi stream, the Rabbi adheres to a Hasidic school—Vishnitz—that is rather different in outlook and practice from Bratslav. In any case, it is also quite distant from the religious practice and outlook of the overwhelming majority of the town citizens, although the primary basis of opposition to the Rabbi points equally to personal as it does to ideological reasons. He has, from the start of his tenure in the town some fifteen years ago, managed to stimulate a level of antipathy that is surprising in its vehemence. He has been accused by various citizens of insensitivity and a tendency to politicize religion beyond the acceptable. He is viewed as a nay-sayer, a man who ever is prepared to forbid and to anathematize. He tried to have the town pool segregated according to sex, he attempted to close the community center on Friday nights, he lends and retracts support to various political figures on the basis of what are perceived as narrow interests. In addition, he is viewed as anti-Zionist—refusing to fly the national flag on Independence Day, and, above all, having never served in the Army. If this were not enough, his personal honesty in financial matters and a certain looseness brought to administrative tasks have been challenged on numerous occasions.

There is no question but that in style, method, outlook, and appearance the Rabbi was and is out of step with the dominant ethos of the community. In a community moving more and more in the direction of a fluid religious outlook, he represents the traditional, not overtly flexible, religion of the shtetl. He is seen by most Yavneelim as a rather unwelcome throwback to a value system no longer shared by them, and this, together with a profound lack of finesse, makes him a veritable model of ineffectuality as well as a lightning rod of communal hostility.

Moreover, the appearance of the Bratslav Hasidim in the town was felt by many to be a conspiratorial move on the part of the Rabbi to "take over" the community. He was widely suspected of having played a key role in the arrival of the Hasidim; and when both the Rebbe and the Rabbi began to speak of their respective roles as complementary, the aura of plot and trickery gathered force. According to their division of religious functions, the Rebbe was the mother figure, the doctor of souls whose task was to guide and solace; the Rabbi fulfilled the role of the stern judge who would interpret the law, adjudicating the permissible and the impermissible.

In this context, attacking the Rabbi and the establishment that he represents might have been viewed by the Hasidim as a bid to create distance from both a figure and an institution that, if not totally discredited in the eyes of the majority, then at least occupies a less than completely salutary role. Breaking the cozy division of responsibility between Rabbi and Rebbe hints at the possibility of undercutting the "thou shalt nots" of the one and replacing it with the warmth, approval, and love attributed to the mothering figure of the other. The attack on the Rabbi was, among other things, a mistaken attempt to demonstrate that the haredi way had a different face from that personified in the Rabbi, and that the Admor was best suited to represent it in the town, if not beyond. It was a delayed recognition of the fact that being associated with the widely disliked Rabbi held no advantage for the Hasidim. Thus, if focusing on an external enemy without much support could both enhance internal cohesion and allow the presentation of themselves as a popular alternative it would seem to be an ideal tactic.

The Hasidim failed to realize, in their bid for "power" in the town, that even if internal aims could be achieved, the latter was doomed to failure. When all is said and done, the Hasidim failed to understand that Yavneelim were not followers of a competing rebbe, of another Hasidic way. Not only were Yavneelim in their majority, whether Sephardi or Ashkenazi, not attracted by whatever spiritual merchandise was being offered by the Hasidim—a newly refurbished mikveh, ultra-kosher meat, study groups for young and old, or even the ministrations of the Rebbe—but they began to resent their neutrality or passivity being taken for enthusiastic acceptance. In addition to resentment, Hasidic claims also tended to renew somewhat quiescent fears about the short- and long-range aims of the Bratslaver. After a year of reading how hundreds were beating a path to the Rebbe's door asking for blessing or advice, or how dozens have requested a deepening and broadening of the services provided the town by the Hasidim, or how a majority of town citizens have found "secret ways" to express their support in the struggle against the dark forces represented by the Rabbi, Yavneelim reacted with a mixture of anger and concern.

But Hasidic claims to popularity were not, I believe, entirely disingenuous. Many in the haredi community believe that they represent the forces of morality, spiritual values, and, in the long run, vision, which has been shown to be absent in Zionism. As a result, they hold that the Israeli population is simply waiting for the proper presentation of these eternal truths, and, indeed, if only the proper devices are found, or the key figures emerge, success is more than assured. When they talk, therefore, about growing popularity for their ideas and leader, it might reflect more their conviction that truth will inevitably conquer error than an exercise in "holy lying." Whatever the non-Orthodox might say, according to the Hasidim, they *know* in their Jewish hearts that the road is straight and the path narrow. Thus, even if true *t'shuvah* or repentance has *not* yet taken place, there can be no serious opposition to the strengthening of haredi institutions and the dissemination of their ideas.

Similarly, the Hasidim seem to have little understanding of the fact that the Rebbe means something different to them than he does to people who have not chosen to follow him. Charisma is not an abstract category, but rather a quality that achieves force because of the existence of individuals or groups who, willingly or unwillingly but rather subjectively, fall under its sway. The lives of the Hasidim tend to revolve about the figure of the Rebbe, who visits the town regularly but sporadically. Most of his time is spent at his yeshiva and "court" in Brooklyn, and although he assures his followers of his dream and goal to move permanently to Yavneel he also emphasizes that for many reasons that time has not yet come.[26] During the time he is in residence in Yavneel, one cannot avoid noticing the transformed atmosphere among the followers. Energy levels reach supreme heights; and Hasidim and others come from all over to seek him out and either gain his ear or simply be in his presence. The Hasidim seem, then, to exist on a different plane from the ordinary, and this is palpable even to the casual observer. The synagogue is packed with local Hasidim and visitors; the Rebbe's talks are attended with undivided attention; and if spirits were lagging prior to the visit, that tends to dissipate through his presence and his words.

The Rebbe's message tends to be simple but at the same time demonstrates a sophisticated understanding of "where his people are." He speaks of the need we all have for understanding, and offers himself as a listening post. He addresses the mystery of the zaddik, attempting to explain how another human being can serve in that role even though he is flesh and blood, not dissimilar certainly in this respect from the follower. He assures believers that faith can overcome all obstacles—even that presented by the fact that he cannot yet joint them permanently in Eretz Yisrael. He speaks with a consciousness that his message will be heard not only by the convinced but by those yet outside the holy community. There is hope even for those who think that salvation has already been achieved by means such as pioneering or political Zionism. In a clever commentary on one occasion, for example, he observed that this "hope" is reflected in the Hebrew slang for a native-born Israeli, which in English is rendered as *sabra,* and in Hebrew as *tsabar.* He noted that the three letters of the Hebrew root *(z, b, r)* should be understood to stand for the following: the grandfather generation were *zaddikim* or righteous souls; the son's generation were *benoni,* or middling compromisers; and the grandchildren are *rashaim,* or evildoers. However, the key, he noted, is that the distance between grandfather and grandson is, in generational and chronological time, so short as to make the possibility of a turn-around a simple matter. The *rasha,* or evil one, can reach back to the very palpable past and reclaim his proper moral heritage with relative ease if the will (and a guiding hand) are present.

Following the presentation of the Rebbe's message on Friday evening, or between afternoon and evening prayers on the Sabbath, the Hasidim all rise and, together with the Rebbe, dance around the prayer hall humming their traditional melodies or *niggunim.* It is a shuffle dance—awkward and without grace—but nonetheless filled with enthusiasm, serving to create as well as support a sense of group. All then come up in a press to wish the Rebbe a good Shabbes, or to kiss his hand, and some thrust their small children forward so that he may bless them.

Clearly the Rebbe fulfills a charismatic function among the believers, but he is perceived in a quite different fashion among Yavneelim, a fact which is not really understood by the enthusiastic followers. They insist that to know him, to merely open oneself to him, would prove irresistible for all but the most unsalvageable diehard opponents. Thus, when they claim that the town is moving toward them, is in fact desirous of rapprochement, they are reflecting, all in one, a pious hope, a misperceived evaluation of the situation, and a crude manipulative assertion of exaggerated strength in an attempt to tip the scales.

The Rebbe expresses conviction that he cannot fail, that Yavneel will become a city of Bratslav once he succeeds in finding or building housing for two hundred families.[27] He explains his targeting of Sephardim as part of the appeal to him of "the fallen and the downtrodden," observing that he has "so much to offer them while they have so little to offer in return other than their natural warmth." He is prepared to encourage intermarriage between the communities, but prefers the pattern of Hasidic men marrying local Sephardic women rather than the marriage of Hasidic women to Sephardi men. These views, recounted to me during a talk in July 1987, are by no means otherwise hidden or unarticulated. One can only surmise that they will not prove effective steps in winning over great numbers of Sephardim locally or elsewhere.

Similarly, the Rebbe's observation that "the farmers are nice people but their ideology is dead and will not sustain or nurture them," will be interpreted as an aggressive appraisal and win few friends or supporters among the Yavneeli settler group. The Rebbe and his followers have, in effect, declared a premature victory and proceeded to act on it. They have taken little or no note of the fact that the rooted life-style of Yavneel is the outgrowth of a lengthy process of development, based on a powerful ideology, and that whatever its present weakening or even disarray, it *does* nurture and does sustain. It is able to elicit loyalty and commitment. It provides warmth and direction. Although it is in flux, it continues to provide a matrix for communal existence.

In moving into Yavneel with first a covert and later overt intention to transform and supplant the reigning ethos, a gauntlet was cast down by the haredim. In appealing to the *edot,* a misreading of the very complex phenomenon of ethnicity in Israel has added to the challenge. Between the communities—the Ashkenazim and the Sephardim—rational discourse seems more than possible. Interests are involved and can be defined within a context of mutual understanding. Not so with the haredim. Here we are truly dealing with another world, a starkly different definition of reality. There exists no ideology of separateness between Sephardim and Ashkenazim: the opposite is the case. The haredim, on the other hand, invoke a fully developed ideology which they believe will prove able to fill the vacuum left by the decline of the Zionist vision. Given the fact that Yavneel has shown no inclination to reject the religion of its fathers, or supplant it with something else, but is rather evolving its own tradition-based, largely folkloristic religious pattern, the attempt to impose or to insinuate a counter vision is threatening and resented as well as feared.

The two worlds of ethnicity are in fact something less than two worlds. They can coalesce and fuse, albeit with much pain and a good deal of pulling and tugging. A new unity of sorts can emerge which does not by definition involve surrender on the part of one group or the other, although it is clear that dominance and subordination will play a role in the eventual outcome. The struggle with the world of ultra-Orthodoxy, which is interpreted by the haredi camps not as a conflict between two worldviews, but rather between a system of true values and a vision lacking any valid truths, is becoming, in Yavneel as in the country at large, an *either/or* confrontation in which there is no possibility for compromise. The ultra-Orthodox claim, that "we are the spiritual generators of the nation," is linked to demands for special privileges, which they believe should be forthcoming without complaint from "all honest folk" who wish to retain the eternal verities of Judaism.

Yavneelim, like other Israelis, I surmise, are not prepared to embrace this outlook. In fact, as the Hasidim began to clarify their stance through various actions, the reactions of many in the town heated up, tending to further bewilder the Hasidim. In March of 1991 a large demonstration was held opposite the Rebbe's house protesting the Hasidic presence in town. Some of the younger people put up a large structure on the mountain made of burlap-wrapped poles spelling the legend, "Shick Out"; then they soaked it in kerosene and set it alight to the cheers of some two hundred residents taking part. Placards were displayed and speeches made excoriating the "interlopers," but the Hasidim, rather than remain passive in the face of a rather strong outpouring of hostility, counterattacked by hooking up large loudspeakers blaring out medleys of eastern music in an attempt to drown out the rally speakers. In retaliation, townspeople climbed a nearby electric pole and cut the electricity for the entire block, which quieted the musical interruption and allowed the rally to continue. All segments of the town's population attended—young and old, veteran and "newcomer," Ashkenazi and Sephardi, although the core group of Ashkenazi settlers was most prominent. And this time, unlike early efforts to prevent the coming of the Hasidim, religious, although not haredi, supporters of the town rabbi also participated. The Rabbi's supporters were incensed by the attacks against him published in *Light of Yavneel,* while the others expressed their anger over what were seen as exaggerated haredi claims of having become "the very heart and soul of the town." The Hasidim expressed shock at these expressions of hostility, attributing them to the machinations of the "boss," the town rabbi. But, they explained, the attacks on the Rabbi were justified because, according to Rabenu (Nahman) as well as the Admor, "false zaddikim must be exposed no matter what the cost."

The rally was the culmination of other actions of the Bratslav group going beyond the harsh and exaggerated fulminations published in *Light of Yavneel.* During the very momentous fourth year of their presence in the town, their numerical strength reached highly visible proportions. They opened a mini-market which not only competed with the two locally owned shops, but did so by undercutting prices. They attempted to gain control of the local government grade school catering to the religious population, here almost exclusively Sephardi, only to be stymied when it was contracted to the Habad movement. They established their own preschool nurseries, thereby undercutting those supported and used by other Orthodox families in the town. They submitted plans for a massive two-hundred-student yeshiva that would dominate the architectural skyline of the town if and when it is built. They talked of plans for a wedding hall and ultimately a religious school for girls. And they floated hints of forthcoming "political" moves that were meant to be threatening to their opponents.

Yavneel, following a period of watchful waiting, was being galvanized into a stance of active hostility to the haredim. For the first time, nasty words were hurled at them in the street such as, for example, "Why don't you go to B'nai B'rak?" or simply "Why don't you clear out?" Some people even advocated violence, and others thought it would come to that without being advocated. The growing sense that the Hasidim were complete outsiders, with no possible justification for being in their midst other than to create mischief, seemed to be gathering larger numbers of advocates.

As if in a desire to solidify this growing suspicion and hostility, or perhaps because of that same inability to properly interpret the convictions of others who do not accept their outlook, the Hasidim of Yavneel took yet one further step on the occasion of the Memorial Day celebration in May of 1991. In the week preceding Memorial Day, ads appeared in *Light of Yavneel* inviting citizens to memorial gatherings that would be held at the town's two cemeteries during the morning hours: to be precise, at 11 A.M. At the designated hour, no one was in evidence other than a group of ten stout sons of the village wielding, each and every one, a heavy club with which they intended to beat any Bratslav followers who would appear: No one came.

# 4

# Whatever Happens Here Will Happen in the Whole Country: It Isn't What We Hoped For

## Memory and Continuity: Memorial and Independence Days

I𝐍 ATTEMPTING TO organize a separate Memorial Day ceremony, which was intended to precede the traditional communal event by five hours, thus overshadowing it, the Hasidim overreached. It is difficult to imagine what was behind their decision to lay claim to *the* central symbolic event in the life of the town. Could they have been unaware of this fact or, more likely, did the move represent a testing maneuver, aimed at the most sensitive sinew of communal existence?

Not only did an essentially "outsider" group attempt to

appropriate the primary mechanism of collective memory, but they did so without even the minimal justification of commitment to the social framework or the very real sacrifices that support it. The Hasidim do not accept either the program or the operative aspects of political Zionism, and they do not, on the whole, put their lives on the line in Israel's wars. Thus the specter of people who do not fight and will be unlikely to suffer the losses of loved ones attempting to run a memorial service for those who do had about it the flavor of bystanders willing to hold the jackets of combatants while the combatants struggled among themselves. The immediate, drastic action on the part of the villagers could have been foretold by anyone who was sensitive to the meaning of the occasion. Either the Hasidim deceived themselves about their true position in the constellation of village life or they deliberately chose to put this position to the test in an almost suicidal fashion.

"Death," as Yves Lambert observed in his study of French village life, "remains the strongest link between the villagers and religion," and in Yavneel as well it proves to be a powerful ingredient in the relationship.[1] The Hasidim are aware that all residents of the town no matter what their orientation to religion—that is, whether or not they define themselves as Orthodox, traditional, or nonobservant—follow a pattern in which life-cycle events in general, and death in particular, reflect some kind of adaptation of the inherited faith. No one is laid to rest in a way other than that sanctioned by the Orthodox religious leadership, and, more important, there is little objection on the part of secularists—although opposition *is* developing—to the prescribed form. While traditional forms are utilized in burial and in mourning, Yavneel has, as part of the developing "bass religion," evolved certain practices that can be considered "adjustments," but they tend to be cosmetic rather than substantive, such as placing many flowers atop the burial mound, which is not a general feature of Orthodox practice. In all other respects, however—preparation of the body, the use of a shroud rather than a coffin, the prayers chanted at the service, the eulogy, the tearing of cloth among the closest relatives—there is little to distinguish between accepted Orthodox practice and that followed by the people of the village.

Among the ultra-Orthodox, who saw themselves as the natural guardians and interpreters of a widely shared set of beliefs and practices, it was probably felt that here at least was an area where consensus would provide a degree of unopposed access to the core of village life. Who better than a highly Orthodox believer could provide a more solid context for marking the occasion and celebrating the memory of those who had died and were laid to rest according to the laws and traditions of the fathers? What better way to demonstrate legitimate involvement in the concerns of the community without compromising religious principles and in fact supplying a sort of patina of continuity with generations past?

Thus, it would seem that the attempt by the Hasidim to run a Memorial Day service apart from and in addition to the communal observance was indeed a maneuver to enhance their involvement in the affairs of the town, although like other moves on their part it reflected a poor understanding of what was truly at stake. Memorial Day for the fallen in Israel's wars does indeed involve the formal religious structure, and does indeed partially take place in the cemeteries that are run fully in accordance with Orthodox practice. But the Memorial Day observances also reflect one of the more highly developed aspects of the community's evolving "bass religion," with their national and group-enhancing qualities taking precedence over and highly coloring the traditional religious content.

In Yavneel, there is a separate small structure devoted to memorializing the town's residents who have fallen in defense of the community prior to 1948 as well as since the creation of the state. It is, in effect, a shrine designed and built rather joltingly more along the lines of a Russian Orthodox chapel than a synagogue or other recognizable "Jewish" structure. The building is windowless and totally bare apart from the photographs, in uniform, of each of the fallen thirty-two sons of the village, with memorial lamps, in icon-like fashion, flickering under each picture. The structure has no chairs or benches (again, as in the Christian Orthodox tradition), and visitors file past or stand in silent contemplation in near darkness before the nave that one faces on entering.

Once a year, on Memorial Day, the building is opened, and the entire community is invited to gather at 4 P.M. on the front lawn for the ceremony, followed by a visit to both of Yavneel's cemeteries. The ceremony follows a ritualized format, which includes paying one's respects before the pictures of the fallen, with two school children, who are relieved by others every fifteen minutes, standing at attention in front of a bank of national flags set up on the left of the entrance. The ceremony is opened by one of the veteran settlers or their descendants, who asks the town choir to sing one or two renditions; the songs are properly somber and the choir is inordinately bad, but no one seems to mind or, indeed, to notice. This is followed by a poetry reading associated with the founding of the nation or the sacrifices of war, and usually a wounded veteran offers a reflection of the meaning of ultimate dedication. *Kaddish,* the memorial prayer for the dead, is chanted by an old settler whose son is among the fallen, which is followed by an additional song or two offered by the choir. Then the crowd silently moves, first, to one and, then, to the second cemetery where identical rituals are carried out.

The two cemeteries of Yavneel are, as I have mentioned, quite beautiful and aesthetically pleasing places. Unlike most Jewish cemeteries in the Diaspora, which seem to reflect a disdain for aesthetics, Yavneel's final resting grounds bespeak much thought and aesthetic concern. The older cemetery in Yavneel nestles high above the town, overlooking not only the village itself but the Sea of Galilee, the Golan Heights, and the distant mountains across the River Jordan. It is cooled by a constant breeze even on the hottest of days and invites rather than repels, which might seem to be an odd attribute of a cemetery but somehow is curiously the case. The other cemetery lies in Bat Gan, and is also shaded by the branches of old trees and enhanced by dozens of flowering bushes, eliciting a similarly pleasant response from the visitor.

Just as the typical Diaspora cemetery, with its tombstones

crowded together and helter-skelter design, hints at tenuous ties to place, even in death, seeming to invoke a need for the security provided by group cohesion, so the relaxed atmosphere of the settlers' final resting place points elsewhere. One has the unmistakable impression that Yavneel reaches out to enfold its cemeteries, to make of them extensions rather than marginal accretions to the life of the community. They are in no way aesthetic attempts to dispel or ignore the reality of death, or even to lighten its finality and associated loss; but rather than denoting defeat they suggest a sort of victory. Here there are no victims, but rather men and women who have overcome passivity and unchosen sacrifice, having lived and died in a manner not particularly consonant with the models that had characterized their forebears through most of Jewish history. Here, rather than learnedness or martyrdom, the tombstones reflect devotion to labor or valor in defense of place, one's promised and deeded place under the sun.

For the Hasidim to attempt to co-opt, or even to actively share, this place or its legitimating ceremony was considered unacceptable by the settler group. It was even less acceptable than the presence of the town rabbi at the ceremony on Memorial Day because of his alleged anti-Zionist stance: he did not display the national flag on Independence Day and, above all, did not serve in the Army. The Rabbi has always refused to take part in the ceremony at the memorial building, asserting that he could not participate in view of the "mixed" choir that constitutes a prominent feature of the event. As a result, a sort of uneasy compromise emerged by which the Rabbi did actively participate in the religious ceremony at the cemetery but stayed away from the preceding event at the memorial building. Yavneelim maintain that they had always been unhappy with this arrangement, but did nothing to change it until 1987, shortly after the arrival of the first group of Bratslav Hasidim. With the tension brought to the surface by the arrival of the Admor, and given the anti-Zionist (or, more correctly, anti-Army service) position attributed to him by many in the community, hostility long harbored against the local rabbi broke forth. There was a growing sense among the townspeople that *their* observances, *their* traditions, *their* consecrations, were under attack by strangers who did not share the basic values of the community. Thus the Rabbi was told that he was unwelcome at the cemetery, and that an Army rabbi had been called in to officiate. Tensions were very high at the first ceremony, where Black Asa insisted that the local rabbi be allowed to participate, and a fight nearly broke out over the grave of a fallen soldier whose parents insisted that the Rabbi was neither needed nor wanted. The discreet presence of police and Border Patrol soldiers probably helped to prevent a melee, and after tempers cooled a compromise was reached whereby *both* the Army rabbi and the town rabbi officiated in the saying of Kaddish, the reading of psalms, and the chanting of the memorial prayer "God of Mercy."

This encounter led to a number of interesting developments. The format of both an Army rabbi and the local rabbi officiating at the cemetery ceremonies has been adopted as a permanent feature of the day. The Rabbi now flies the national flag from his home on Memorial/Independence Day and appears as part of the participating audience at the memorial ceremony. The growing sense of threat seen in the arrival of the Hasidim and their steady growth in numbers has led both rabbi and townspeople to step back an inch or two in recognition that little profit was to be had from their growing rift. The townspeople recognized that the Rabbi might be an irritant, but in the absence of a strong following he was not a threat. The Rabbi recognized that whatever the distaste or hostility demonstrated by his opponents among the townspeople, it was mild in comparison to what he could look forward to at the hands of a competing figure from his own world. A bit of compromise from both sides was indicated, and this, in fact, is what has occurred.

The townspeople *could* have done without the Rabbi had they chosen to do so, but they did not. The religious dimension, in its official as well as unofficial garb, is part and parcel of their lives and of their self and communal definitions. They will go far indeed—believer and unbeliever alike—in what they are willing to imbibe from the cup of revealed faith before calling a halt. Thus they recognized that while the Rabbi might protest this or that act, or attempt to interfere in areas which are deemed beyond his brief, he is, when all is said and done, "under control," responsive to community concerns—and pressures. On the other hand, both rabbi and townspeople see the Hasidim as subject to the will of only a single person, to whom they are totally and, it is believed, fanatically dedicated. Although both rabbi and Hasidim can be defined as haredi, or ultra-Orthodox, and both follow the Hasidic way, for the Rabbi it is a personal choice without wider repercussions, while for the Hasidim the implications of group action color all aspects of response.

The unexpected alliance was created between reluctant townspeople and a somewhat inflexible rabbi when it was realized that the Rabbi could be convinced to play a role in the context of the communal "bass religion," which was far from rejecting key aspects of traditional orthodoxy. The Rabbi in many respects represented a degree of marginality, but was nonetheless seen as being within the community. The Hasidim were perceived as outsiders, and dangerous outsiders at that, but bearing an undeniable claim to Jewishness, thus making their outright exclusion unthinkable. The villagers are prepared to see the integration of the Hasidim into the community, and very much on what they imagine would be their own terms, but they are not prepared to stand idly by when the core values and symbols that frame their lives are threatened. For the Hasidim to participate in the Memorial Day functions would have delighted the Yavneelim, and defrayed their opposition; to have attempted to co-opt it raised the specter of *Kulturkampf* from which the villagers would not shrink.

The weaving of collective memory among the villagers occupies a place of central importance. Telling and retelling the collective story takes place both formally and informally and provides a basis for both the creation and strengthening of community. This sense of community in Yavneel, as in the country at large, remains fragile, and the reasons are not hard to discern. In terms of the two major groups, the Sephardim, in large measure, suffered personal *and* collective trauma in their uprooting from what were still essentially traditional societies and their propulsion into the strange world established prior to their arrival by Jews fulfilling a different agenda than their own. The ideologically dominant Ashkenazi group is suffering the communal trauma of seeing dreams unfulfilled and, above all, threatened or unraveling. Thus the deeply important function of building and sustaining memory, approached in diverse ways, acts as a cohesive and a balm. Old men from both communities can be heard to compare their pasts under the Arabs in North Africa or under the British in Palestine, with the key linking word being "under," meaning subordination, rather than the distant and diverse conditions of oppression being described. And in discussions in the synagogue courtyard on Tisha b'Av, people of both groups agree that "Jeremiah didn't really write Lamentations; it was the people who wrote it," thus elegantly slicing through to a link involving all with all over time.

But the two major groups do not yet relate to remembered events in the collective past uniformly, nor do they mark these events in the same way. Memorial Day is still largely a veteran settler occasion, while Independence Day is celebrated, as it were, together and apart. Though the Sephardim do not attend the Memorial Day ceremony in anything like their proportion of the total population, they still recognize the event as a central link to the community. As they experience a greater degree of rootedness it is clear that they will embrace it more strongly, a process that cannot be expected of the Hasidim who are not committed to integration on any basis other than their own absolutist outlook.

The inability of the Hasidim to legitimately integrate into the Memorial Day events is even more pronounced in the celebration of Independence Day. Israel has evolved an interesting linkage in celebrating Independence Day contiguous with Memorial Day. In what has been sometimes regarded as a scarcely tenable combination of disparate emotional expression, deep reflection and sadness is followed immediately by the expectation and reality of often raucous joy and celebration.

The Independence Day celebrations, which begin in the evening at the conclusion of Memorial Day, following in this the religious practice, continue to reflect the religious and ethnic split of the earlier commemoration. The communtiy celebrates with performances by entertainers from outside, the youth band of the village, the communal choir, and dances by grade-school pupils. In addition the council head or mayor generally makes some pertinent remarks. Here, too, in 1987, participation was overwhelmingly by the core group, Ashkenazi and non-Orthodox. In asking some members of the *edot* why they were so little in evidence, I was given to understand that it was a sort of spontaneous boycott brought on by the sense that *their* culture was not represented, the Ashkenazi culture being not only dominant but exclusive. A sense of *their* Independence Day celebration rather than *ours* has festered among the *edot* over the years, gaining expression in a quasi-boycott on this occasion. On the following day, too, expression was given to this heightened sense of longstanding communal segregation: certain undertakings were of the *edot,* others were Ashkenazi, while nothing of an ultra-Orthodox nature was evident. For example, the annual adult basketball game was played on this day by and for an almost exclusive audience of veteran settlers in the lower town. In the upper town, a key event was a soccer game that was almost exclusively played by and for the *edot*. Both groups were aware of the segregated nature of the celebrations, and they tended to explain matters in cultural terms—for example, the settlers viewing basketball as a middle class, Western game in Israel, and the *edot* seeing soccer as the poor man's game. However, the Ashkenazim envisioned the *edot* gradually moving toward their dominant mode with time and westernization. The *edot* viewed their differences with the Ashkenazim as hardened by cultural and class inclinations and choices, and by an unstated but palpable distancing practiced by the core group even in what should have been a communal ritual of unification and unity. The day concluded with what has become a widespread Independence Day practice—cookouts, family picnics, and the gathering of friends at home; in this one could again witness widespread segregation of groups.

Thus, Memorial-Independence Day 1987 clearly reflected what Victor Turner referred to as phases of "breach" and "developing crisis" in a community, in this instance centering around the growing religious rift and ethnic tensions that were festering for over thirty-five years.[2] Polarized feelings of "us" and "them," increasing resentment and expressions of "anti" sentiments, were all present in heightened and dangerously explosive form. Masks that had been worn for over three decades fell, revealing that indeed "something was rotten in the village." If a split with its accompanying disintegration and possibly violent aspects was to be avoided, some form of healing, of bridging, of what Turner refers to as "redressive action," was clearly required. And the catalytic agent for this redressive action was provided by a force from outside the community—the recognition of a common enemy, more threatening and dangerous, and less capable of assimilation, than any challenge from within.

## CAN WE LIVE WITH STONES BEING THROWN IN WADI ARA?: THE "DAY OF PEACE"

The "Day of Peace" was organized by the Association of Arab Villages in Israel. It resulted in some acts of violence against the state and its representatives, including, in a few instances, the stoning of vehicles, raising of the Palestinian flag, and verbal expressions of identity with the wider Palestinian cause. Rage was the predominating emotion among all segments of Yavneel's population in response to what was seen as this revelation of the Israeli Arabs' true colors. They, it was widely said, were part and parcel of the Intifada launched by their cousins in the West Bank and Gaza against us, and their aim was the same—the destruction of Israel. At the very least, it was noted, we—the religious, the *edot,* the veteran settlers—are all Jews, all Israelis; the enemy, the real enemy, was to be found elsewhere.

On the day following the "Day of Peace" I spent a number of hours at the local filling station, and for the first and last time in the course of my study of the community I confronted firsthand an almost surrealistic outpouring of emotion concentrated on one single topic—the Arabs in our midst. Without asking questions, or making any attempt to direct the course of conversation, I was made to function as a sort of audio mail-drop; and the townspeople, whom I had come to know as garrulous interlocutors who generally took care to temper their more aggressive responses with a variety of caveats and a high degree of adjectival reticence, let go with a torrent of rage and barely suppressed fear. People representing the entire range of the town's population with the exception of the Hasidim flowed in and out, and without any stimulus addressed themselves to me and to others, close and far, about "them." "The Arabs are not to be trusted," they opined; "they have shown us once and for all who they really are"; "they must be gotten rid of"; "they should be transferred"; "we must take a strong stand," and so on. One of the villagers who had taken a very strong stand against the Hasidim observed that "Shick is not the enemy; it's the Arabs who are the enemy." Another remarked, "We must stop employing them and get them out of our gas stations and restaurants and from now on employ only Jews." Even people who had previously identified themselves as sharing left-wing attitudes, and who continued to maintain that violence against Arabs could not be justified, expressed feelings of betrayal and hopelessness.

At one particularly tense moment a beat-up old station wagon occupied by four Arab men drove in for gas. While the gas was being pumped a group of four Yavneelim, including the filling-station attendant, exchanged opinions on what was to be done with the Arabs. "They have lived here for forty years and have gotten all sorts of benefits from the state and now this: it is time to throw them out." The driver of the vehicle was standing outside alongside the car and remained silent, a small, nervous smile on his face. The three other men in the vehicle sat in silence and stared ahead, not moving their heads. Not a word passed between the Arabs and the clearly enraged

Jews. When the car pulled out I asked if it wasn't apparent that these people were Arabs and heard every word being said about them. I was told, "Yes, we know they were Arabs, and it's time to tell them what we think. In Russia they would have known how to deal with them; there they wouldn't have lasted one day. It's only here that they can riot and later come in for gas and a cold drink." As one villager drove out of the station he yelled at me, "Read Haim Levyakov—he'll tell you what an Arab *really* is like."* A few expressed their willingness to participate in any effort to put the Arabs on buses and drive them over the Jordan River, "free without charge." The only person during the course of a very long morning to express a degree of moderation and understanding was a middle-aged woman who had "married into the community" and felt that things were getting out of hand. The lady grew up in Tel Aviv, I was told, and didn't really know or understand Arabs. When one villager, almost in a state of shock, revealed that "they even demonstrated on Herzl Street in the middle of Jaffa," he was told "We have to break their bones."

These comments, as I mentioned, were typical. One man, with whom I had spent a great deal of time and who I came to like and respect, not least for what I perceived as his levelheadedness and kindness, in response to demonstrations at a large Arab town—Um El-Fahem—said that "The Army should have lined up in front of the town and shelled it." Another resident, with his two pre-adolescent sons sitting in the back of the car and well within earshot, opined: "They have demonstrated that they are not part of the state, and we should shoot them down each time they raise their arms in revolt." Said another, "In Tunis, where I come from, the French knew how to deal with them. They built walls around entire villages and stopped demonstrations before they even began. We should have drawn artillery up in front of the larger Arab villages, and with the first stones we should have opened fire." One of the

---

*Haim Levyakov is a popular Israeli folklorist who is a native of Yavneel.

town's most respected elders announced that he "doesn't believe in collective punishment, and doesn't favor the reintroduction of military government in the Arab sector." Nevertheless, a "strong hand" is needed, he said. "Security is sacred and we cannot allow the guilty ones to go wild. As far as the territories are concerned, we can argue, but when it is this side of the green line, we can't. There must be control and all signs of anarchy must be eliminated."

The events of Peace Day had thrown the community—and the country—into a state of shock and disarray. Some reactions verged on panic. A few people were heard to express fears for the future of their children in this land. Never had I seen so many grim faces or heard so much anger expressed—anger, it should be added, which lacked only a spark before, it would seem, it would erupt into blind violence. It was not a matter of left and right, religious and secular, Sephardi and Ashkenazi: it was *us* and *them*.

The explosive reactions to the Day of Peace took place, it should be emphasized, in reaction to the actions of a few hundred people out of an Arab population of some 700,000 souls. Stones were thrown in only about four or five places in the entire country, and yet the Israeli response suggested mass revolt on the part of people who neither had a legitimate complaint nor could be trusted to stop at this kind of protest. Clearly the unease brought about by the Intifada and the fear that it might represent simply the first act in a drama that could engulf the entire country, not only the disputed territories, were powerful catalysts motivating the reactions of Yavneelim.

The villagers tended to appraise Arab disaffection much as, internally, Ashkenazim interpreted Sephardi resentment: with little willingness to notice, let alone sympathize with, the objective facts of their existence. They see Arabs sending their children into their fields to harvest tomatoes and peppers, aware that being there means they are not in school, but they make no connection between this and the conditions that make it either necessary or possible: it is simply a fact of life. They know that their roads are paved and their schools have indoor plumbing, in contrast to neighboring Arab villages, but that is attributed to differing levels of group development. There is a widespread conviction that the Arabs, or a very high proportion of them, have grown rich and prosperous as a result of Jewish rule, and in any case, "they are better off here than in the Arab countries." People point to Arabs benefitting from Social Security, observing that they get this *and* medical care notwithstanding the "fact" that they massively avoid paying taxes and do not serve in the Army. "Yes," it will be admitted, "there are disabilities attaching to their minority status—how could it be otherwise given the fact that they want us out of here to take back what they lost." "Don't let us delude ourselves—the Arabs will never become Zionists," a Yavneeli declares. "Only forty years have passed since we fought for our freedom against them. In their hearts they are against us even if their conditions are better here than in the Arab countries—in their hearts they are against us. They are just not digestible."

Yavneelim believe that Arabs as a group understand only force, only power. "If you let down your guard they will put a knife in your back. If you educate them, they will think you are weak. If you give them Social Security and hospitalization, they will take advantage. They are getting too much and as a result are demanding much more. They must be dealt with strongly." Ilan, a veteran settler who has fought in three of Israel's wars and who defines himself as a moderate with respect to the Arabs, observed that "I have lived with Arabs all my life and if I have learned anything it is that they respect strength. I understand them, and I understand their pride and the fact that they want to take back what we took from them. It's understandable, but it is a matter of who is going to be stronger—us or them. America, Poland—everybody had to fight a long time for their independence and we will have to as well. I have lost one son in war, and I have two more who are in reserve combat units, but if war it must be then war it will be." Meir, another veteran Yavneeli, opined that "this just proves again that when the Arabs see weakness, they will attack us: we must survive, we must live through our power. We wanted to develop them in the hope that when they became more advanced they would understand us and accept us: this was our mistake." Another third-generation farmer, in a particularly bitter reaction to the events of the "Day of Peace," gave vent to a particularly harsh, almost hysterical, sense of frustration when he said, "We have to burn them because they want to burn us. They have a bigger share of the national wealth than I do, and they are freer than I am. *He* can wander in my village at night, but *I* cannot do it in *his* village—if I want to live. This will become Belfast. Can I live with stones being thrown in Wadi Ara?"

Within a few days of these events, however, the answer as to whether or not the villagers, and indeed the country, could live with "stones being thrown in Wadi Ara" was apparently affirmative—on the behavioral if not the rhetorical level. On the very day following the "Day of Peace," a van whose license plates marked it as coming from the West Bank parked on the main street and, its loudspeakers blaring, invited Yavneelim to sell used clothes and unwanted appliances "at good prices." The vendor did not lack for custom, and the banter and bargaining which usually accompany transactions of this kind were, if not overly warm, then entirely civil. There were no theats, no audible nasty asides, and no visible air of tension or even discomfort.

That very day I witnessed an Arab-Jewish encounter that suggests the ambivalent, almost surreal mechanism for dealing with it, which could point to future possibilities of "working things through" or else a bloodbath. On the basis of the following incident, it is unclear which path will be taken.

## A Yavneel Story

While sitting in Yehoshua's living room talking over the events of the previous day there was a knock on the door. Yehoshua rose, opened the door, and in fluent Arabic invited three grizzled middle-aged men who were standing on his doorstep to enter. He invited them to be seated, introduced me, and we all sat down. The host exchanged what I assumed to be pleasantries with his guests, and after a few moments went off to prepare coffee. The guests talked quietly among themselves, and when the host returned with coffee, all partook and the conversation continued with occasional chuckles and many smiles. All in all, it was clear that a general atmosphere of good will and civility was present. The men, it transpired, had come to conduct business with Yehoshua, but from the general context it was clear that more than business was being transacted, and, interjecting in Hebrew, I asked if they were discussing the "situation." Yehoshua cheerily said, "Yes, indeed they were," and I then asked what he had said to them. He answered that he told them that "the only good Arab is a dead Arab"—and he smiled. Shocked, I asked what they had said in response and he answered that they said "The only good Jew is a dead Jew"— and smiled again.

Like dominant groups elsewhere in speaking of disdained or feared minorities with whom they live, Yavneelim maintain that they truly know and even like the subordinate group and enjoy intimate friendships with many of its members. Among the older Sephardim in the village one is often privy to quite positive appraisals of Arab culture, or certain presumed facets of this culture, such as "the Arab will share his last crust of bread with you and give you the best he has," or "when times were bad, Arabs never hesitated to supply us with flour and cheeses and other dairy products which they make so well." Some even suggested their suitability to act as bridges to the Arabs, when peace comes, because of their knowledge of and respect for their language and customs. Most of the older Ashkenazi settlers and their second-generation descendants *did* live cheek by jowl with Arabs in the region, and a high proportion spoke or at least understood Arabic. They were clearly rivals in the larger national sense, but in times of quiet—and there were many such times—they were also neighbors and fellow farmers who struggled jointly against the ravages of poor crops, lack of water, and other shared devastations associated with a marginal agricultural existence.

It may be true, as Nigel Barley observed, that "it is one of the more depressing discoveries of the anthropologist that almost all peoples loathe, fear and despise the people next door,"³ but it appears equally true that living "next door" can just as often have a tempering effect on these baser passions. Although Jews and Arabs are without doubt enemies who have killed in the past and might well do so in the future, there exist between them curious networks of relatedness, which either foretell more vicious combat or perhaps the creation or enhancement of memory forged in a very different mold from that which binds the diverse strands comprising the Jewish community. A Yavneeli tells this, again, ambivalent and cautionary tale:

> Is there a question of our right to be here? A few years ago one of our workers from the Triangle invited us for lunch on the occasion of the festival of Id el Fidhr. We had a nice talk about Torah and the Koran and the place of Eretz Yisrael in our religions. So one of them said to me—"what are you talking about? Even in the days of Abraham, who is our father too, you discriminated against us. Yitzhak was given the blessed land, and Hagar and Ishmael were sent into the desert." That had been a serious mistake, I answered—if Abraham had known that the desert contained oil, he would have sent us and given *you* the blessed land.

Arabs and Jews are in and out of each other's lives in the village, although it is clear to both who is dominant and who occupies a lower rung in the relationship. There exists an awkward and precarious network of relatedness combining, on both sides, intimacy, ease, fear, and disdain. Somehow or other, however, the element of fear seems more characteristic of the dominant Jewish majority than of the Arab minority. This might reflect the very real fact of overwhelming Arab population and resource superiority in the region, or the unifying function of this fear in buttressing Jewish solidarity. In any event, the matter does reverberate with a certain ambivalence so that Yavneelim experience a sense of security which is as fragile as their sense of community. But this last point should not be exaggerated: The villagers lose little sleep over the nightmare specter of being overwhelmed tomorrow, nor do they feel a lack of deep relatedness to each other, which is, after all, what community is all about. Though the "religious issue" may act as a divisive factor among the Jewish groups living in Yavneel, with anger directed against those who, it is feared, wish to push the community in a direction that the majority do not prefer, it is also a powerful unifying factor, serving to distinguish between *us* and *them*. Similarly, with regard to the gulf between Sephardim and Ashkenazim, who, when all is said and done, both desire the creation of stronger communal bonds rather than fragmentation and difference.

With regard to the perceived challenge from the Arabs—those within as well as outside the national borders—this complication does not exist. Here, the sense of a common enemy acts only to unify. There may exist disagreement as to what is to be done, and with what degree of liberality or harshness, but almost no one inclines to define the issues in other than the most consensual fashion, pitting the beleaguered Jews against the irreconcilable Arabs. Somehow it is hoped that internal religious differences will work themselves out, or at least stay within acceptable bounds. The local rabbi *can* be convinced that displaying the national flag on Independence Day will not irreparably sully the purity of his religious principles, and the Hasidim *can* be restrained when they exceed acceptable norms of village behavior. But Arabs throwing stones in Wadi Ara represent a danger to the community that is viewed as existential by nature, eliciting a degree of fear and rage that other challenges simply do not provoke. In the face of this threat, all internal conflicts are laid aside as "family matters": Arabs, after all, "will not become Zionists."

Within ten days of the "Day of Peace," Yavneel had returned to the "normal" pattern of relationships between themselves and the Arab population. The filling station was again a place of meeting and interaction between Jews and Arabs featuring a ready degree of surface camaraderie and fairly good-natured banter. Arab workers carried out their tasks as construction workers and field laborers. Arabs sitting together, or at times together with villagers, could be seen drinking coffee at the local kiosk, passing the time of day, or even talking about current events. Indeed, later on and during the Gulf war, conversation between Arabs and Jews shifted to talk about whether or not "we"—Arabs *and* Jews—would be hit by "germs" delivered by the missiles so promiscuously launched from Iraq.

But the collective "we," with respect to Jews and Arabs, is circumscribed by limitless caveats. There exists no powerful impetus from either side for the evolution of shared memory other than on the rather superficial level of pragmatic civility or, from the perspecive of the villagers, to buttress the status quo, which is seen to be workable if not ideal. The fear among the villagers that the Arabs hold to a resolute agenda that would, if it came to pass, destroy the village *and* the country is palpable, and not very far from consciousness. The Hasidim represent a challenge to a way of life, even deeply held ideological commitments, but they are not perceived as life-threatening. For the Yavneelim, the menace they feel coming from the Arabs in their midst has about it a biblical cadence which resounds of Esau hating Jacob; while that perceived as coming from the Hasidim raises questions of Jewish legitimacy, continuity, and, not least, defeat of the Zionist ideal of the new Jew that has been a core value in the village.

## Bringing Back the *Galut:* The Pull of Exile, the Push of Zionism

While it is certainly true that the Arabs are not likely to become Zionists, yet another issue besets the villagers: Will the Zionists remain Zionists? The appearance of a large contingent of ultra-Orthodox believers in Yavneel brought to the fore the villagers' doubts as to the very viability, the present and future strength, of the ideology that supported their existence. There is no doubt that Yavneelim felt uneasy about the presence in their midst of a numerically significant group of Hasidim, but their response would have been considerably less anxious had they felt surer about the health and vibrance of their own ideology. A combination of their sense of having been invaded by opposing forces bearing aloft symbols of a counter-image of high legitimacy together with the waning vibrance of their own Zionist vision provided the context and reason for their strong objections to the ultra-Orthodox presence.

Zionism, much like other powerful ideologies to have emerged in the latter part of the nineteenth century, is a multifaceted, complex phenomenon subject to varied and sometimes contradictory interpretation and understanding. For some adherents it was a logical response to the seemingly endemic persistence of anti-Semitism as an ineluctable feature of European civilization; simply put—removal of the irritant, the Jews, to their own national home would prove a solution to the problem of Jew hatred, *Judenhass*. For others, it evolved from a recognition that, unless they created their own response to a world gone mad with nationalistic strivings, the Jews would be crushed in the head-long stampede toward ethnic, historical, linguistic, and cultural restructuring of the societies where at best they were a tolerated anomaly. Still others, recognizing the growing movement toward secularization, saw a need for a parallel development among Jews that might insure their group cultural viability while rescuing them from the dead hand of religious obscurantism. Some viewed it as a political solution to the essentially political challenges of the postrevolutionary age, while others saw it as a movement for cultural renewal and a preparatory framework for entrance into a world characterized by modernity, secularism, national autonomy, and economic independence.[4] It is a movement that has produced its mystics and saints as well as its bureaucrats and adventurers—Martin Buber and Asher Ginzburg (Ahad Ha'am) as well as David Ben Gurion and Josef Trumpeldor, A. D. Gordon as well as Theodor Herzl.

Shlomo Avineri calls Zionism the most fundamental revolution in Jewish life because, among other reasons, it attempted to answer the dilemma of identity brought to the fore as a result of the French Revolution.[5] The Revolution brought in its wake not only the ideas of liberalism and secularization but also nationalism, which, instead of invoking a comprehensive idea of universalism that could have embraced masses of willing Jews, rather evoked a new national identity characterized by ethnicity, language, and common past history. Thus the Jew was propelled into a dilemma of national identity, and could not fully participate in the various nationalist undertakings without first embracing the encapsulating Christian faith that still constituted the backdrop to the emerging new political and cultural dispensation. Zionism was one answer to this dilemma. It substituted, says Avineri, a secular for a religious self-identity; it changed a passive commitment to Zion to an active one; and it revitalized a language, which must form the basis for any national movement of self-realization. In all three of these changes, we do indeed see elements of "a fundamental revolution in Jewish life," bearing wide-ranging repercussions in its wake.

These themes were not universally apposite among all Jews. As Daniel Elazar has observed, the Zionism of the Ashkenazim was *revolutionary,* a desire to change the Jews as well as their objective situation, while the Zionism of the Sephardim was *redemptive,* a desire to change the Jews' situation, to fulfill but not to change them; it was continuous rather than a break.[6] The basic themes and patterns, the guiding ideology of Yavneel, as well as of the broader society of Israel, drew primarily from the regnant Ashkenazi vision, and in its formative stages only marginally and minimally from Sephardi roots. Differences following from these discrete visions are still visible among the two groups in the village and wider afield. The legitimacy of all forms of religious traditionalism is, by and large, unquestioned among the Sephardi residents of Yavneel, so that opposition to the presence of the Hasidim, when it appears, tends to be based on matters such as their refusal to share the national burden of Army service, or signs of interference in personal, as opposed to communal, life-styles. The haredi pattern of religiosity might be slightly exotic, perhaps a bit foreign, but for the Sephardim it does not constitute a threat to any firmly held ideological predisposition or affirmations.

For large numbers among the core group of Ashkenazi settlers, however, there does exist a sense of threat, and it goes beyond the fear of religious coercion or the presence of not easily assimilable practices. It involves a challenge not only to what may transpire in the village today or tomorrow, but in fact reflects on what happened in the town almost a hundred years ago, suggesting a type of retroactive cancellation of core Zionist values that underlay not only the town's founding but the national enterprise as well. Although Zionism has had many faces, the theme of the new Jewish person occupied a central place in what transpired here on the ground, as it were, if not in the more theoretical writings produced by the movement.

The early years of Zionist settlement in Palestine without a doubt reflected a wide-ranging desire to throw off the behaviors and life patterns thought to be typical of the Diaspora, the *Galut. Galut* was conceived of as not alone the objective situation of minority existence in a particular place, but also as a state of mind, a pattern for action (or inaction), a web of culture, a psychology of being—all of which was given a negative valence by the Zionist settlers. To a startling degree the *chalutzim,* or early pioneers, absorbed and acquiesced in the definition of the Jew promulgated by the often hostile cultures among whom they lived, and sought, in effect, to "become like the nations." "Jews," their enemies averred, "do not fight." In Zion we will reclaim the ancient martial tradition and demonstrate that Jews can indeed soldier with the best of them. "Jews," it was said, "are middlemen, 'handlers,' nonproductive manipulators of markets where all is subject to the cash nexus." In Palestine it was to be shown that ties to the soil and productive labor in factory and workshop call to the Jews as to other peoples when the opportunity presents itself. Jews were *luftmenschen,* people of spirit, "up in the air," with all suggestions of physicality denigrated as the mere shell covering true substance. In Palestine we would develop muscles, engage in sport, and apotheosize beauty in all its expressions. In place of a certain portability we would here reclaim deep ties to place; instead of dependency, independence; rather than sufferance, sovereignty.

Notwithstanding a remarkable degree of success in carrying forth elements of this program—and Yavneel shines forth as an exemplar of ranking importance—there exist lingering deep fears with respect to the power and durability of what has been achieved. Farming is in decline, and the grandchildren of the founders in their majority are going to university and entering business and the professions. Although never fully absent, distinctions based on wealth and material possessions have reasserted themselves in rather crass form, the richer residents building large villas for themselves or their children while the poorer live in visibly less comfortable circumstances. Not a few of the younger generation have left the village for the attractions of city life, and some have left the country altogether, thus willfully reclaiming the previously despised status of *Galut* Jew. More and more, one sees the hard physical work of construction and crop harvesting being done by Arab hired laborers rather than by the Jewish yeoman farmers.

There exists unease in Zion, fear that the era of the "new Jewish person" might have been a mere passing phase in a fleeting moment of a history patterned according to a very different agenda. Forty years—even a hundred years—are not sufficient to root out, it would seem, the norms and values established over a period of a thousand years. There are fears among Yavneelim that the roots established here are perhaps ephemeral, and that the challenges that inspired the founding generation, and their sons and daughters, will not engage the convictions of the present generation and those to follow. One old farmer proudly recounted the fact that the birth of each of his children was coterminous with war and conflict—one daughter born during the 1929 riots, another during the 1936 riots, a son during World War II—not, as tradition would have warranted, during the Feast of Tabernacles, or on the eve of Rosh Hashanah, or at the Fast of Gedalia, as if there had evolved a new Jewish calendar or mode for marking the passage of time. But one daughter lives in Cleveland, Ohio, and the other in Tel Aviv, and his son no longer earns his living from the land, and he himself feels as if he were an actor "in a play which ran for just a month and then closed as darkness enveloped the theater."

The appearance of the Hasidim represents to many an insult to the lives they have chosen to live. The haredi claim to legitimacy raised or, more correctly, underscored the villagers' doubts about the viability of their concept of how things should be. The claims of the Hasidim to continuity with the Jewish past and legitimacy as keepers of the flame cannot too easily be contested; but they stand in firm opposition to almost all of the founding values, resulting in the paradox of their integration in the community representing a defeat for what had been so assiduously reformulated.

Yavneelim are aware of the pull exercised by the rejected value system of their forebears and exemplified in the haredi community. They understand that Jewish history has not for the first time demonstrated a tension between the attractions of marginality and the demands of sovereign responsibility; and in opposing the haredim they are, in effect, fighting for their lives. It is as if a mirror were held up to the faces of the villagers, and rather than the weather-beaten face of the farmer seen in their mind's eye, a Jekyll-Hyde projection of a bearded Talmudist stares back at them instead. A farmer explains it in his own words:

> Look—as to why they are unacceptable to me, I could give you a whole speech. I think the haredi world symbolizes for me everything negative and objectionable in the Jewish religion. The haredi world as I see it was born in the towns of eastern Europe during the eighteenth and nineteenth centuries. When the emancipation began there, and people began to think of a new way, and non-religious men of vision rose and wrote of ways to fashion a new Jewish nation and people began to dream of Zionism—then the haredi movement thought to build a barrier against everything the Zionist movement represented. The haredi world is a world recognizable through its uniform, which differentiates them not only from other religious Jews but from everything positive in the world. The haredi thinks that the one and only thing he has to do in this world is to worship God. What do I have in common with him? They think that if they worship God they have done all that they need to do in this world: I will work the land and *he* will work for God. He permits

himself to enjoy the fruits of my earthly labor—and that of everybody else.

The haredim represent, uphold, and symbolize in what they do *not* do the very essence of what Yavneelim see as the culture of *Galut*. They do not go to war, they do not farm, they do not work in construction or in factories, they are not nurses or doctors, they are not scientists or university professors, they do not drive trucks or taxis, they do not paint pictures, mold sculptures, or create literature. They represent also a return to a type of dependency typical of the threatened lives of Jews in an often hostile world. When the venerable haredi leader Rav Eliezer Shach appeals for compromise on the matter of territories, it is "not for love of Mordechai but for fear of Haman": he is afraid to arouse the wrath of the omnipotent and always hostile "goyim." The haredi world, like the departed world of the shtetl, knows how dangerous life as a Jew can be and is prepared to do what must be done to endure, to survive, but always on the assumption of moral and spiritual superiority linked to physical and material weakness. Thus maneuver, rather than straightforwardness, is the hallmark of haredi action, and fear and suspicion the backdrop, rather than confidence and an aggressive spirit.

All of this could be considered a mere hangover from a rejected and departed past, which in time would fade away, but for the fact that it not only exhibits a high degree of vibrance but does so at a time that the dominant new culture seems unable to aggressively compete. The haredim are not merely a group of Jews living their lives in a fashion unacceptable to the villagers, who for some reason or another wish to live quietly alongside them: they want the Yavneelim to leave what they are and return to being what they think they should be. Almost every value upheld by the villagers is condemned by the haredim as inadequate, wrong, sinful, and non-Jewish in any legitimate sense. It is either/or. If the vision of Jewish life upheld by the haredim is correct, then the life of the Yavneelim is not an alternative; it is a lie. The Yavneelim recognize the legitimacy of the haredi way as having deep roots in the Jewish past and a defensible and legitimate role for those choosing it in the Jewish present. But the reverse is not applicable. For the haredim, the values and life-style of the Yavneelim represent a breach, and a break with legitimacy, and will, they believe, in the long run, disappear as did other ephemeral deviations in the past.

For many villagers, however, there remains a nagging, underlying concern that the pull of *Galut,* in both its cultural and geographical manifestations, is still relevant and attractive, and provides a fundamental challenge to all that had been achieved under the banner of Zionism. There seems to be evidence to the effect that *Galut* patterns of life that had been eulogized as having been irretrievably overcome are in fact very much alive. The pioneering values of simplicity in material lifestyle and a lack of concern for frills, together with the deeper positive values of physical labor, self-defense, and rootedness in place are seen to be in eclipse, if not totally in retreat. The concern, when all is said and done, which truly grips the people of the village is not really whether or not the vision of the haredim or their own is correct. They understand that *some* vision is required as a baseline in life and as an inheritance for those to follow, and that the *Galut* vision as embodied in the Hasidic newcomers has demonstrated a preternatural vibrance, viability, and longevity, while their own, it is feared, may not prove up to the mark.

## The Decline of Commitment: Israel as a Failed Utopia

In an impressive wall mural entitled "Israel: The Unfulfilled Dream *(Yisrael: Chalom v'Shivro)*" at the main entrance to the University of Haifa, the late Israeli painter Avraham Ofek sums matters up in a most gripping fashion.[7] Triumphs of the human spirit and great feats of will are celebrated in panels depicting the Jewish people's ancient tie to the land where its creative skills were shaped and honed, and where this people made its move to re-enter a history embedded in space as well as time. The achievements of the Yishuv, of the pioneers in farming and building and settling and reclaiming, are displayed in muted colors but very strong lines, adding up to a picture of great accomplishment. But there is a snake in the garden. This is, after all, not a depiction of the new "Soviet Man" winning out against all odds, slaying dragons to the left and to the right, and emerging pure, untroubled, and free not only of blemish but of doubt. While dreams have been realized, reality in the sense of all the sinful relativities that afflict mankind as a whole, and no less the Jewish people, has crept in, demanding our humility if not our attention. Greed, avarice, cheating, causing pain are, if not our fate, certainly our sometime lot. Ofek uses the Latin terms for these negative qualities as if in an effort to warn us, but not unduly alarm us or turn us away from the harsh truth, which use of the Hebrew language—a language of hope and revelation but also of higher chastisement—might effect. It is almost as if he wants this dimension of reality to seep in, rather than blaring forth. He perhaps thought that while we had to hear, we needed also to be cushioned so that our dream would remain a holy dream—of scripture, of prophet, of pioneer, of sage, and of artist—while our reality, in the form not of sacred but profane history, is perforce of this world.

Not alone for the artist but for so many of lesser sensibilities as well, the dream is, if not broken or shattered, as Ofek says, then at least tarnished or lessened. What has happened to the city on a hill? Where are the dreams of social justice, of unity, of constantly renewed hope? Even for those among us who dreamed little, an image of something larger than our narrow individual existence still insinuated itself into consciousness. After all, rebuilding Zion is heady stuff and a far cry from mere self-determination or the renewal of sovereignty.

For the people of the village, as well as for many among the country's citizens, it has become clear that the building of the state has caused so much to be undermined, so much to be lost. Pride and satisfaction with achievements wrought against great odds combines with disappointment and doubt about present and future developments: something more, it would appear, than just a state was envisaged. The current enterprise is experiencing difficulty in evoking the kinds of deep loyalties characteristic of the early state-building period, and as Horowitz and Lissak have suggested, might be showing signs of being "overburdened," when, they say, "the system's capacity to mobilize instrumental resources and normative commitments lags behind the concrete demands placed on the political center."[8]

Some of the mystery and wonder has begun to recede, as inevitably it had to, and is being increasingly replaced by a sense of the commonplace. Distinctions, whether of class, origins, political orientation, or religious inclination, which had been submerged or tempered or contained in the excitement of creating a new conception and reality of Jewish life, have re-emerged to prominence and begun to exact a toll. "A city-state," says Yi-Fu Tuan, "loses its cohesiveness and its standing as a permanent and natural unit when its citizens begin to question its institutions and values, not necessarily because these are oppressive but rather because the citizens have come to recognize their own separate identities."[9] With the weakening of a sense of dependence on "eternal verities" ordained by a higher force, he argues, the personal and the individual and the parochial will fill the vacuum left. When a commitment to a transcendent ideology fades, it will result in much the same weakening of loyalty to the center.

Why, it might be asked, given the impressive achievements of the Zionist idea in so many of its targeted goals, is there at this juncture a growing malaise and disappointment in the land? There is no questioning the remarkable triumphs of not only agricultural production and the successful reclaiming of a most unforgiving land, but of the emergence of the Jewish farmer demonstrating a skill and genius previously unsuspected as being possible among the people of the book. The drama of the "ingathering of the exiles," while not total or complete, has reached a level that few among even the most utopian of Zionist visionaries could have foretold not too long ago. An industrial framework has grown so that in four decades

Israel has moved from a society that had to import almost everything heavier or more complicated than a lathe to one that manufactures everything from razor blades to jet airplanes and enjoys export levels reckoned in billions of dollars per annum. Pride in these achievements is palpable and essentially unshaken.

There is pride also deriving from the embedded and enshrined doctrine that Jews must assume responsibility for their own fate. If enemies seek to undermine or attack the national home, others will not be called upon to defend the enterprise: "we will do it ourselves," paying whatever price is required. This notion of Jews taking full responsibility extends beyond the borders of the state to include Jews oppressed or threatened anywhere in the world. When Jews were threatened in Ethiopia, an impressive, difficult, and dangerous airlift was organized to fly thousands to the country in one weekend. When Jews—not just Israelis—were threatened in tones and words reminiscent of the Holocaust during the Entebbe hijacking, the Israelis, in a complicated and daring operation, flew four thousand miles into Africa, fought a short battle on the ground, and brought the endangered passengers to Israel and safety.

But other developments have occurred alongside those dramatic achievements which have elicited so much pride and so high a sense of accomplishment and change. In a society that had assumed as one of its goals the maintenance of relatively modest gaps between those earning the most and those earning the least, a chasm has opened up so that Israel is second only to the United States among "western" countries with respect to the distance between the top and the bottom of the economic scale. Poverty, or those living below the poverty line, is in excess of half a million people, about 20 percent of the population, again placing Israel close to the United States.

While Israel must be seen as among the most politically stable of the countries to have achieved independence following World War II, and one of the few to have maintained a democratic framework, there is nonetheless a great sense of political impotence, both internally and externally. Israel's economic and political dependence on the United States has assumed almost legendary proportions, leaving in its wake an uncomfortable feeling as to whether Israel is an independent state at all, or perhaps on its way to becoming an unrecognized fifty-first state. Internally, Israelis are badly governed, partly a function of the absence of a viable political tradition, and partly the result of a seriously divided electorate for whom making "deals" rather than "rational decision making" forms the operative principle of governance.

Although Israel is democratic in a formal and perhaps more than a formal sense, there is no gainsaying the sobering fact that its population, in origin at least, stems overwhelmingly from places with no tradition of political democracy. Most Israelis come either from the more authoritarian sectors of East and Central Europe or the Middle East and North Africa, where self-governance is and was a foreign conception. Too often for comfort one is told in Yavneel and elsewhere that a good part of what ails the country can be attributed to "too much democracy," which somehow is confused with anarchy. Telling the truth about things—especially matters with serious political or social implications—is often thought to be not only unwise but dangerous and destabilizing. After giving a lecture in Yavneel about the problems of emigration from the country, I was told by two women that they found the talk good and to the point, but "thank God there were so few young people present." The feeling was that an objective analysis might "put ideas into their heads," or justify "certain tendencies already festering." Somehow the idea has taken root that love of democracy and love of homeland are two contrary doctrines, so that, according to a villager, "too much democracy has caused young people to denigrate and debase the idea of homeland, *moledet.*" Teaching democracy in the schools (an exercise that in any case might be doomed) is not seen as an unvarnished good because "expressing oneself too freely is dangerous." What is being reflected here perhaps is a widespread lack of faith in the good will of one's neighbor, which may be a function of disparate origins and a veritable babel of tongues, or, simply, one of the birth pangs associated with a still young national culture. It might also be a byproduct of the widespread lack of trust that Israelis have in their political leadership, which is seen as corrupt and unresponsive. Again, partly because of the absence of a political culture and partly because of the political system that holds sway in the society, there exists little responsiveness on the part of government to expressions of dissatisfaction with society or the political structure. Following the widespread disgust expressed in the political process itself, following the fall of the unity government in March 1990, and the unseemly wheeling and dealing that marked the formation of a new government, over 200,000 citizens marched and rallied in Tel Aviv to demand change. The government and the various political elites were able to completely ignore this rare outpouring of wrath with the insouciance generally brought to bear in turning a page. Phenomena of this kind do not enhance a sense of political potency nor, for that matter, faith in the accountability associated with democratic governance.

Additional problem areas, such as the growing rate of emigration from the country, the continuing gap between those of eastern and western origin and their descendants, the growing impress of crime and deviance, higher levels of family instability, and more, add to what might be called the "overflowing plate" syndrome in Israeli society. The plate is just too crowded with problems that seem to elude repair or solution, certainly including the everpresent challenge of war, which has about it a quality of overriding permanence and inevitability, delaying and sidetracking solutions to other pressing issues.

Israel is not the only society to be beset by deeply rooted problems, nor is the society unique in the pervasive malaise and disappointment that seems to penetrate public and private domains alike. A key difference, however, present in the case of Israel and largely absent in other societies with which Israel compares itself, is to be found in the problem of legitimacy, which is associated with the conditions of its birth in war and the displacement of an indigenous population *and* the rather unique constellation of factors underlying its national movement. Most of the nation-states achieving independence and national expression in the preceding century emerged from liberation movements, or already existing natural formations based on language, propinquity, history, and a common culture. In this respect, Israel must be seen as being an anomaly if not quite "abnormal." Rather than liberation from a foreign yoke, Jews were *brought* here for purposes of *founding* a national home that had not existed for two millennia. I know of no other case of an idea of this kind being kept alive for so long and ultimately resulting in the hope being fulfilled—which in itself, it might be added, provides cause for inevitable disappointment. When the reality is measured against the expectations embodied in a dream of such gripping magnitude and duration—how could it not fail to measure up? Even when it does measure up, as in the case of the revival of Hebrew as a language of everyday discourse, it does not suffice. In an unparalleled fashion, by an act of national will, Hebrew was transformed from a language of prayer and study into an everyday, conventional language. There are few cases of equal success with which this achievement can be compared, but in numerous ways one sees the effects of the absence of an organic continuity of usage preventing the kind of flow and richness of expression required in complex societies. This has opened the door to widespread dependency on English, with repercussions for a sense of cultural autonomy which could be surmised.

Israel is succeeding, I believe, in creating a national culture, which like other cultures that evolved more "naturally" or less "anomalously" reflects indigenous impulses and uniqueness, but also seems to be uncommonly under the sway of what occurs elsewhere, especially in the United States. This dependency, which extends from the material to the cultural, has given rise to a perception of Israeli society as a periphery to the center represented by America. The more Israel moves away from the forming notions of its founding, the more it appears to reject its own orbit for one promising more access to a dominant mainstream, thus weakening, though not defeating, its ability to evolve a new culture with a binding vision that can elicit a high level of commitment from its citizens.

The powerfull *will* called forth in the creation of this "anomalous" national undertaking has given rise to a society which might be described as a national *intentional community,* with its attendant strengths and weaknesses. The intimacy and sense of purpose, the heightened energy levels, one finds especially in the early stages of intentionally formed or utopian communities is without parallel. But when these falter or decline as the enterprise unfolds and develops, moving from the founding to succeeding generations, alternative visions are sought and sometimes found, but only rarely do they supply similar levels of commitment.

Rosabeth Moss Kanter has observed that communities, and by extension, nations, fall or hold together insofar as they are committed; and she suggests the centrality of six commitment mechanisms in this process that she identifies as sacrifice, investment, renunciation, communion, mortification, and transcendence.[10] All of these qualities enjoyed high resonance in the founding stages of Israeli society, and all have undergone a process of decline over the years. Sacrifice, in its lesser sense of the willing acceptance of austerity in personal life-styles, as well as the willingness to invest resources, time, and energy for the common weal no longer have quite the same claim on Israelis as they did in the past. Similarly with communion, which Kanter sees as the expression of a strong "we" feeling together with sharing a sense of brotherhood, which also has altered to fit a very different conception of society than that of the early vision. Perhaps, above all, change of a radical and significant nature is to be seen in what Kanter calls "transcendence," quoting Buber to define it as "the need to feel his own house as a room in some greater, all-embracing structure in which he is at home, to feel that the other inhabitants of it with whom he lives and works are all acknowledging and confirming his individual existence." It is a seeking after a certain "rightness" that "cannot be realized in the individual but only in human community," and involves attaching a certain degree of charisma to the group as a whole, a kind of "institutionalized awe" which can be symbolized by a leader or by tradition.

The years of Yishuv, the pre-state settlement and the early years of the state, which had at the helm larger-than-life figures like Weizmann, Ben Gurion, and Begin, were marked by the force of these individuals' personal charisma and the power of their vision. But the last decade has witnessed a precipitous decline in this kind of leadership. If a sense of something beyond personal quixotic desires is required to elicit commitment to a larger entity, then clearly it will not come from the formal political leadership of the country. The natural fallback to the gap left by the absence of charismatic, or even powerful, leadership figures points inevitably to what Kanter has called tradition as a transcendence-facilitating mechanism. "Tradition defines what is as what should be, and preempts the ability of those not yet involved with the tradition to offer alternatives and suggest changes," she writes. "It asks members to submit to principles that have 'stood the test of time.' The aura of history surrounds it."

Of the two major ideological systems underlying Israeli society—secular Zionism and religious traditionalism—only the latter retains serious efficacy and motivating energy. All societies require justificatory myths, but in a society such as Israel's that attempted, as it were, to create itself, the need for validation and legitimacy is perhaps more cogently felt than in the more ordinary undertakings of state or society building with which it might be compared. The insecurity experienced by Israelis, with its accompanying sense of having failed to maintain and expand the Zionist vision, bears more relationship to what might be seen in a declining "intentional community," with its problems of motivating the second and third generations, than in a modern state. Insofar as one can look at Israel as an "intentional nation," commitment mechanisms, while robust, have provided a type of energy and enthusiasm which lent it strength. With their decline, as inevitably they must, and in the absence of needed structural and ideational change, as well as the further growth of an "at homeness" in place that comes only with time, the society is threatened with a fate that has overtaken other social organisms that failed to elicit commitment in necessary degree.

Because of their intuitive recognition of the truth of this perception, Israelis in Yavneel and elsewhere see no replacement for a vibrant religious tradition. The "bass" or popular religion, whose clear outlines are visible in Yavneel, may well be the development of the future, but traditional Orthodoxy and even the haredi claim to exclusive legitimacy will not be frontally challenged except in the face of the most extreme provocation. When this occurs, when the forces of religious tradition, even those that have "stood the test of time," attempt to overturn the emergent value system of an opposing and evolving secular tradition, weakened as it may have become, battle lines will be drawn.

## And What of the Village?

More than four years have passed since the Bratslav Hasidim first appeared in the village, and although much has changed, much has stayed the same. The bucolic attractiveness of the town has been unaffected by the atmosphere of crisis stimulated by the "invasion," and the ties that bind Yavneelim to their small place in Galilee are as deep as ever they were. The crisis in agriculture continues to cause grave concern not only among those still farming but among those who refuse to envision Yavneel as other than a beacon for the triumphant return of Jews to the soil. The failure to attract small-scale industry to the community persists, as does the related concern that there might exist little to hold the current generation of teenagers in the village when they come of age.

The divisions that characterize the social fabric of the community based, as they are, on distinctions between veterans and "newcomers," Ashkenazim and Sephardim, farmers and other workers, continue to hold sway. Veterans are convinced that the Sephardi "newcomers" have nothing or almost nothing to complain about, and Sephardim, whether landholding or not, are equally convinced that they have been and are being dealt with badly.

The core values of the villagers, for whom physical labor and service in the defense forces assume something of a quasi-religious coloration, is undiminished in strength and continues to form a powerful underpinning to the hostility felt toward the ultra-Orthodox community in their midst. The pattern of relationships between the haredim, on the one hand, and the villagers, on the other, pursues a cycle of active conflict followed by periods of watchful waiting. At times one is almost unaware that hostility or suspicion is present, while at other times the air veritably crackles with it. The town rabbi has begun to show somewhat more flexibility than he has demonstrated in the past, but he remains a marginal and largely disliked figure to most residents of the community. A "divorce" does not seem imminent or indeed possible, and the different parties have settled into what has become a marriage of little convenience and small alternative.

If one word could be used to symbolize the prevailing spirit of the village it would be "disappointment." As Shimon put it, "It's not turning out right." Faith in the country's *and* the village's institutions has faltered, reflecting a growing feeling that "our" point of view—whatever it might be—is not being adequately represented. "I feel like a rag," one Yavneeli said to me, and "for this we are all to blame. We have been tied down. I have nobody to follow or to go with. I have lost my faith in people." The disappointment is tied to a sense of impotence, the inability to influence, let alone control, events. "If I had to vote today," said another resident, "I wouldn't know who to vote for and am not sure I care. They destroyed all that I believed in." The "they," in cases where the word was used, refers to vague forces somehow or other associated with the various establishments dominant in the country, primarily the political.

The people of the village feel control slipping from their hands with regard to almost all matters large and small. They cannot control the drift of the economy that is anachronizing them at a rapid rate. They cannot control the mechanisms that have deemed that a haredi rabbi will be in charge of the formal religious structure, which does not reflect their emergent popular religion and in fact stands in active opposition to it. They cannot control the settlement in the town of a group representing a powerful religious counter-image to the still fragile identity that has developed among them over the years. There is certainly little that they can do about the endless wars with the surrounding states, or about the Intifada, which appears to have assumed a similar mien of permanence. Nor can they affect the pervasive unresponsiveness of the national political structure, and the growing gulf that seems to characterize the relationship between elite decision makers and the people of their rather remote village.

Impotence, a sense of slipping or absent control, can be a very dangerous, explosive factor in any social context, and those who feel the sense of deprivation or of frustration may strike out at perceived causes of their discontent. Can one therefore expect that the village will lash out at selected targets who they rightly or wrongly perceive to be at the root of their dissatisfaction? Will serious conflicts emerge between "veterans" and "newcomers," the ultra-Orthodox and the non-Orthodox?

There is, in fact, no evidence that this is probable other than in the most extreme of unforeseen circumstances. When all is said and done, conflict in Yavneel, although by no means benign, is still very much within the bounds of "family trouble." The Sephardim will continue to interact and intermarry at an increasing rate with Ashkenazim, as the various conditions of the gap between them narrow. Non-haredi Orthodox believers will continue to see themselves, and be seen by others, as full participants in village life, sharing with the majority of residents, even in the religious dimension, much more than they do not.

Finally, the village, while not articulating the matter, has become increasingly aware of its strength and discipline as well as of its fragility. One hundred years in place might be enough for certain changes to set in and for certain cultural patterns to solidify—but not for everything. The ties to the land are indeed deep, but, clearly, only time, much more time, will tell how lasting. The values evolved over millennia can be tempered and altered—even, under revolutionary circumstances, abrogated—but the price is inevitably high and the results unpredictable.

# NOTES

## Introduction

1. Victor W. Turner, *Dramas, Fields, and Metaphors: Symbolic Action in Human Society* (Ithaca, N.Y.: Cornell University Press, 1974), p. 34.
2. Everett Carll Ladd, "Secular and Religious America," in *Unsecular America,* ed. Richard John Neuhaus (Grand Rapids, Mich.: Eerdmans, 1986), p. 23.
3. Daniel Bell, *Sociological Journeys: Essays 1960–1980* (London: Heinemann, 1980), p. 353. See Chap. 17, "The Return of the Sacred? The Argument on the Future of Religion."

## Chapter 1   A Small Place in Galilee

1. Bernard Lewis, *History: Remembered, Recovered, Invented* (Princeton, N.J.: Princeton University Press, 1975), pp. 11–12.
2. Elias Canetti, quoted in Yi-Fu Tuan, "Thought and Landscape," in *The Interpretation of Ordinary Landscapes: Geographical Essays,* ed. D. W. Meinig and J. B. Jackson (New York: Oxford University Press, 1979), p. 94.
3. Eudora Welty, quoted in Orville Vernon Burton, *In My Father's House Are Many Mansions: Family and Community in Edgefield, South Carolina* (Chapel Hill: University of North Carolina Press, 1985), p. 7.

4. Mordechai Naor, *Yavneel: 1901–1981* [Hebrew] (Tel Aviv: Milo, 1982), p. 79.
5. Maurice Godelier, "Work and its Representations: A Research Proposal," *History Workshop* 10 (Autumn 1980): 164–174.
6. Everett Cherrington Hughes, "Work and the Self," in *Social Psychology at the Crossroads,* ed. John H. Rohrer and Muzafer Sherif (New York: Harper & Brothers, 1951), p. 314.
7. Howard Newby, "The Work Situation of the Agricultural Worker," in *The Experience of Work,* ed. Craig R. Littler (New York: St. Martin's Press, 1985), p. 76.
8. Naor, *Yavneel: 1901–1981* [Hebrew], p. 183.
9. Lee Braude, *Work and Workers: A Sociological Analysis* (New York: Holt, Rinehart & Winston, 1975), p. 127.
10. Maurice Godelier, "The Object and Method of Economic Anthropology," in *Relations of Production: Marxist Approaches to Economic Anthropology,* ed. David Seddon, trans. Helen Luckner (London: Cass, 1978), p. 63.
11. Simcha Haruvi, "Society in Development—the Agricultural Settlement, Yavne'el: 1911–1917" [Hebrew], *Kivurim* 18 (1983): 104.
12. ICA is the Jewish Colonization Society; PICA is the Palestine Jewish Colonization Society.
13. Newby, in *The Experience of Work,* ed. Littler, p. 75.
14. Barbara A. Hanawalt, *The Ties that Bound: Peasant Families in Medieval England* (New York: Oxford University Press, 1986), p. 5.
15. Abraham Kosnitsky, *B'terem Ha'ir Ha-Boker* [*Before Daybreak*] (Jerusalem: Israel Ministry of Defence, n.d.).
16. Jamaica Kincaid, *A Small Place* (New York: Penguin, 1988), p. 54.
17. Yi-Fu Tuan, *Space and Place: The Perspective of Experience* (Minneapolis: Univ. of Minnesota Press, 1977), p. 202.
18. Richard Whipp, "'A Time to Every Purpose': An Essay on Time and Work," in *The Historical Meanings of Work,* ed. Patrick Joyce (Cambridge: Cambridge University Press, 1987), pp. 234, 214.
19. Andrew Delbanco, *The Puritan Ordeal* (Cambridge, Mass.: Harvard University Press, 1989), p. 224.
20. David Graybeal, "What Happens in the Village," in *Continuities and Discontinuities: Essays in Psychohistory,* ed. Shirley Sugerman (Madison, N.J.: Drew University, 1978), p. 77.

21. Ibid., p. 78.
22. Bialik quoted in Naor, *Yavneel: 1901–1981* [Hebrew], p. 1.

## Chapter 2   And Prophecy Departed from Israel: Yavneel's Religion

1. The two leading strongholds of ultra-Orthodoxy in the country—the first in Jerusalem and the second outside Tel Aviv.
2. Abraham Kosnitsky, *B'terem Ha'ir Ha-Boker [Before Daybreak]* (Jerusalem: Israel Ministry of Defence, n.d.), pp. 342 ff.
3. Ibid.
4. *Davar,* 9 April 1990, p. 24.
5. Charles S. Liebman and Eliezer Don-Yehiya, *Civil Religion in Israel: Traditional Judaism and Political Culture in the Jewish State* (Berkeley: University of California Press, 1983), p. 165.
6. Natalie Zemon Davis, "From 'Popular Religion' to Religious Cultures," in *Reformation Europe: A Guide to Research,* ed. Steven E. Ozment (St. Louis, Mo.: Center for Reformation Research, 1982), p. 322.
7. Liebman and Don-Yehiya, *Civil Religion in Israel,* p. 136.
8. Robert N. Bellah and Phillip E. Hammond, *Varieties of Civil Religion* (San Francisco: Harper & Row, 1980), p. 92.
9. Ibid., p. 93.
10. Ibid.
11. Ibid., pp. 92–93.
12. Ibid., p. 93.
13. Ibid., p. 90.
14. Liebman and Don-Yehiya, *Civil Religion in Israel,* 20, 21.
15. Ibid., p. 165.
16. *Jerusalem Post,* 12 December 1989.
17. See Ephraim Tabory, "The Identity Dilemma of Non-Orthodox Religious Movements: Reform and Conservative Judaism in Israel," in *Tradition, Innovation, Conflict: Jewishness and Judaism in Contemporary Israel,* ed. Zvi Sobel and Benjamin Beit-Hallahmi (Albany: State University of New York, 1991), pp. 135–52.
18. See Charles S. Liebman and Steven M. Cohen, *Two Worlds of*

*Judaism: The Israeli and American Experiences* (New Haven: Yale University Press, 1990).
19. See A. Ben Meir and Y. P. Kedem, "A Measure of Religiosity for the Jewish Population of Israel" [Hebrew], *Megamot* 24 (1979): 353–62. See also Liebman and Cohen, *Two Worlds of Judaism*, p. 141.
20. See Liebman and Cohen, *Two Worlds of Judaism*, p. 141.
21. Ibid., p. 139. See also Ben Meir and Kedem, "A Measure of Religiosity for the Jewish Population of Israel."
22. See Liebman and Cohen, *Two Worlds of Judaism*, p. 139.
23. I use "assert" and "claim" in view of the fact that an eye-check over a two-year period suggested much less than the reported observance.
24. Will Herberg, *Protestant, Catholic, Jew: An Essay in American Religious Sociology* (Garden City, N.Y.: Doubleday, 1955). For a definition of "Hansen's Law," see pp. 30 and 257.
25. Janet O'Dea Aviad, *Return to Judaism: Religious Renewal in Israel* (Chicago: University of Chicago Press, 1983), p. 141.
26. Ferdynand Zweig, *Israel: The Sword and the Harp* (London: Heinemann, 1969), pp. 70–80, especially Chap. 7, "The Basic Myths of Israel".
27. See M. J. Aronoff, "Civil Religion in Israel," *Royal Anthropological Institute News* 44: 2–6.
28. John Updike, *Roger's Version* (New York: Knopf, 1986), p. 85.
29. See Carl Mayer, "Religious and Political Aspects of Anti-Judaism," in *Jews in a Gentile World: The Problem of Anti-Semitism*, ed. Isaque Graeber, Steuart Henderson Britt, et al., (New York: Macmillan, 1942), pp. 311–328.

## Chapter 3   A City of Bratslav: The Hasidic Invasion

1. Admor is a contraction of the Hebrew term "Adoneinu v'morenu," "our master and teacher." It is not an official title such as "Rabbi," but an honorific usually bestowed upon a religious leader, such as a rebbe, by his followers.
2. Some sources list his death as occurring in 1811. See Louis Jacobs, *Hasidic Thought* (New York: Behrman House, 1976), p. 57.
3. Harry M. Rabinowicz, *Hasidism: The Movement and its Masters* (Northvale, N.J.: Jason Aronson, 1988), p. 94.

## Notes

4. Rabinowicz, pp. 94–95.
5. I base my appraisal of Nahman on the following works: Martin Buber, *On Zion: The History of an Idea,* trans. Stanley Goodman (New York: Schocken, 1978), pp. 89–108; Gedaliah Fleer, *Rabbi Nachman's Fire: An Introduction to Breslover Chassidus* (1972), 2nd. Revised edition (New York: Hermon Press, 1975), and *Rabbi Nachman's Foundation* (New York: Ohr Mi Breslov, 1976); Arthur Green, *Tormented Master: A Life of Rabbi Nahman of Bratslav* (Tuscaloosa, Alabama: University of Alabama Press, 1979); Louis Jacobs, *Hasidic Thought* (New York: Behrman House, 1976), pp. 57–65; Harry M. Rabinowicz, *Hasidism: The Movement and its Masters,* and *Hasidism and the State of Israel* (East Brunswick, N.J.: Associated University Presses, 1982), p. 45–55.
6. Quoted in Louis I. Newman, *The Hasidic Anthology: Tales and Teachings of the Hasidim* (1934; rpt. New York: Schocken, 1963), p. 454.
7. See Zvi Sobel, *Migrants from the Promised Land* (New Brunswick, N.J.: Transaction Books, 1986), pp. 38–55 ("Commitment and Completion").
8. Buber, *On Zion: The History of an Idea,* 94.
9. Ibid., 100.
10. Ibid., 104.
11. Ibid., 107.
12. Ibid., 104.
13. Ibid., 90.
14. Verses 5 and 6 from Psalm 126 are presumed to be the basis for the selection of Yavneel. In the Hebrew of verse 6 the circled letters are an acronym for Yavneel: *Bo (Y)avah (B)erinah (N)osaia (Al)umotav:* "They that sow in tears shall reap in joy. He that goeth forth and weepeth, bearing precious seed, shall doubtless come again with rejoicing, bringing his sheaves with him." (The Bible, King James Version)
15. Sermon, April 1987.
16. Rabinowicz, *Hasidism and the State of Israel,* p. 53.
17. Among the "practical" considerations, two stand out: the fear of his flock being "raided" by other haredi groups during his frequent absences from Israel; and the attempt to move far away from the hostility of other Bratslav groupings who resent his assumption of Nahman's authority. As is well known, Nahman has not been, and orthodox outlook suggests, can never be,

replaced. Rav Shick spends most of his time in New York and visits for periods of two or three weeks at least five or six times a year. This might be useful in some ways, for example, by maintaining a degree of distance, making fewer mistakes, "imitatio Nahum," and so on, but it does have, in a context of sectarian charisma, decided drawbacks as well.

18. Under joint sponsorship, the leading Sephardi sage Ovadia Yosef *together* with the leading non-Hasidic haredi Rav Eliezer Shach together have organized a political party called Shas, with educational and social affiliates.

19. At the Shuvu Banim Yeshiva for the newly penitent in Jerusalem, which is run by an opposing branch (to Rav Shick) of Bratslav, there is also a majority of Sephardim.

20. Baba Sali was a Moroccan rabbi and charismatic religious leader who, before his death a few years ago, had become *the* dominant popular living "saint" and wonder worker for large numbers of Israelis of North African background.

21. See the annotated bibliography by Sammy Smooha, *Social Research on Jewish Ethnicity in Israel, 1948–1986* (Haifa: Haifa University Press, 1987).

22. Harvey E. Goldberg, "Historical and Cultural Dimensions of Ethnic Phenomena in Israel," in *Studies in Israeli Ethnicity: After the Ingathering,* ed. Alex Weingrod (New York: Gordon and Breach, 1985), pp. 189, 190.

23. The Mitzvah Tank is a mobile home turned into a sort of traveling propaganda van that encourages the unaffiliated to try religious practices such as prayer with phylacteries or lighting candles in celebration of Hanukkah. Habad, an acronym for *Hochma, Bina, Daat,* is the official name for the followers of the Lubavitch Hasidic movement.

24. For a description of a similar process occurring in Islam, see Michael Gilsenan, *Recognizing Islam: Religion and Society in the Modern Arab World* (New York: Pantheon, 1982), pp. 129–130.

25. The following are samples of Shimon's graffiti:
    (a) There is a creature,
    offer it a finger—
    it would demand the whole hand.
    The parasite latches onto living things.
    For some idol worship provides a living, and
    the understanding will understand.

- (b) Citizens of Yavneel:
  The wise men of Bratslav lost decency, truth, and common sense: Will the finder please send them to P.O.B. 289 (the group postal box in town). Are shame and integrity orphans?
- (c) Wise men of Bratslav:
  Torah without labor leads to idleness and sin.
  The understanding will understand.
- (d) If you believe that the Messiah is coming, run to the gate where his donkey awaits. What a tale for children and "wise" men.
- (e) Hear o wise men of Bratslav:
  He who works the land will gain bread and the idle will gain nought.

26. Among the "suspected" reasons for the Rebbe's failure to settle permanently in Israel, it is thought by some that his wife and some of his children oppose the move, and also that his base of financial support remains largely American, requiring his presence.
27. Personal interview with the author, July 1987.

## Chapter 4  Whatever Happens Here Will Happen in the Whole Country: It Isn't What We Hoped For

1. Yves Lambert, "From Parish to Transcendent Humanism in France," in *The Changing Face of Religion,* ed. James A. Beckford and Thomas Luckman (London: Sage Publications, 1989), p. 58.
2. Victor W. Turner, *Dramas, Fields, and Metaphors: Symbolic Action in Human Society* (Ithaca, N.Y.: Cornell University Press, 1974). See Chap. 1, "Social Dramas and Ritual Metaphors," especially "redressive action," pp. 39–41.
3. Nigel Barley, *A Plague of Caterpillars: A Return to the African Bush* (New York: Viking, 1966), p. 72.
4. See S. N. Eisenstadt, *Israeli Society* (London: Weidenfeld and Nicolson, 1967).
5. Shlomo Avineri, *The Making of Modern Zionism: The Intellectual Origins of the Jewish State* (New York: Basic Books, 1981), p. 13. See especially "Introduction: Zionism as a Revolution," pp. 3–13.

6. Daniel Elazar, "The Place of the Zionist Vision and the State of Israel in the Sephardi World," *Forum* 60 (Summer 1987): 17–25.
7. This is not a literal translation but comes closest, I feel, to the thrust of the Hebrew title. "Dream and its Destruction" would be more precise, but somewhat awkward in English translation.
8. Dan Horowitz, *Trouble in Utopia: The Overburdened Polity of Israel* (Albany: State University of New York Press, 1989), p. 239.
9. Yi-Fu Tuan, *Segmented Worlds and Self: Group Life and Individual Consciousness* (Minneapolis: University of Minnesota Press, 1982), p. 4.
10. Rosabeth Moss Kanter, *Commitment and Community: Communes and Utopias in Sociological Perspective* (Cambridge, Mass.: Harvard University Press, 1972). See especially Chap. 4, "Live in Love and Union: Commitment Mechanisms in Nineteenth Century Communes," pp. 75–125.

# GLOSSARY

*Admor:* "Our master and teacher," an honorific often bestowed on a religious leader by his followers.

*Apikoras:* Skeptic, freethinker, or heretic.

*Arak:* Alcoholic beverage popular in the Near East and Mediterranean.

*Aruchat eser:* Morning tea.

*Ashkenazi* (pl. *Ashkenazim*): Jew(s) of European descent.

*Ba'alim:* Owners or bosses of enterprises, or dominant figures in a political and social context.

*Baal Shem Tov:* "Master of the good name," Israel Ben Eliezer is the founder of Hasidism; also referred to as the *Besht*.

*Ba'al t'shuvah:* A penitent, or returnee to Orthodox religious observance.

*Ba'alut:* Ownership, suggesting a propertied class or individual.

*Bar Mitzvah:* Religious coming of age for male youngsters at age thirteen.

*Batlan:* Loafer or idler.

*Bat Mitzvah:* Relatively recent and not universally accepted equivalent of Bar Mitzvah for females.

*Bilu:* Movement founded in Russia in 1882 to sponsor and encourage agricultural settlement in Palestine.

*Black Panthers:* Movement founded in the post–Six-Day-War period by disaffected youth of North African background in order to protest prejudice and Ashkenazi dominance of Israeli society.

*Chalutz* (pl. *chalutzim*): Pioneer, especially in agriculture in Palestine and later in Israel.

*Chevrah Kadishah:* Voluntary religious association responsible for burial of the dead.

*Dati* (pl. *datiim*): Religiously observant or Orthodox.

*Diaspora:* Jews living outside Eretz Yisrael, the land of Israel.

*Dunam:* Unit of land approximately equivalent to one-quarter of an acre.

*Edot ha-mizrach:* Groups of Jewish immigrants to Israel originating in North African and Middle Eastern countries. Often shortened to *edot.*

*Eretz Yisrael:* The land of Israel.

*Galut:* Exile, the condition of the Jewish people in dispersion.

*Galutiut:* The spirit or essence of *Galut.*

*G'dud:* Brigade, as in the army or other disciplined formations.

*Gematria:* Interpretation of Hebrew words according to the numerical value of the letters.

# GLOSSARY

*Grush:* Coin, of low value, in use during the mandate and early independence era of modern Israel; generally the equivalent of a penny.

*Habad:* Acronym for *Hochma, Bina, Daat,* or wisdom, understanding, knowledge; the Hasidic movement often and alternatively referred to as Lubavitch.

*Haganah:* The major underground force of the Jewish community formed during the period of the British mandate in Palestine.

*Haggadah:* Ritual recited in the home on Passover eve during the seder.

*Hakafot:* Ritual dancing with the Torah scrolls on the holiday of Simchat Torah, marking the conclusion of the yearly cycle of Torah reading.

*Halakha:* An accepted and binding decision in rabbinic law.

*Hanukkah:* A holy day commemorating the victory of the Maccabees and the rededication of the temple.

*Haredi* (pl. *haredim):* Ultra-Orthodox Jew(s), including both Hasidim and non-Hasidim, characterized by rejection of the values of modern society and the strictest observance of Jewish Law.

*Hasid* (pl. *Hasidim):* Followers of the Hasidic way.

*Hasidism:* Religious movement of revival and renewal, founded by the Baal Shem Tov in eighteenth-century Poland.

*Hatzer:* Court of a Hasidic rebbe or leader.

*Hazan:* Cantor in the Ashkenazi tradition, and among Sephardic Jews a respected religious figure.

*Heder:* Primary school for the teaching of Judaism and Jewish practices to youngsters.

*Hiloni* (pl. *hilonim):* Secular or nonobservant Jew(s).

*Histadrut:* Major labor federation of Israel founded in 1920.

*Hitbodidut:* Isolation for personal communion with God; a central practice of the Bratslav Hasidim.

*Hofshi* (pl. *hofshim*): Freethinker(s).

*Id el Fidhr:* Moslem three-day feast marking the end of Ramadan.

*Issachar/Zevulun:* Two of the twelve tribes of Israel, used to symbolize the relationship of spiritual and material pursuits. According to biblical exegesis (Deuteronomy 23:18), Zevulun's profits in trade made it possible for Issachar to study Torah.

*Kaddish:* Traditional mourners' prayer for the dead.

*Kalashnikov:* Submachine gun of Russian design in wide use by Arab regular and irregular forces in conflict with Israel.

*Kapote:* Long outer garment or coat traditionally worn by Orthodox Jews in Eastern Europe.

*Kasher:* Ritually acceptable food; *also* kosher.

*Kashruth:* Jewish dietary laws.

*Kibbutz* (pl. *kibbutzim*): Israeli communal settlement originally based exclusively on agriculture, but lately expanded to include industry.

*Kiddush:* Prayer recited over wine or bread on festivals and the Sabbath.

*Kippah* (pl. *kippot*): Skullcap worn by observant Jews; also yarmulke.

*Knesset:* Israeli Parliament.

*Ma'abara:* Temporary community comprised of tents and huts used for housing new immigrants to Israel in the 1950s.

## Glossary

*Ma'aser:* The tenth part of an offering set aside for the temple priesthood; tithe.

*Masorti:* Traditionalist; generally refers to a person who is observant on a selective basis.

*Melamed:* Teacher in a religious primary school or *heder*.

*Mezuzah* (pl. *mezuzot*): Portions from the Bible encased in a small tube or box and affixed to the doorposts of Jewish homes.

*Mikveh:* Ritual bath.

*Minyan:* Quorum of ten adult males required in Orthodox practice for communal prayer.

*Mishnah:* Codification of Jewish oral law.

*Misnagid* (pl. *misnagdim*): Opponent(s) of Hasidism.

*Mitzvah* (pl. *mitzvot*): Religious commandment(s); good deed(s); merit.

*Mizug galuyot:* Integration of Jews coming to Israel from diverse countries of the Diaspora.

*Moshava* (pl. *moshavim*): Settlement where agriculture is practiced on individual farms and where land is privately owned.

*Niggun* (pl. *niggunim*): Wordless melody(ies) or tune(s) hummed especially by Hasidim as part of formal and informal religious observances.

*Ol Ha-Torah:* Yoke or heavy obligation of carrying out the commandments of the Torah.

*Omer:* Forty-nine days elapsing between Passover and Shavuot.

*Oriental:* Sometimes used to refer to Jews of North African or Middle Eastern origin; see also *Sephardi(m)*.

*P'shot:* Of the four types of biblical exegesis, *p'shot* is the first, meaning literal or simplest meaning. The others are *remez* (hint), *d'rash* (homiletical interpretation), and *sod* (mystery, or esoteric interpretation).

*Rabash:* Person primarily responsible for security and arms in an Israeli village or settlement.

*Rebbe:* Hasidic leader or zaddik who may or may not be a rabbi in the sense of ordination *(smicha).*

*Rotel:* Turkish measure, equivalent of 2.5 kilos.

*Sabotnik* (pl. *sabotnikim):* Nineteenth-century Russian peasant converts to Judaism; the term comes from sabbatarian. Some emigrated to Palestine at the end of the nineteenth century and were among the first settler groups in the Galilee, including Yavneel.

*Sephardi* (pl. *Sephardim):* Jew(s) of Iberian descent, but commonly applied to Jews coming from North Africa and the Middle East. Israeli Jews are basically referred to as either Sephardi or Ashkenazi, with some groups (Ethiopian) falling between the cracks.

*Shas:* Israeli political party comprised and supported overwhelmingly by Sephardim. The leadership is Orthodox, though its voters tend to a mix between Orthodox and traditional.

*Shavuot:* Pentecost; Festival of Weeks.

*Shed:* Devil or evil spirit.

*Shmita:* Sabbatical year; religious law dictates that land is not to be worked during this period.

*Shomer* (pl. *Shomrim):* Guard(s); member(s) of an organization founded in Palestine in 1909 for Jewish self-defense.

*Shtrayml:* Fur-edged hat worn by Hasidim on Sabbath and festival days.

*Shul:* Synagogue.

## Glossary

*Simchat Torah:* Holy day marking the completion of the annual cycle of reading the Pentateuch.

*Sukkah:* Booth erected for the festival of Sukkot, when for seven days observant Jews eat, and for the most observant, sleep in the *sukkah*.

*Sukkot:* Feast of booths, one of the three pilgrimage festivals.

*Talmud:* Compendium of debates and discussions based on the Mishnah; the basis of Orthodox teaching of which there are two locational streams, the Babylonian and Palestinian, or Jerusalem, Talmud.

*Tefillin:* Phylacteries, small leather cases containing passages from scripture, placed on the forehead and arm by male Jews during morning prayer.

*Tehilim:* Psalms.

*Tel:* Ancient mound that marks the remains of settlements from historic and prehistoric periods in the Middle East.

*Tisha b'Av:* Ninth of Av, fast day marking the destruction of the First and Second temples.

*Treyf:* Forbidden; non-kosher according to Jewish dietary laws.

*T'shuvah:* Return to faith.

*Tsabar:* Jewish native-born Israeli; also sabra.

*Vidui:* Confession of sins.

*Western Wall:* Also called the wailing wall, or *kotel,* all that remains of Herod's Temple. It is believed to have been an outer retaining wall of the Temple Mount.

*Yishuv:* Jewish community of Palestine in the pre-state period. The pre-Zionist community is called the "old Yishuv," while that dating from approximately 1880 to 1948 is referred to as the "new Yishuv."

*Zaddik* (pl. *zaddikim):* Saintly figure, generally applied to a Hasidic rebbe or leader; see *Rebbe.*

# Index

A, Rabbi, 168
Abraham, 110, 206
Abuchatzera, Baruch (Baba Baruch), 85
Abuchatzera, Sali (Baba Sali), 85, 158
Agriculture, 23-28; and conflict over land, 26, 31; decline of, 20, 21, 23, 224; and nature, 17, 51; ideological and historical meaning of, 15-17; and ownership, 24-26, 31-32, 39; work in, and national renewal, 13-17. *See also* Land; *Moshavim; Yeomanry*
Anti-Semitism, 209
Arabic (language), 43, 145, 204, 205
Arabs, 91, 197; and "Day of Peace," 199-208; and Israel, 43, 93, 125-26, 132, 200-3; and Jews, 145, 162, 200-8; and Palestinian refugees' desire to return, 119; standards of living of, 202-3; and Yavneel, 4, 6, 13, 14, 31, 33, 36, 37, 132, 212
Ariel (disciple of Rav Schick), 170, 173-76, 178
Asa (interviewee), 41-51, 104, 121, 176, 195
Ashkenazim, xi, 10, 12, 18, 28, 94, 117, 149; and Arabs, 200-1, 203-8; current attitudes of, in Yavneel, 22-23, 157, 225; and "ethnic" groups, 164, 224; and Hasidim, 158, 162, 164, 173, 176, 177, 210-25; and Hasidism, 177-79, 207-8; as landowners, 24-26, 28, 175; and Sephardim, 28, 80-81, 136, 157-59, 161-64, 175-76, 187, 198-99, 207; Zionist vision of, 210
Asian Jews, 12
Association of Arab Villages in Israel, 199
Avineri, Shlomo, 209-10

*Ba'alim,* 161, 168, 169
Baal Shem Tov (the Besht), 141, 142, 144, 174
*Ba'alut,* 28, 136
Bar Mitzvah, 77, 78, 97, 99, 101, 103, 111-12, 132
Baruch, Baba. *See* Abuchatzera, Baruch
Bat Mitzvah, 78, 97, 99
Bedouin (Kadar), 13, 44
B'eer Sheva, 85
Begin, Menachem, 223
Beit Alpha, 115
Beit Gana, 33
Ben Gurion, David, 83, 209
Ben-Menashe, 36
Ben-Shimon, Menashe (interviewee), 32-36
*Bet Din,* 57

Bet Gan, 2, 4–7, 26–27, 29, 32–34
Bet Jen, 33
Bet Midrash, 155
Bialik, Chaim Nachman, 51–53
Bible, 44, 69, 76, 79, 91, 96, 121, 122, 174; as justifying return to Palestine, 120, 126, 129
Bilu movement, 13, 13n
Binyamin, Rav, 75
Black Panthers (of Israel), 165
B'nai Brak, 54, 138, 178, 189
Border Patrol, 195
Bratslav, 135, 141–44, 151, 152, 156, 166–69, 173, 174, 177, 178, 180, 182; aim of Hasidim to replicate eighteenth-century, 137, 151, 153. *See also* Bratslav Hasidim; Hasidim
Bratslav, haredi Hasidim of, and Yavneel, 133–89, 194. *See also* Hasidim
Bratslav Hasidim, xiii, xvi, xvii, 135–89; background of, 166–67, 174–75; the "ethnics" and, 156–70; goals of, 141–56; communion with God by, 137, 143; and worldviews in conflict, 177–89. *See also* Haredim, Hasidim
British, x, 31, 36, 42, 197
Brooklyn, 135, 155, 168, 169, 174, 184
Buber, Martin, 144, 148, 209, 222
Buddhism, 101
Burial Society, 113
Busso, Leah (interviewee), 81–95

Catholicism, 105
Caucasus, 32
Central Europeans, 219; and Yavneel, 12, 17
Chagall, Marc, 2, 3
*Chalutzim,* 211
*Chevrah Kadishah,* 238
Christianity, converts to, xi, 10
Circumcision, 105
Conservative Judaism, 65, 66, 78, 97, 104, 108
Cook, Chief Rabbi Yitzhak HaCohen, 58–59

*Datiim,* 54, 66, 68, 99
"Day of Peace," 199–208
Dayan, Moshe, 42
Days of Awe, 122–23
Diaspora, 66, 80; continuity with models of, in Israel, 49, 50; non-Orthodox Jews of, 72; orientation of, 65, 103, 105; religion of the, 94, 96, 103–5, 158; separation of, 15, 16, 29, 40, 215; way of life of, vs. Zionist vision, 208, 211, 212, 214, 215. *See also Galut*
Durkheim, Emile, 63–64

East European Jews, 165, 219; religion of, 61, 94–96; and Yavneel, 8, 10, 12, 17
*Edot ha-mizrach. See* Sephardim
Education, 57–60
Egypt, 36, 110
Ein Harod, 35
Elath, 29
Elijah, 123, 145
English (language), 221
Eretz Yisrael, 43, 44, 71, 73, 131, 150, 185, 206
Esau, 38, 74, 208
Esther, Book of, 91
Ethiopia, 218

F, Rabbi, 162
Farmers Union, 24
Fast of Gedalia, 212
Feige (mother of Rabbi Nahman), 141
Fichman, Yaakov, 51, 52
First Temple, 63
Freethinkers, 10, 12, 53, 62, 66, 68, 99, 104, 105, 108–10, 115–16, 127–28, 132–33; and Rav Shick, 153, 155–56. *See also* Secularists
French Revolution, 209

Galilee, 96, 123, 150, 153, 177, 274; building stone of, 6–8; Jewish agricultural settlements in, 13; Lower, 10, 14, 26, 36; Sea of, 2, 8, 145, 193; Upper, 26
*Galut,* 29, 36, 50, 208ff. *See also* Diaspora
Gaza, 199
*Gematria,* 175

# INDEX

Gilead, 2, 3

Ginzburg, Asher (Ahad Ha'am), 209

God, attitudes toward, 60–62, 69–70, 77–78, 82, 89, 92, 101–4, 108–11, 113, 127–28, 130–32, 147, 171, 173, 213–14. See also Judaism; Religion

Godelier, Maurice, 15

Golan Heights, 2, 3, 5, 193

Gordon, A. D., 209

"Ground bass" religion, 64–76, 80, 101, 102, 112–14, 133, 137, 191–92

Gulf war, 207–8

*Habad,* 167, 168, 171, 189

Hadera, 59

Hagar, 206

Haifa, 96, 117, 145, 161, 164

*Hakafot,* 70

*Halakha,* 56, 59, 63

Haman, 214

Hanukkah, 78, 97, 99–101, 105, 110, 171; celebration of, 167–70

*Haredim,* 12, 71, 114, 144, 168, 170, 173, 178, 226; of Bratslav as infiltrating Yavneel, 133–41, 150, 154, 156, 178, 183–84, 187–89, 213–14, 225; claims of, 213–15, 224; and the non-Orthodox, 123, 132–33, 156, 184, 187, 213; and Sephardim, 156, 169, 176, 210. See also Hasid

Hasidim: accusations against, 19–20, 178, 213–14; and agriculture, 23, 214; comparison with Arabs, 200; attack on Yavneel's rabbi by, 180–84; and belief in reincarnation, 151, 172; definition of, 174–75; dress of, 136, 213; element of, in Yavneel, 10–12, 19–27, 49, 55, 94, 104, 113, 133–34, 153–56; the "ethnics" and, 156–70, 173–76; goals of, 140–56, 177–78, 214; intolerance of, 117, 120, 134, 149, 177–81, 210; and defense of Israel, 20, 120, 177, 191, 211, 214; model of life of, 19–21, 29–30, 47, 67, 134, 136–41, 156, 177–78, 214; the future in Yavneel and Israel and, 148, 176–77; and the land, 147–48; organized opposition to, 178–79, 188–89, 225; as outsiders, 96, 137, 190–91, 196, 199; problems caused by, of Bratslav in Yavneel, 135–41; 147–56, 177–84, 189–92, 194, 196–97, 214, 224; reasons for choice of Yavneel by, of Bratslav, 149–56; and Sephardim, 156–58, 162, 166–67, 174–75; threat to Yavneeli tradition, 124–15, 133–35, 140–41, 149, 154, 177, 178, 183–84, 187–89, 195, 208–11; work ethic and, 15, 16, 19–20, 120, 177, 213, 214; resistance to, 67, 154, 177–79, 183, 186–89; results of invasion of Yavneel by, 154, 176–77, 189–92, 194, 196–97; return to faith and, 169, 177–78; and "taking over" Yavneel, 189–90; view by, of conflict with non-Orthodox, 187; view of the Rebbe of, 180 184–85; and Zionism, 137–41, 147–49, 154, 156, 176–79, 183–89, 207–8, 213–15. See also Bratslav Hasidim

Hasidism, 141; of Eastern European origin, 156; reasons for conversion to, 170, 172–76

*Hatzer,* 155

*Hazan,* 67, 116

Hebrew (language), 43, 58, 86, 174, 185, 205; revival of, as a national language, 216, 221

*Heder,* 57–58, 162

Herzl, Theodor, 120, 126, 209

Herzog, Chaim, 74–75

Hillel (school of), 104

Hirsch, Baron, 26

Histadrut, 74

Holocaust, 171, 218

*Hovevei Tzion* (lovers of Zion), 13

Huran, 13

ICA (PICA after 1924), 26–27, 31, 36, 57

Id el Fidhr, 206

Immortality, belief in, 101

Independence Day (in Yavneel), 123, 182, 194, 197–99, 207

Intermarriage, 90, 93, 186, 226
Interviewees. *See* Ariel; Asa; Lea Busso; Menashe Ben-Shiman; Mendel; Rivka Ovadia; Shimon; Simon
Intifada, 199, 202, 226
Iraq, 208
Iraq, Jews from, 167
Isaac, 110
Isaiah, 120
Ishmael, 206
Israel, 42, 51, 52, 74, 174; agricultural success of, 217; absence of anticlerical movement in, 113–14; Arab-Jewish conflict in, 119, 165, 200–8; burial practices in, 191–96; leadership in, 223; as a democracy, 218–19; economic divisions of, 218; "ethnic" conflict in, 160–64; faults in government a weakness of, 219–20; as holy, 84, 85, 180, immigration to, 32, 160, 169, 178; industrial growth of, 217–18; legitimacy of, 220–21, 223; as creating a national culture, 221–23; population of, 29; religious political parties in, 98, 113, 156; religious beliefs and practices in, 95–105; as a religious or secular society, 93–96, 99–102, 112–14, 156, 223–24; role of, in preserving Jewish religious tradition, 96–99; dependence on United States by, 219, 221–22; as a failed Utopia, 215–24; wars of, 118, 190, 203, 226; and Western Wall, 112
*Israel: The Unfulfilled Dream* (Avraham Ofek), 215–26
Israelites, ancient, 1–2
Issachar/Zevulun, 19, 49, 96
Istanbul, 145
Italy, 64–66, 103, 105

Jacob, 36, 74, 92–93, 110, 208
Jaffa (Yaffo), 32, 33, 58, 145
Jeremiah, 197
Jerusalem, 29, 35, 93, 96, 138, 139, 145, 155, 165n, 173, 175; Bratslav Hasidim in, 178; significance of, to Jews, 1, 144, 146, 147
Jesus Christ, 110

Jewish Agency, 5
Jewish Brigade, 42
Jewish national renewal, 225; value of agricultural work in, 13–17; and Zionism, 208–15. *See also* Zionist vision
Jordan, 119
Jordan River, 193, 201
Jordan Valley, 2, 14, 116, 160
Joshua, 48, 129
Judaism, 8, 129; effect of United States on, 106–7; conflicts over, 158; integration of, into life in Yavneel, 104, 112; and secular vs. Jewish state, 94; survival of, dependent on Israel, 96–97. *See also* Conservative Judaism; Reform Judaism
Judea, 1

Kaddish, 153, 193, 195
Kamieniec, 144
*Kapote*, 136, 168
*Kasher. See* Kosher
Kashruth, 99, 102–3, 113
Katzir, Ephraim, 98
Kfar Tabor, 26–27
Kibbutz, 16, 168, 169; attitudes in, 30
Kibbutz Alumoth, 2
*Kiddush*, 77, 91, 132, 133, 171
*Kippah* (pl. *kippot*), 68, 90
Knesset, 160
Koran, 206
Kosher, 67, 77–79, 90, 92, 171, 183, 240; observance of, in Israel, 99–100; observance of, in Yavneel, 102–3, 111, 113, 117, 132
Kosnitsky, Avraham, 36

L, Rabbi, 64–65
Labor party (Israel), 10
Land, significance of, 30–32, 36–38, 44–51. *See also* Agriculture; *Moshavim*; Yeomanry
Levyakov, Haim, 201
Libyan Jews, 167
*Light of Israel* (publication), 180, 188, 189
Likud, 138
Lubavitcher Rebbe (Brooklyn), 168, 169

# INDEX

Ma'abara, 160
Ma'aser, 63
Maimonides, Moses, 142
Masorti, 66–69, 99
Matzot, 111
Masada, 123
Mayer, Carl, 129–30
Mea Shearim, 54
Medical care, 203
Medvedevka, 142
Medzibozh, 141, 144
Melamed, 57–58
Memorial Day (May 1991 in Yavneel), 189–97
Menachemya, 26–27
Mesopotamia, 48
Messiah: attitude toward, of Rabbi Nahman, 142, 152; expectation of, 15, 16, 42–44, 93, 101, 107, 123, 141, 150, 152, 173; mountain of, 3, 5, 155
Metulla, 13, 36, 59
METV (Middle East Television), 160
Mezuzah, 59, 77–79, 101, 105
Migdal, 33–35
Mikveh, 57, 87–88, 92, 155, 175, 183
Minyan, 16, 54, 89
Mishmar Hashlosha, 2, 4, 5; appearance of, 6–7; Hasidim in, 135; history of, 6–7
Mishnah, 44, 62, 121, 150
Mitzvot, 56, 66, 90, 92, 109, 112, 115, 129, 167, 168
Mordechai, 214
Morocco, 85, 165n; Jews from, 12, 18, 158, 167
Moses, 108–9, 120
Moshavim, 5, 16, 26, 33, 54
Mount Carmel, 145
Mount Sinai, 101, 108, 130

Nafta, 91, 92
Naftali, tribe of, 4
Nahman, Rabbi (1772–1811), 141–48, 151–54, 172, 173; journey of, to Holy Land, 143–47, 150–51; attitude toward Messiah, 142, 152; teachings of, 142–43, 146, 147, 153, 174, 175, 188

National Land Authority, 160, 163
New York, 91, 168, 171
Niggunim, 167, 185–86
North Africa, 219; Jews from, 5, 10, 12, 158, 162–63, 166, 197; and Yavneel, 12, 22, 158

Odessa, 145
Ofek, Avraham, 215–16
Orthodoxy, 105, 169–70; beliefs of, 99–100, 102, 177; demands of, 114–15, 133–34, 137–38, 140, 178, 210; fear about, 208–9; and politics, 98, 118, 138, 140, 153–56; and standards of propriety, 97–98, 102, 103; resistance to, in Yavneel, 115–18, 133–34, 136–40, 154–56, 177, 225; secularists and, 156, 177, 226. *See also* Religious traditionalists
Ovadia, Rivka (interviewee), 81–94

Pagnol, Marcel, 30
Pale, the, 148
Palestine, 36, 57, 58, 126, 144, 146, 148, 197, 211
Passover, 77–79, 100, 105, 110–11, 113, 127, 144
Persian Jews, 167, 169, 173, 176
Petah Tikva, 34
PICA. *See* ICA
Podolia, 148
Poland, 67, 145, 146
Population, 7–12; from Eastern Europe, 10, 17, 18; from Russia, 10, 32, 158, 169; Hasidic element of, 10, 15–16, 19–21, 23, 25, 29–30, 47, 49, 55, 67, 104, 113, 120, 130–91; heterogeneity of, 11–12, 17–18, 158; newcomers, 9, 10, 12, 17–18, 23, 25, 37, 73, 80, 112, 116, 119, 158–60, 176, 224–26; religious range of, 10, 66–70, 105, 107, 109–10, 114, 135–40; veterans, 9, 10, 12, 17–18, 23, 25, 28–29, 37, 39, 73, 80, 112, 118, 124, 149, 158; Yemenite element of, 10, 39, 81, 88, 89, 158
Poriah, 2, 3, 82, 84, 87, 88

249

Pork, attitude toward, 95, 102–3, 105, 113, 127, 132, 133, 171
Porush, Menandrum Rabbi, 62–63
*P'shot*, 1
Purim, 78, 105

*Rahash*, 47
Rabbi: role of, in American Diaspora, 97; of Yavneel, 152, 180–84, 194–96, 207, 225, 226
Ramat Gan, 29, 139
Rebbe, 135–37, 149–58, 162, 168, 169, 175, 176, 182–84, 186–88; demonstration against, 188; Hasidic view of their, 182–87, message of, 185–87. *See also* Shick, Eliezer (the Admor)
Rechovot, 82, 83
Reform Judaism, 65, 66, 71, 78, 97, 104, 108, 117
Reincarnation, belief in, by Bratslav Hasidim, 151, 172
Religion, 53–134; atheist and believers in, 105–18; and attitude toward rabbis, 98–99, 103, 148; and belief in immortality, 101; belief in spirits, by Sephardim, 81, 84, 94, 95; in Yavneel as compared to Israel generally, 95–105; changes in, 58–59, 107; as comfortable, 104–5, 118, 121; conflict of secular Zionism and religious traditionalism, 121–22, 136–40, 224; conflicts over, 115–16, 121–22, 136, 150, 156; education and, 57–59; "ground bass" of, 64–76, 80, 101, 102, 112–14, 191–92, 194, 224; and idea of resurrection, 101; importance of, 107–9, 113–14, 121–22, 131; as inseparable from Jewish selfhood, 130, 131; integration of, into life in Yavneel, 104–5, 114; Israeli context of, 79, 89, 93–101, 109, 113, 124; Jewish context of, 78–79, 93–94, 103, 105, 109, 113; Jewish state vs. secular state, 93–94, 97–98, 121–22; justification in, of Israel for return to Palestine, 119–23, 125–26, 128–33, 223; as a legitimating force, 114, 118–34; mix of politics and, 113, 118, 156; movement from more, to less, 57–58, 60, 107; Orthodox, in official practice in Israel, 97–99, 103; Orthodox religious parties and, 98, 118, 138, 156; toward a popular, 56–64, 70, 73; range of, 66–70, 105, 107, 109–10, 114, 135–40; real, vs. legal, 65, 70, 75, 76, 114; secular Jewish nation without Jewish, not sufficient to legitimate return to Palestine, 120–22, 128; and the seven synagogues of Yavneel, 54; similarities of Ashkenazim Sephardim in, 94–95; spatial rather than temporal communities and, 65, 71, 78; stress on links to past and continuity, 59–60, 62, 63, 72–73, 75, 76, 78, 79, 106, 118; as syncretistic concoction or Durkheimian conception, 63–64, 97; as a unifying force, 72, 75, 77, 97–100, 109. *See also* Ashkenazim; God, attitudes toward; Hasidim; Orthodoxy; Religious traditionalists; Sephardim
Religious traditionalists, 10, 12, 44, 49, 53–57, 65–67, 71, 79; as a compromise between true Orthodoxy and freethinking, 68–69, 99–100, 102, 109–10; defined, 99; and lack of Zionist vision or work ethic, 18, 107; as largest group in Israel, 100; practices of, regarding burial, 191–96; as reinforcing legitimacy of Israel, 223, 224; resentment regarding, 50–51, 75–77, 79, 80, 154–56, 226; Sephardim as more likely to be, 81; vs. Zionist vision, 121–22, 223–24, 226
Resurrection, belief in, in Israel, 101
Revelation, 109
Romania, Jews in Israel from, 10
Rosh Hashanah, 212
Rosh Pina, 13, 33, 36
*Rotel*, 34

# Index

Rothschild, Baron, 26; and Yavneel, 26, 36, 57
Russian Jews, 10, 32, 169

S, Rabbi, 168, 169
Sabbath observance: formal, 54–56, 67, 79, 89–92, 99, 115, 117, 132, 136; for the non-Orthodox, 54–56, 77, 79, 99, 110, 113, 132, 139, 155, 171, 180
*Sabotnik* (pl. *sabotnikim*), 13
Safed, 93, 139, 145, 160, 172
Saham Julan, 36
Sali, Baba, 85, 158
Satan, 87, 152
Second Temple, 63; destruction of, 72
Secularists in Israel, 99, 105, 108–10, 137; as connected to Zionist desire for the new Jew, 209; religious practice of, regarding burial, 191–96; and ultra-Orthodox, 156. *See also* Freethinkers
Sejarah, 34
Sephardim, xi, xii, and agriculture, 23, 39; and Ashkenazim, 80–81, 158, 161–66, 174, 176, 187, 202, 226; and Haredim, 156, 169, 176, 210; attempts by Hasidim to represent downtrodden, 154, 156, 167–70, 173–76; attitude of, toward work, 15–19; definition of, 10; degree of assimilation of, in Yavneel, 18, 37, 137; goals of, 22–23; example of fusion of traditions of, and Ashkenazim, 167–70, 175; examples of discrimination against, 160–64, 198; as fearful newcomers, 37; folk religion of, 80–95; Hasidim of, background in Yavneel, 136; identification with Hasidim, 78–79, 156–58, 179; immigration of, in 1950s, 10, 22, 72, 158–60; traditionalism, 157, 181; many of, and Mishmar Hashlosha, 7; as more likely to be landless in Yavneel, 24–26; from North Africa, 5, 10, 12, 158, 162–63, 166; as potential followers of Hasidim, 150, 174–75, 177–78; religious Orthodoxy of, 61, 81, 189; resentment of, toward establishment, 157, 159–64, 198, 225; similarities and differences of, vis-à-vis Hasidim, 156–57, 167–70; syncretism of religion of, with that of Hasidim, 157–58, 167–70, 174, 175, 211; view of, by themselves as deprived, 159–64, 174, 198, 224–251, Zionist vision of, 18, 210
Shamir government, 62
Shammai (school of), 104
Sharona (a moshav), 2, 3
*Shavuot*, 78
Shed, 84–88: dealing with a, 84, 85, 87, 88
Shellfish, attitude toward, 102–3
Shick, Rav Eliezer (the Admor), 94, 135–37, 139, 156, 168, 200, 214; and attack on rabbi, 152; belief by, Hasidim in ultimate triumph of, 152, 186; conciliatory tactics by, 155–56; goals of, 149–56, 174–75, 186; message of, 185–87; as patron of Sephardim, 156–57, 186; reasons for choice of Yavneel by, 149–54; role of, in Yavneel, 180, 182–87; two disciples of, 170–77
Shikun, 5, 8, 16, 22, 54, 86, 159–60; Hasidim in, 135; population of, 5, 7; as a social problem, 5, 29
Shimon (interviewee), 41, 45–52, 153, 176
Shinto, 64
*Shmita*, 57, 63
*Shomer* (pl. *Shomrim*), 26, 59
*Shtrayml*, 136
*Shul*, 8, 77, 115
*Shimchat Torah*, 70–72, 140
Simon (American disciple of Rav Shick), 170–73
Six Day War, 165n
Smadar, 2, 4–5, 37, 54, 161; Hasidim in, 135
Social Security, 203
Song of Songs, meaning of, 1
Sternhanz, Rabbi Nathan, of Nemirov, 142–43, 151, 172

251

*Sukkah,* 101, 243
*Sukkot,* 78, 100–1, 105, 212
Switzerland, 41
Syria, 119

Talmud, 44, 48, 50, 62, 130
Tammany Hall, 113–14
*Tefillin,* 67, 112
*Tehilim,* 60, 88
Tel-Aviv, 17, 96, 201, 212, 220
Ten Commandments, 69, 108, 127
Tiberias, 46, 57, 93, 145
*Tisha b'Av,* 68, 72, 197
Torah, 43, 61, 66, 68, 69, 92, 101, 112, 130, 173, 206; as assuring the existence of the Jewish people, 129
Tozar, 92
*Treyf,* 180
Trumpeldor, Josef, 209
*T'shuvah,* 44, 136, 168, 169, 171, 184
*Tsabar,* 185
Tuan, Yi-Fu, 40, 217
Tunis, 162, 201
Tunisia, Jews from, 12, 81, 91, 111, 116, 158
Turks, 31, 34, 36

Udel (daughter of the *Baal Shem Tov*), 141
Ultra-Orthodox. *See* Orthodox
Um El-Fahem, 201
Uman, 142, 153
United States, 66, 72, 91, 97, 137, 165, 175, 176, 218; dependence of Israel on, 219, 221–22; expectations of Jewish immigrants to, regarding religion, 106–7

Vishnitz school of Hasidim, 181–82

Wadi Ara, 199, 204
War of Independence, 42, 111, 117
Weber, Max, 71
Weizmann, Chaim, 223
West Bank, 199
Western Wall (in Jerusalem), 11, 112, 122–23
Work (in Yavneel), 12–23; and Arab laborers, 212; changing attitudes toward, by all of younger generation, 18, 20–21; Hasidim and rejection of work ethic, 15, 16, 19–21
World War I, 4
World War II, 42, 212, 218
Worldviews in conflict (in Yavneel), 177–89

X, Rabbi, 111

Y, Rabbi, 111
Yavneel: achievements and failures in, 216–17, 224; agriculture of, 7, 9, 23–25, 27, 224; appearance of, 2–9, 51–52; Arabs and, 4, 6, 13, 14, 31, 33, 36, 37, 132, 212; atmosphere of, 4–5, 7–9, 11–12, 24, 51–52; beginnings of, 12–13, 26; buildings of, 7–8; changing attitudes younger generation in, 22, 224; as a city of Bratslav, 173, 186; division of, along "ethnic" lines, 154; education in, 8, 21–22, 57–58; emergence of Jewish yeomanry in, 27–41; future of, 176–77, 227; golden age (1960s–1980s) of, 23–24; historical development of, 3–9, 26–28, 36, 107; industrial zone of, 8–9, 24, 224; location of, 10; as not a religious settlement, 48; outer communities of, 2, 4–8; politics of, 10, 74, 138–40, 153–56; rabbi of, 152, 180–84, 194–96, 225, 226; religious range in, 10, 12, 53, 134–36; social problems of, 5, 24–26, 31, 39, 135–41, 159, 160, 220; as typical of much that is Israeli, 9–11, 136, 139–41, 150, 177–78, 190–227; and water supply, 27–28, 144; work in, 7, 12–23. *See also* Agriculture; Education; Hasidim; Independence Day; Memorial Day; Population; Religion; Work; Worldviews in conflict; Yeomanry; Zionist vision
Yemenites: and Mishmar Hashshlosha, 7; and Yavneel, 9, 12, 18, 22, 26, 39, 54, 81, 88, 89, 158, 162–63
Yeomanry, 10, 28–41; and their land, 30–31, 36–38, 40–42, 49, 118–19, 226–27; change for, only in technology, 38; characteristics of, 30–31,

# INDEX

36–37, 40–41; conflict caused by sense of rootedness of, 29–31, 39; differences of, from Israel's largely urban population, 29; differences of, from Kibbutzniks, 30; emergence of a Jewish, 28–37; importance of Yavneel to, 29, 37, 40; view of themselves, 10–11, 36–37, 39, 42, 49, 118–19

Yiddish, 43, 58, 174

Yishuv: achievements of, 216; later, 6, 58; old, 58

Yitzhak (Isaac), 206

Yom Kippur, 42, 59, 68, 77, 78, 88, 89, 90, 100, 105, 111, 127, 132, 133

*Zaddik,* 85, 87–88, 137, 139, 141–43, 145, 151, 152, 158, 170, 173, 174, 185

Zemach, 83

Zimmerman, Shmuel, 13–14, 21

Zionist vision, 1, 9, 11, 13, 17, 58, 111, 147; achievements and failures of, 216–18; and anti-Semitism, 209; and national identity, 209–10; coupled with religion, 125–27, 131, 147, 169–70, 187, 208–12, 214–27; and "ingathering of the exiles," 217; of Jews as fighters, laborers, farmers, and athletes, 211, 215, 217; and Hasidim, 140, 177, 184, 185, 191, 213; and Sephardim, 18, 161; and the new Jew vs. *Galut* way of life, 208, 211, 214, 215; political, 120, 121; and religious traditionalism, 121–22, 169–70, 213–14; results of, 147, 177–78, 210–12; as revolutionary in Jewish life, 209–10, 217; and Sephardim, 18, 161, 210; of a unified Jewish people, 176, 208

Zweig, Ferdynand, 121